THE

KINGSPORT STRIKE

Books by Sylvester Petro

THE

KINGSPORT STRIKE

by

Sylvester Petro

ARLINGTON HOUSE
New Rochelle, N.Y.

To

MIGUEL A. DE CAPRILES

Great Fencer,
Law Teacher and
Law Dean

PREFACE

THIS BOOK has two purposes: first, to tell the story of a long
and immensely significant strike; second, on the basis of the sad
and tragic facts disclosed in that story, to stimulate a re-examination of the labor policies of the United States. For the tragedy of
this strike was produced by those labor policies and by the ideas,
mainly fallacious, which underlie them.

This book is not intended as an attack upon any person or
group of persons. *Ideas* are the object of my criticism, not union
members or their leaders, and not the members of the National
Labor Relations Board—despite the active role they have all
played. If any human beings were to be regarded as the sub-
jects of criticism, they would have to be the people of the United
States and the intellectual community whose views rule the
country, directly and indirectly, and who, therefore, have created
the conditions in which alone the deplorable results of the strike
at the Kingsport Press could have come about.

The reader may wish to compare this book with the study
recently published by Professor Philip Ross, *The Labor Law
in Action* (1966). That study, supported by the National Labor Relations Board with public funds, concludes that the Labor
Board has well and faithfully administered the national labor
policies, and that if the Board has fallen short in any way the
deficiency has lain in a tendency to deal too lightly with intransi-
gent employers.

Coming to a contrary conclusion on that point, this book holds
that the Labor Board has considerably changed and distorted
the national labor policy declared by the only governmental

authority competent to make such policy, namely, the Congress of the United States. It holds, moreover, that the Labor Board's distortions have all been of one kind; that they have all imposed heavier burdens and tighter restraints upon employers than Congress intended; and that the result has been, naturally, to stimulate arrogance and irresponsibility among some of the leaders as well as among many of the members of trade unions.

Going further, this book does not stop with the assumption that the labor policy declared by Congress is a correct policy for the United States. On the contrary, the present book takes the position that though our basic labor policy is different from and better than the Labor Board's version, it is nevertheless fundamentally defective and out of touch with reality; that it is based on myths and errors; and that it is accordingly bound to lead to anti-social and inhumane results of the kind described in this story of the strike at the Kingsport Press.

The philosophy of labor relations and the analysis of labor law contained in this book are substantially the same ones developed in my previous books, most notably *The Labor Policy of the Free Society* (New York: Ronald Press, 1957). The difference between this and my previous books lies in the wealth of factual material gathered by direct observation which this one presents. The others could be done in a study and law library, with only my earlier experience in unions and industry as an empirical base. But the bulk of the material for this book came from direct personal inquiry at the scene of the strike. For the funds with which to support those researches I am indebted to the Master Printers Section of the Printing Industries of America. Needless to say, it was understood that every word, idea, and conclusion stated in the book was to be mine; the Master Printers Section was not privileged even to examine the manuscript prior to publication. I am not sure that the Master Printers Section is in accord with the result of my researches and writing, but I must nevertheless acknowledge its help with gratitude, since I should not otherwise have been able to spend the time in Kingsport, Tennessee, necessary to gather directly all the information which has gone into the book.

The strike began in March of 1963; as of January, 1967, it continues. In March of 1966, reversing a previous decision, the New York City Board of Education adopted a resolution boycotting textbooks manufactured by the Kingsport Press. This resolution seemed so plainly beyond the Board's legitimate authority that the Corporation Counsel of New York City, Mr. J. Lee Rankin, was unwilling to defend it in an injunction suit brought by the Press. Bowing to a court order, the Corporation Counsel finally did defend the Board. When in October of 1966 Mr. Justice George Postel of the New York Supreme Court ordered the Board of Education to rescind the boycott resolution, however, the Corporation Counsel declined to appeal. Thus the Press has won a clean-cut victory against one of the unions' most significant boycotting attempts.

However, the situation for the Press and its workers remains complex and hazardous. The unfair-practice charges with which the unions have harassed the Press for a long time are still pending, prolonging the strike and delaying a clean-cut resolution of the issues—a significant commentary on the boast that an expanded administrative law would bring to society swift and fair decisions.

The original charges were dismissed in the Labor Board's regional office after a full investigation. The unions then appealed the dismissal to the Board's General Counsel in Washington, where the charges inexplicably hung fire for many months, only to be withdrawn by the unions "without prejudice" before the General Counsel came to a decision. Later the unions refiled charges, and when they were again dismissed in the regional office, appealed once more to the office of the General Counsel, where they were finally dismissed—only to be followed by other charges which were dismissed in the regional office and are pending now on appeal to the General Counsel.

The striking unions have an intense interest in keeping the charges hanging fire as long as possible. As long as the charges remain unresolved, the Press and its present employees will be unable to get new elections, and the unions will remain bargaining representatives of the striker replacements, that is, of employees whom the unions are determined mainly to injure economically. If new elections are held, the replaced strikers will be ineligible to vote. With only non-strikers and striker replacements voting, it is not likely that the unions would win. They would probably be "decertified" and could therefore no longer continue either their harassing strike and boycott activities or their mockery of "collective bargaining."*

For it must never be forgotten that the main thrust of the unions' current "collective bargaining" is to compel the Press to reinstate the replaced strikers, even though this would probably require firing the striker replacements. Theoretically, the national labor policy, like the common law, requires a bargaining agent to deal fairly, ethically, and morally with the employees it represents. Thus the Press's current employees, since the unions are currently their bargaining representatives, have a legal right to get fair representation. Instead the representatives whom they are forced by the law to accept are preoccupied with a course of action likely to harm them, and this ugly travesty of justice will continue as long as the Labor Board and its General Counsel refuse to dispose of the unfair-practice charges which have been festering so long in Washington, D.C. A labor policy which can produce such a result should be discarded, whatever the cost to the myths upon which it is based.

Sylvester Petro

New York
January, 1967

* Late in January 1967 the Board ordered elections which will probably be held in February or March 1967.

CONTENTS

THE

KINGSPORT STRIKE

1

THE SETTING

MARCH CAN BE bright and balmy in Kingsport, but it can be gray and chilly, and volatile, too, with little previews of all the seasons scurrying in quick succession across the valley, the hills, and the sky. Natives there brag about the weather—how nasty and unpredictable it can be in the winter and spring— almost the way Chicagoans do. Monday morning, March 11, 1963, was so particularly bad, with rain and cold and wind, that it might have served for years to come as an example of the mean tricks that Kingsport's weather could play. It might have, I say, except for *the event* which that day's dawning brought with it. People in Hiroshima do not talk about the weather that prevailed on August 6, 1945. For much the same reason, people in Kingsport, when that morning in March of 1963 is the subject, do not think of the weather, notably bad as it was. What they think about and talk about is the strike at the Press.

Some Problems and a Mystery

That there was a strike at all was remarkable enough. The Press was a "native child" of Kingsport, having been born and bred in town. Its owners and officers had had a great deal to do with the founding of the town itself. Highly social-conscious, they were active in all the humanitarian movements, from education to public welfare, which have made Kingsport the very model of the "progressive American city." The Press's current president, also its largest stockholder, Mr. Edward J. Triebe, has headed almost every do-gooding organization the town has ever known: among many others, the Salvation Army, the Public Welfare Commission, and, recently, the Committee to Fluoridate Kingsport's Water Supply. An admirer of Mortimer J. Adler, he has participated in "Great Books" reading courses. So far as I have been able to tell—and I might add that I have done a great deal of inquiring about this—Edward Triebe might very well even today walk away with any popularity contest among the people who struck his firm back then in March of 1963. Dozens of strikers spoke to me warmly and admiringly of him. One said: "What a hell of a striker he would have made. I only wish we had him on our side!"*

The Press was one of Kingsport's best known and most admired firms. It was one of the biggest hard-bound book manufacturers in the country, one of the few to conduct a fully integrated book-manufacturing operation, all the way from the raw paper to the final binding and the mailing to individual book-purchasers. Its equipment was the most modern available, its research and development program among the most heavily financed in the industry, the quality of its products unsurpassed. It is easy to see why people in Kingsport, in fact all over East Tennessee, spoke familiarly and proudly of "the Press," or even just "Press." Getting a job there was an object of high aspiration for people in the surrounding area.

The strike which started on March 11 was memorable for a number of other reasons. It was the first sign of serious "labor trouble" that the Press had ever displayed in the forty years of its existence and in the more than twenty years that it had bargained, apparently amicably, with the unions which called the strike.

The strike has proved to be even more remarkable for its pure

* In May of 1963, when the strike was in the most turbulent state it ever reached, a stockholders' meeting was held at the Press. According to the *Kingsport News,* "The biggest stockholders vote ever cast at Kingsport Press yesterday gave 100 per cent support to company officials in the current labor dispute." The remarkable thing is that of the ninety stockholders present, ten were on strike at the time of the meeting. See *Kingsport News,* May 10, 1963, page 1.

duration. As of the spring of 1966, while this book is being prepared, the strike continues. Three years! And the prospects of a
settlement still seem dim.

Perhaps most remarkable of all are the activities which have
attended the strike—the violence, the assaults, the bombings,
the bitterness, the coercion, the nationwide boycott that the
unions have sought to impose in an attempt to strangle this so
widely admired company.

But there is a mystery, too, about this strike—pervasive, profound, and challenging. Some of the aspects that we have already
seen are components of the mystery—the pride in the Press,
its peaceful labor history, the desirability of a job there. But
these, while remarkable, only hint that there might be a problem involved in understanding the strike. The commanding,
imperious mystery—the baffling element in the whole situation
—bursts out when one begins to pursue those hints; when one,
brought to a state of wonderment, asks the strikers: *Why did
you strike?*

Then one finds that the ultimately remarkable thing about the
strike at the Press is the mystery which surrounds its motivation. All disinterested persons who have investigated the affair
on the scene, including some extremely astute labor journalists,
have, as has this writer, found confusion and a curious flabbiness
of motivation among the strikers. Despite the obvious reasons
for exaggerating their grievances against the company, the strikers on the contrary complained only half-heartedly about the
wages and working conditions at the Press—and scarcely at all
about the Press management. Indeed, the Press management,
especially the top management, was more praised and admired
than censured.

Often hard feelings increase with proximity; the closer we are
to some things, the more intensely we come to resent them.
Strangely, the opposite is true of the Kingsport Press affair.
There the people furthest from the Press management seemed to
have the strongest feeling against it. Animosity toward the Press
management was displayed not so much by the strikers, but by
the national union leadership; and, at that, by the leadership

which had had the least to do with the Press management. As we shall see, at least one highly placed union official—a man of great ability and experience who has known and dealt with the Press management for many years, and who has proved on countless occasions to be the Press's most skilful opponent—this man, Mr. John S. McLellan, General Counsel of the International Printing Pressmen and Assistants Union (IPP&AU), has never used the Press management as a punching bag. He has opposed and continues to oppose the Press. He has given the Press management many an anxious hour, made great inroads upon what would otherwise and normally be sleeping time. Like many an outstanding man of strong personality and lively mind, Mr. McLellan has a name for everything. His name for this affair is the "Press Mess." But one of the most interesting things about him is that he does not join the other union leaders in their name-calling game. He does not accuse the Press management of being alone responsible for the "mess at the Press."

We shall devote a substantial part of the rest of this book to exploring the mystery of the motivation of the strike at the Press. Let us continue here to place Kingsport, the Press, and the strike in their most relevant setting.

Kingsport and Appalachia

Kingsport lies in a high Appalachian Mountain valley on the northeastern edge of Tennessee, almost at the southwestern border of Virginia. It is only a few miles from Kingsport to a number of other states—Kentucky, West Virginia, North Carolina, and South Carolina. If you look at a map you will see that Kingsport is close to the middle of "Appalachia," the scene of the current "War on Poverty." If you look again, you will observe that it is in fact not far at all from the town which is itself called Appalachia, in Virginia. I have made it driving leisurely in an hour, and I have been told by men who drive daily from Appalachia to Kingsport that they do it consistently in less than that.

Kingsport is a "bright jewel in an Ethiop's ear," a trim, fast-moving town, bursting with vigor, in the middle of a murky, tranced, retrograde environment. It is a bustling, prosperous city, its broad, straight streets lively with traffic and framed in spare, clean architecture of contemporary style. Banks, hotels, office buildings, and large stores line Center Street, its main drag, also known as U.S. 23. Massive industrial plants and factories loom at the margins and borders. Its residential districts are easily as modern, comfortable, and attractive as those of the more prosperous towns of the North, including those in the well known suburbs of Chicago, Los Angeles, or New York. Comparable houses cost on the average a quarter to a third less, but they are at least as well constructed in Kingsport as in Westchester County, New York. Land values are, if anything, higher, perhaps because real estate taxes are so low, relatively.

As one moves out from Kingsport, in any direction, the prospect changes abruptly. Soon one finds oneself in forlorn country. The older frame houses in Kingsport are for the most part handsome and well maintained. Its new construction runs to neat, cheerful ranch houses and split-levels, with here and there a gracious colonial—all usually in brick. Just a few miles out, however, the Appalachia of the "War on Poverty" begins. Black, ugly, unpainted, weatherbeaten, crumbling shacks litter the rugged countryside. Dismal relics of coal-mining days carve the sky and the hills. They are bad enough on a sunny day. On an overcast day they are morbid; in the rain, downright depressing.

The cause of Kingsport's prosperous condition is the prolix productivity of its industries. It is the home base of Tennessee Eastman. A giant chemical firm affiliated with Eastman Kodak, Tennessee Eastman stretches for a mile or more along the Holston River, the historic stream which runs along one side of Kingsport. The biggest single productive unit in all of Tennessee, Eastman employs about 10,000 men and women. Its Kingsport payroll alone is well over $70,000,000 a year.

Kingsport has a number of other large and nationally important firms, as well as a multitude of bustling small ones. American-Saint Gobain Corporation, third largest flat glass manufacturer in the country, has its headquarters and two major plants in Kingsport. The Mead (paper) Corporation, employs 1,200 in its Kingsport plant, just across Center Street from the Press. The nation's second largest textile manufacturer, J. P. Stevens Company, employs almost 1,000 in its Kingsport plant. Mason & Dixon Lines, Incorporated, one of the country's biggest motor carriers, employing over 2,000, was founded and is still headquartered in Kingsport, and dispatches its far-flung operations from there.

I have mentioned only a few of the larger Kingsport employers. There are many others, industrial, commercial, and transportation firms—utilities, banks, railroads—so many that one wonders how this metropolis-like variety of productive activity can be contained in a city which numbered only 14,000 inhabitants in the 1940 census and which, despite its growth since, is still probably under 40,000. The point, of course, is that Kingsport's industries provide employment for people not only in the city itself but also in its attractive suburbs and, as already mentioned, from outlying areas at least as far away as Appalachia, Virginia. This has been the product of the enduring war on poverty which the American enterprise system started in Kingsport around the turn of the century, when New York capitalists began investing there, attracted by its resources and its sturdy hill people.

"Press Is Hiring"

Next to Tennessee Eastman, the Press is Kingsport's largest employer. When the strike was called, the Press was employing about 2,200 men and women. As one of the largest, if not the largest, of the fully-integrated book manufacturers in the country, it has also been Kingsport's most widely known firm. Wage rates at the Press were not *all* as high as those in the New York City printing establishments, but they were well above those prevailing in other towns of similar size and location. More important, Press wages and working conditions were easily among the highest and most attractive not only in Kingsport, but in the whole southeast. Anthony J. DeAndrade himself, president of the Pressmen's Union, recognized as much. And the *people,* who always know their relevant labor market better than anyone else —far better than labor economists have generally given them credit for—were infinitely more vividly aware of the desirability of a job at the Press than Mr. DeAndrade was.

News that "Press is hiring" has always been welcomed by all within hearing distance. "Press is hiring" called people magically from the smoky valleys lost in eastern Kentucky. It drew them from Virginia, the Carolinas, from nearby Bristol and Johnson City. Hillbillies brushed up on their reading and writing, put on their shoes, started up their jalopies, and took off for Kingsport whenever they thought there was a chance of getting on. It was the difference between hard scratching on a stony ten acres in Scott County, Virginia, or Harlan County, Kentucky, and one of those trim ranch houses, the good schools, the fine churches, a college education for the kids, and a new Chevy under the carport in Kingsport.

If one got on and stayed on the Press payroll, he might eventually get to master one of the aristocratic printing trades. He would then be "somebody." He might even join one of the private clubs where Press workers and those at the Eastman and the other high-paying firms had all the fun, living it up.

I remember sitting up late one night in my room at the Holiday Inn, on the outskirts of Kingsport, talking with one of the strikers. He was Hugh Reece, born a farm boy near Boone, North Carolina, and still speaking in the gentle accents of North Carolina although he had been working at the Press since 1940. Mr. Reece was one of the top journeymen in the Press bindery when the strike was called. This straightforward, clean-cut man had been out on strike for two years when I talked with him in the spring of 1965. Although he had obviously been hurt badly by the strike, although the future which had once seemed so promising, so secure, was then clouded and obscure, Mr. Reece talked about the strike calmly and for the most part far more objectively than one might have expected. He is the man who spoke so admiringly of the Press president, Edward Triebe, who said that Triebe "would have made a great striker," who wished that Triebe "had been on our side."

Hugh and I were drinking beer as we talked, beer that he had supplied, for it is not readily available, at least for out-landers, in Kingsport. Midnight was approaching, and Hugh, after a spirited discussion of the strike, suddenly turned sad. He was thinking, he explained, about the effect of the strike on the private clubs, his own in particular.

The Press journeymen were the backbone of many of the clubs. Some were still on strike, some had gone back to their jobs. The instances in which men from both categories had tried to maintain their club relationships together had not been happy; there had been violence, bitterness, bad feeling. A friendly, com-panionable relationship was no longer possible. Neither the strikers alone nor the men who had gone back, even together with the striker replacements, could keep the clubs on the old footing. What kind of future did the clubs have? Probably the same as the future for the bitter-end strikers: vague, obscure, unpromising. It was sad and worrisome, Hugh said. I had to agree.

The discussion hanging there, our visit fell apart. We had both enjoyed analyzing the strike and its issues. I had learned a great deal from Hugh Reece about the problems of principle raised by strikes, at least as seen by a strong union man of good character and sound personality. Hugh had done a lot of thinking during the two strike years, and he was passing much of it along to me. One of the things he said which most impressed me was that the strike weapon must be used only after the most searching deliberation, and then only as a desperate last resort. This he had learned the hard way, through the bitter lessons taught by a long strike, the thousands of big and little trials and tragedies which had filled his days and troubled his nights. By that time, however, along toward midnight, as I have said, there seemed no point in going on. Hugh was too mournful, with neither desire nor aptitude for vocal mourning. Real suffering must always be in silence. We said good-night.

2

UNRAVELING THE QUESTION: WHY?

It Is Not So Simple

THE SIMPLEST ANSWER to the question "What caused the strike at the Press?" is that the Company refused to concede the demands of the five unions representing its employees. The trouble is, however, that as this answer would apply to every economic strike that has ever been called, it tells us very little about the strike at the Press, the unique phenomenon in which we are interested. It fails to advance our understanding or to satisfy our curiosity about this specific case.

We want to know more. We want to know not only why the strike was called in the first place, but also why it has lasted so long. We want to know the basis upon which the union formulated its demands, and what relationship those demands had to the felt grievances of the workers.

We seek an answer to the really formidable question: What induced particular men to go on strike? For it must be remembered that a union decision to call a strike and a worker's decision to go on strike can be two distinct things, sometimes sharply distinct. If we really want to know what brought about *this* strike, therefore, we must seek information not only from the men who conceived the union strategy, but also from the men who walked the picket line.

Solid answers to questions of even more universal public interest will come only if we go still deeper. In a very general way, it is true that the strike at the Press was brought about by management resistance to the unions' demands. Yet managements do not always resist union demands. The vast preponderance of the 70,000 or more collective agreements in the United States are re-negotiated year after year without strikes, although they almost always involve additional concessions from the employers. Kingsport Press had been one such employer. It had made concessions to the unions continually from 1940 to 1963. Indeed, it offered substantial concessions in the 1963 negotiations. What made it refuse then to go as far as the unions wished it to go?

Finally, and perhaps most important of all from the point of view of the public interest, we must try to determine what gave this strike its particularly damaging character. Why was there so much violence? Why did the unions engage in all kinds of boycotts, lawful and unlawful? Why did the unions find it necessary to engage in such conduct? What happened to the legal controls which are designed, in a decent and free society, to keep some men from assaulting and abusing other men?

Such are the questions which occurred to me in my investigation of the strike at the Press, and which directed my inquiries. I intend to present the direct evidence which will provide the basis for answering some of the questions I have posed. This direct evidence comes in the main from interviews with the people involved—strikers, union officials, company officials, and other persons close to the strike. In a few instances I have been compelled to rely on hearsay. This is regrettably true in respect to Mr. DeAndrade, president of the Pressmen's Union, probably the key union in the five involved. I tried several times, but was never able to arrange a meeting with him. Still, the ideas and remarks I attribute to him were made and reported publicly, and so far as I know he has never disavowed them. Moreover, as we shall see, those ideas and remarks have been confirmed by some of his associates.

Some Notes on Methodology

Not all of the questions I have just posed can be answered in one chapter. Moreover, some of the questions are of the kind that can never be answered by a mere accumulation of fact.

Action is one thing, purpose another. A man can tell you that he walked the picket line, or that he went back in to work after walking the picket line for a while. Explaining why he struck, why he picketed, why he decided to quit picketing, however— these "whys" are considerably more obscure and complicated. After the man has explained himself as fully as he can, you find that there are still things that he hasn't explained, things that you must fill in one way and another, relying largely on that universal solvent, that ultimate identity, the quality that makes us all brothers under the skin—our common human nature. Beware of the man who tells you that he will explain—fully explain—any complex human action or event by resort to "coldly objective," "empirically verifiable," "statistical data." He is deceiving himself, and perhaps seeking to deceive you.

For in the first place we do not all see the same event in exactly the same way, let alone interpret it the same way—not even events which do not involve the complicating factor of human purpose. If I ask three men, "How fast was the car going?" I shall more than likely get three different kinds of answers. The poet will say, "swiftly as a bird," or, maybe, "like a shot." The physicist will say, "so many miles per hour," or, "so many meters per second." The man less sharply tuned to the incident will say, "I don't know," or, maybe, "fast," or, "slowly," if he is a grammarian.

That was a simple question, one of the simplest conceivable. Think of the complexity of the questions we have set ourselves! Consider how hopelessly pretentious it would be for this writer or, for that matter, any writer, to suggest that his answers to such questions were both conclusive and objectively demonstrable. "Objective" a *man* may be, if only he be capable of keeping his prejudices and predilections under control—which means, first, that he must be aware of their existence, and, second, that he has disciplined himself. But to provide objectively *demonstrable answers*—that is another matter. A man may be objective and still make mistakes. The mistakes may be either in the telling, or the hearing, or the interpretation. The man you interview may have made mistakes in observation, correlation, or interpretation; unfortunately, it is all too possible, also, that he has deliberately lied or sought to mislead. The man doing the interviewing may make similar mistakes of observation, correlation, or interpretation; he too may deliberately lie or misrepresent.

"Not the devil himself knoweth the mind of man." The motives of our acts are deep, complex, obscure, difficult to separate out and evaluate. The more complicated the act or the human event, the more difficult the unraveling becomes. The writer who wishes to keep faith with his readers must do his work in such a fashion as permits him to say, honestly: "I have studied the situation with great care; I have prepared myself well; I have asked the questions which I thought would help most in reaching the most relevant and interesting truth, though it be, as Byron said, a gem which loves the deep; I have presented the evidence as fully as the exigencies of accurate explanation seemed to me to require; and, finally, when ambiguity or conflict or contradiction called for interpretation, I have been as fair as I can be."

The main requirement for reader and writer alike, as I see it, is that they guard constantly against the "statistics" fallacy. Men seeking to interpret complex human events are not mere recording machines. They observe some things; they do not observe others. What makes the difference is the equipment they themselves bring to the situation—their own already formed ideas, theories, and ways of interpreting life. They ask some questions; they do not ask others. Again, it is their own rational equipment, their own theoretical framework, which tells them what questions to ask. Finally, in putting together a comprehensive and coherent set of answers to a complex set of human problems, it is the logical structure of the human mind, not the miscellaneous concatenation of parallel or successive events, that counts. The inquiries and observations which I have made, the answers which I shall offer, have all been formulated in full consciousness of these considerations.

3

TWO STRIKERS

Jack Rhoten: One Who Stayed Out

JACK RHOTEN, pressman first class, is one of the most appealing persons I met in Kingsport. He is quiet, soft-spoken, friendly, a bit on the retiring side, yet as direct as one can reasonably expect an essentially gentle person to be. The first time I met him, early in 1965, I took him for a man in his late twenties, and I was astonished when I learned that he was thirty-eight. However, rest can do much to erase the years, and Jack had had a great deal of rest at the time. By the spring of 1965 he had not done his regular job at the Press for two years.

Although well rested physically, and youthful, Jack was reserved and troubled. Back behind his eyes there was a haunted look, and the corners of his mouth were tight. There was a good reason. He had been through a profound and devastating crisis, and his was the look which you are likely to find on the face of a man who has dragged himself through a deep trial, not knowing just how it came about, expecting it all to end from one day to the next, only to find it going on, apparently forever, without end, without conclusion, without decision. It is what happens to a man who runs into a problem which will not resolve itself, and which he is incapable of resolving. He feels himself an endless loser. I think that is how Jack Rhoten felt, and I think that is what accounts for the haunted quality which enfolded this tall, good-looking, and very decent young man. It is bad enough that now, in 1966, he has not done the make-ready on one of the majestic presses since the strike was called three years ago. Much worse, he does not know when or even *whether* he will ever be running one of the big presses in Kingsport again.

Banal as it may sound, Jack loved his work; felt good near a printing press, and felt good in the right way, for all the right reasons. There are few machines in this world to equal a great, smooth, four- or five-color press. It is big and that is important. It runs with a purr of controlled power which hints at any moment of the possibility of a furious roar. But it is fussy and delicate, too. Set right it will turn out thousands of beautifully printed pages, in hours, in beautiful, glowing colors. Set wrong, "out of register," and it can drive you crazy.

Jack was a pressman who did good work, so good that the Press management, which continues today to speak highly of him, often gave him supervisory authority, and it had really been a question only of time before he would have been a regular pressroom foreman. Moreover, he was not a man who had other interests, passions, or delights which might make his job just a way of earning a living. He was a good family man, played some with the kids, occasionally took a correspondence course in order to keep his mind active, went regularly to church and to union meetings, but without becoming a fanatic in either connection.

No, the big thing in Jack's life—other than his family—was his job and his future at the Press. It is not really strange that it should be so when you consider that he had practically grown up among the presses. He had started to work at the Press when he was only seventeen, in 1944, and went back immediately after a thirteen-month stretch in the Navy. He had never given a thought to any other work. By 1949—still only twenty-two—he had his "papers"; he was a journeyman pressman at an age when many others were not even apprentices.

We never forget the events which we consider really important. That is axiomatic. When I asked Jack Rhoten, in 1965, what his first press was, the answer came immediately, slid right off the

top of his brain. It was a Miller 2-color, 41-inch flatbed. I had
the impression that he could describe every event connected with
his assumption of responsibility that day.

In March 1963, when the strike was called, Jack at thirty-six
years of age was at the top of the pressmen's heap. He had a
steady day job after working second and third shifts for years. As
first pressman on a 5-color giant, he was entitled to the day
shift's top pay,* a cool $3.38 per hour. With premium pay for
overtime work, fringe benefits, and the profit-sharing plan (one
of the best, if not the best, in the industry), Jack had an income
of at least $10,000 a year virtually insured. And there was the
supervisory probability before him, too.

It is necessary to re-emphasize that, although he had joined
the Pressmen's Union in 1946, had attended its meetings more
regularly than most, and had voluntarily maintained his membership without interruption, he had never been a militant unionist.
As we shall see in a moment, Jack was anything but a union
zealot even during the period of greatest agitation preceding the
strike. He has proved the hard way that he is a good union man.
He has adhered loyally to what he considers his union commitment; he has been one of the "bitter-enders" during the strike;
he has served as chairman of the allied unions' "hardship committee." And these are the more remarkable because of the
great, the overwhelming personal cost to him that they have involved. Yet, despite all this, I still believe it fair to say that Jack's
sympathies and interests lay more with the Press than with the
unions. I wish to make it clear that Jack never said this in so
many words, but my strong conviction is that he identified more
intimately with his employer than with his union before the
strike.

Why, then, did Jack Rhoten strike? And why has he stayed
out so long, years after many of his fellow-pressmen—men who
were far more interested in striking than he was—have returned
to their jobs at the Press?

To put squarely and briefly what came out in bits and pieces
during hours of discussion: Jack Rhoten did not ever, actively,

* There is a premium for second and third shift work.

wish to go out on strike. He told me that before the strike some of the men in the pressroom were a little aroused—"upset" was his word—over upgrading (promotions) and personal grievances. There was no serious feeling at all about wages. "The strike was not over money," he said. He himself had no gripes at all. He felt that he was doing fine at the Press, that he was well on the way to a permanent supervisory position. His lips curled in a boyish smile, half embarrassed, and his eyes lightened a bit as he said that the others expected him to "stay in" when the strike was called.

I asked how his thinking had gone in the days and weeks preceding the strike. The unions, I knew, had been talking strike for weeks. A strike vote had been taken. What had been Jack's position then?

The answer, apparently, is that Jack had simply not developed a position. He did not think it necessary because he was confident that he would not be called upon to make any decision. To the very end he was sure that there would be no strike. He had even left his tool box in the plant on the last working day before the strike was supposed to begin. The biggest shock of his life came, he said, when he approached the plant at his regular time on Monday morning, March 11. Only then, seeing the "howling mob" blocking the plant entrances, did the reality come home to him. Stunned, sick, stiff in the knees, the brutal fact hit him hard. The strike was actually on.

This was Jack's big moment, perhaps the most critical he had ever faced in his life, or ever will. If not his whole future, certainly a good many years were to be determined by the decision he made, all unprepared as he was, that dark Monday morning. "I wasn't prepared to make a big decision right then, on the spur of the moment. I was prepared only to go in, to go to work as usual. I hadn't even taken my tool box home. It was still there in the plant."

Unprepared, he was in no position to make a reasoned decision; and yet he had to act, nevertheless. The choices were terrifyingly clear-cut: go in or stay out—no other alternatives. He repeated that it was a bad moment, a terrible, belly-grinding moment. He did not have to elaborate. The choice was a terrible one because Jack wanted to go in but was morally and emotionally incapable of challenging the hundreds of belligerent pickets posted all along the ways leading into the plant.

He made up his mind. He had to. The pickets played the dominant external role in the immediate decision, but it will not do to say that the pickets decided for him, as one hears so often in such situations. The fact is that Jack Rhoten's personality and character were the ultimately determining agents. The fundamental truth is that Jack Rhoten was not tough enough inside to enter the plant, much as his mind and his calculation of his long-run best interests may have urged him in that direction.

It was not just a matter of physical courage, though doubtless that was involved, too. Jack said that he might have been capable of the physical act of crossing the massed picket line, if that had been all there would have been to it. What he shrank from was the longer-run prospect, the sustained act of living as a "scab" in a community in which a large proportion of his acquaintances either stood on that picket line or had family members there. He told me frankly that he would rather there had been no strike, yet that he just could not bring himself to cross the line. In his slow, soft, wistful way he said that things might have been different for him at that hard moment had it all occurred in a big city. "But here in Kingsport everybody knows everybody else. People are always running into each other." He would have had to have been more stiff-backed and stiff-necked than he could ever be. An enormous implication rests in this one statement of his: "Not a single other Pressman went in—only supervision." What would have happened if just a few Pressmen had gone in?

Jack Rhoten was not going to be the only Pressman to go in. He would certainly have been a pariah, and only perhaps a hero. But Jack is in any event not the hero type, just a very decent fellow who feels more comfortable when he is not attracting any particular attention.

A strike vote had been held on March 4, just a week before the strike; the "ayes" had won by a great majority. And a strike

rally had been gathered on Sunday, March 10, with much com-
motion and fiery speeches by both national and local union leaders. They had announced with vigor and determination that the
strike was on for the next morning. I asked: "What about the
strike vote, Jack? How did you and the others feel about that?
And what about the strike announcement on Sunday? Didn't
that prepare you? Why should you have been so stunned the next
morning?"

The strike vote was by secret ballot. Among the Pressmen, at
least, there was no hint of pressure or coercion. Pressmen officials aren't the type, and Pressmen themselves wouldn't stand
for it—not in Tennessee, anyway, where by law a man does not
need to belong to a union in order to hold a job. The "Right-to-
Work Law" sees to that. Still the vote was a lopsided 300 to 30,
in favor of the strike. Jack said, however, that the vote in favor
of striking was understood by all the men to be really intended
only to give the Union a firmer bargaining position. The men did
not think, Jack said, that their vote in favor of striking was the
same thing as a strike announcement. They thought that by voting in favor of striking they would induce the Press management
to take the unions' demands more seriously. I might add here
that the phenomenon is well understood in the labor relations
trade. Union leadership will often ask the men to authorize a
strike—not necessarily in the belief that a strike will actually be
called—but simply in order to induce the opposing management
to *believe* that a strike will be called if the Union demands are not
met. Hence there is nothing unusual about Jack's interpretation
of the motivation of the Kingsport Press strike vote.

There is this additional fact, which Jack pointed out. He and
most of the other Pressmen, he said, felt that this strike vote
would come to nothing just as the ones in previous years had
been no more than "collective-bargaining maneuvers." There
had been favorable strike votes before, but there had never been
a strike at the Press before. Indeed, in the immediately previous
negotiations, Jack recalled, there had been both a favorable
strike vote and an actual strike announcement. Precisely as in
1963, there had been a strike announcement for Monday. But it

had come to nothing because an agreement had been reached on Sunday night. He had felt sure that the same thing was going to happen this time. He was therefore not greatly disturbed when the decision to strike was announced on Sunday morning, March 10, 1963. Most of the people he knew felt the same way, he said. The moral seems to be that "it" *can* happen here. Do not believe that merely because "it" has not happened that "it" *will* not happen.

Jack Rhoten bore no personal grudge against the Press management then; though his life is falling to pieces all around him, he bears no grudge against the Press now. "They fought a fight they had a right to fight," he told me.

I saw bitterness and harshness in Jack Rhoten only once in the hours I spent with him. That was when we got to talking about some of his fellow Pressmen who abandoned the strike. Let us be clear about one point, for we owe it to him to establish with precision the extent and firmness of his decency. Jack bears no grudge against all those who went back. He is much too discriminating, too humane, to condemn human beings categorically. He does not resent the return to work of those Pressmen who had never wanted to strike in the first place. He despises and condemns only those who agitated vehemently for the strike before it happened—and then went back to work soon after the strike started.

As we shall see, a fair look at all sides may produce justification for even men of that kind. Still, in the absence of powerfully extenuating circumstances in their favor, I do not see how anyone can find fault with Jack Rhoten's reasoning, or even deplore his attitude toward them. After all, much as the national union leadership may have wanted to call a strike against the Press for unique reasons of its own, the decision to call the strike must have been at least *strengthened* by those working at Kingsport who were vocally strong for a strike. A union can only *call* a strike. Working men must do the striking. It seems unlikely to me that any union leader today—let alone the leadership which one encounters generally in the printing trades—will call a strike when the men themselves are genuinely dead-set against it.

Hence, if it is true, as Jack said, that "the biggest strike agitators were the first to go back," those men seem to me culpable. And if it is also true, again as Jack said, that they went back quickly because "they saw a way to advance themselves," then their culpability is even graver.

One of the more serious mistakes to be made today is to put the blame entirely on union leaders for the quite obviously defective conditions which prevail in labor relations. I am no great admirer of union leaders as a class. Still, there is no point and, what is more important, no accuracy in putting all the blame on them. Others are responsible, too, and not the least responsible are the kind of working men who have aroused Jack Rhoten's animosity. Men of that kind have caused a great deal of harm to society in general. In particular, they have grievously injured such persons as Jack Rhoten, who never wished to strike at all, but who, once having struck, has borne it out even to the edge of doom.

Jack told me that among the thirty who voted *against* authorizing the Union to call a strike were some of the best and most loyal union Pressmen. "Men are still walking the picket line who never thought a strike should have been called, and even voted against authorizing the union to call a strike." I was on the verge several times of asking how *he* had voted. Something held me back, and I never did put the question. My suspicion is that he was among the thirty, not among the 300. This suspicion is based in part on the warmth with which he referred to the thirty and in part on the bitterness he expressed against the "strike agitators." It is based to a great extent on my reading of his character. Jack Rhoten is in my opinion an exceptional man. He goes his own way when he can, gets his ideas from inside himself, lives a life of his own. Such men are more likely than not to be found in the minority. In the secrecy of the vote, Jack could express his individuality, uninhibited by that reluctance to confront the mass man which permeates the character of gentle folk—and which kept him from crossing the picket line that Monday morning in March, 1963.

Charlie Heffner: One Who Changed His Mind

Charles John Heffner, born in Egypt, Pennsylvania, in June of 1919, the son of Austrian immigrants, lively, pugnacious, aggressive, a star high school athlete with letters in football, baseball, and basketball, a professional baseball player for several years before settling down at the Press—Charlie is another kind of man. I am more nearly certain that he voted to authorize the strike than I am that Jack Rhoten voted the other way.

But I do not mean by this to suggest that Charlie Heffner was one of the "strike agitators" who returned speedily to their jobs "in order to advance themselves." On the contrary, up to a certain point Charlie was among those who argued most strenuously against striking. In fact he almost came to blows several times with the "strike agitators" during some of the arguments among the Pressmen in January and February of 1963, when the negotiations were going on between the unions and the Press. Another thing: he stayed out for almost six months. It was late in August before he went back to his job at the Press.

Charlie brought the months preceding the strike into vivid focus for me. Something new and sharp was in the air. Union meetings were being held at Skoby's, the cavernous restaurant on the outskirts of Kingsport, where, although you have to bring your own bottle, you can get steaks and seafood that rival the best in New York. The excitement stirred up at Skoby's flowed outward. Talk in the pressroom was all about the negotiations, and you heard the word "strike" more often and more seriously than it had ever been heard before at the Press. The national union leadership was taking a stern, tough stance. For the first time in the more than twenty years of collective bargaining at the Press, the five unions (Bindery Workers, Electro-Typers, Machinists, Pressmen, and Typographers) were negotiating more or less as a unit. The top leaders announced that they were not going to let the Press, this time, use what they called the "divide and conquer" tactics it had used in the past. They would all hold out together and strike together, if necessary.

Charlie Heffner did not like the strike talk at all. Some of the younger men seemed to him to be going off half-cocked, and he was not the man to keep still in the face of such nonsense. "I told them it was downright silly to go on strike for a few cents an hour. It would take years to make up the money lost in just a month or two of striking." One young man told Charlie as they were changing clothes in the locker room—"You're a lousy union man." Charlie, with one leg tangled in his working pants, looked up and said: "Listen, you squirt, I've been in the union here seventeen-eighteen years, and you've just started."

Charlie might have backed up his testy reply, too. He was forty-four in December of 1962, but compact, tough, and still muscular. Only five feet eight, he weighs 165 pounds, and he carries no more fat now than he did when he was making a living out of baseball.

Charlie takes no guff from anyone, and it is impossible to conceive of him as a diplomat. I had a long talk with him in one of the cubbyholes at the Press. The location did not inhibit him at all. He spoke fast and candidly about his fellow workers, the Union leadership, his supervisors, and the Press management. He had salty, straightforward things to say about them all.

About his fellow Pressmen, he echoed Jack Rhoten's view that most of the men had no serious grievances; that, certainly, like himself, the average mature Pressman would not have dreamt of striking over "money." "Some of the younger fellows, maybe; but not any that had any sense."

Charlie did change, and so did many others. However, that was not till the Union leaders, apparently sensing that the men could not be aroused sufficiently over wages, began spreading the rumor that the Company was going to try to strip the older men of the benefits acquired through seniority. This news, according to Charlie, changed his attitude. "What, exactly, was being said?" I asked. Charlie said: "They tried to put some fear into us. They'd say you finally got a day job. Your supervisor didn't like you personally and would say: 'We need your services on nights,' and back to night shift you'd go. That's what the Union tried to do."

This kind of rumor was perfectly calculated to get Charlie's back up. He was working nights at the time, had been continuously for thirteen long years, and was "fed up to the ears" with it. What hit more sharply than anything else was that by virtue of his seniority he was directly in line for a steady day job. Not having had one for so long, the prospect looked attractive to him in the highest degree; hardly anything gave him more pleasure to contemplate. When he heard it said that the Company was insisting on watering down seniority rights, he was furious. He became as vehemently in favor of striking on the seniority issue as he had been against it on the wage issue. "I assumed that our local and international officers were telling us the truth about the Company's position on seniority. I'd strike again if the Company tried to take my seniority away."

So Charlie went on strike full of conviction, and he put as much pep into his picketing as he had in his work and in his athletics. Clifton Fritschle, the Press's embattled vice-president in charge of labor and public relations, is now, after three years, able to look back with relative calm on the first months of the strike. But those days were tougher on him than on anyone else in the Company—except, perhaps, his second-in-command, Homer Clevenger, manager of the Company's public relations. Both went largely without sleep for the first six months of the strike. The mass picketing, the assaults, the bombings, the blockading of the plant, the almost infinity of forms of harassment to which the unions submitted the Press—all these affected everyone who was trying to keep the Press going, but they seemed to hit Fritschle and Clevenger the hardest. To be called up in the middle of the night was standard procedure for both. They were understandably fed up with the strike, the strikers, and the pickets. Even today, though Homer Clevenger, wry and sophisticated, will crack wise about it now and then, they still see very little to smile or joke about.

Except when talk turns to Charlie Heffner. "Charlie was a good picket, even a great one," Fritschle said to me, with one of his rare smiles. Homer Clevenger amplified: "Charlie out there on that picket line never kept his mouth shut, but still never used any foul or even nasty language, either. He was out there to keep up morale. He was his old baseball self, like a shortstop keeping the chatter going to raise his own and the others' spirits."

Charlie admits to having been a noisy picket, especially in the early days of the strike. But as the weeks stretched out, he turned fidgety, uneasy. He began asking questions, first of himself, and then about the strike issues. The more he learned about the negotiations, the more uncertain he became about the justice and prudence of the strike, and about his own judgment in advocating and supporting the strike.

His peppery independence, his lively sense of his own interest and responsibility, kept him in a constantly questioning frame of mind. He is the kind of man whose very soul quivers when he suspects that someone is taking advantage of him. Moreover, at no time, not even during the earliest days of the strike, did he tie himself very closely to the Union, either mentally or physically. "Many of the guys would hang around Carpenters' Hall [the strike headquarters] all day long. I never did. Oh, I'd check in daily, but never hang around for more than maybe five minutes. I'd see those other birds sitting around that place, soaking up the Union propaganda, and I knew I had to get out and get some air, get doing something."

One of the things Charlie did was a lot of umpiring. As a matter of fact, he said, he averaged about $50 a week. That together with the $50 weekly strike benefits gave him a fair income throughout the period he was on strike. He was not having a bad time financially. He did not go back because he was starving. Something else was involved.

Charlie spent a lot of time, too, in traveling among the larger cities of the middle South, looking for work as a pressman as he umpired. He never could find anything to compare with the wages and working conditions at Kingsport Press, at least not in cities where life was as pleasant and the cost of living as bearable as in Kingsport. He told me that he thought he could have earned more in New York or Philadelphia—more per hour, anyway, though the total annual income might be less. But the cost of living, he felt, would erase any possible gain. Besides, he was extremely attached to his life and his home in Kingsport. The fact is that Charlie has a handsome home on a half-acre of land in one of Kingport's better residential areas. Clifton Fritschle, out-ranking Charlie at the Press by a long measure, says he wishes he had a house as nice as his neighbor's, Charlie Heffner.

Charlie's uneasiness about the strike was sharply increased by an incident which occurred while he was poking around, looking for work in Allentown, Pennsylvania, near where he was born. He had dropped in on a high school friend who was running a printshop in Allentown. He said: "The fellow asked me a lot about Kingsport Press, especially about the pay. When I told him that I averaged $10,000 a year and often made $11,000, and when I told him about our profit-sharing plan—which I heard DeAndrade describe as the best in the industry—my friend said, 'What the hell are you striking about?' That shook me up!"

Charlie was even more shaken, he said, when, along in May, he acquired some new facts about the negotiations between the Press and the unions on the seniority issue. He found out then for the first time that as of the time when he and others had been told that the Press wanted to destroy their seniority privileges, that is, February of 1963, Clifton Fritschle (for the Press) and Claude E. Smith (president of the Pressmen's local union) had already jointly initialed a new seniority agreement. Moreover, he said, the new agreement was more favorable to the men than the old one.

This discovery not only shook Charlie; it just about tore him loose from his union moorings. Remember: he had never wanted to strike over money; seniority had always been his single concern. To learn after more than three uneasy months on the street that there had never been any threat to his seniority was shocking. "I trusted them, and they lied to me," he said.

From then on Charlie's relationship with the Union, the strikers, and the picket line became increasingly distant. Soon he let it be known that he thought he had been played for a sucker. During Union meetings, when the old seniority fear was raised, Charlie would vociferate. "You don't know what you're talking about," he would tell his fellow-strikers.

Charlie Heffner is perhaps unfamiliar with that most momentous of all dicta: "Ye shall know the truth and the truth shall make ye free." But the more he learned about his Union and what he understood finally to be its "real" strike objectives, the closer he came to being freed of any sympathy with either the Union or the strike. He told me that along in June he heard some of the Union officers threaten to "bust" the Press if it didn't make the concessions they sought. At first, he said, this threat puzzled him no end. He went around asking people: "What good is it going to do us or Kingsport or anyone else to bust the Press?" But other things he heard helped to advance his understanding. One item of information he picked up was that a number of Northern book manufacturers were working only three days a week while the Kingsport Press was working six days a week, three shifts around the clock. But the most enlightening information of all, according to Charlie, was that Mr. DeAndrade was pressuring the Press because *he* was under pressure from the Northern shops.

Putting all these facts together, Charlie says that he finally could make some kind of sense out of the alleged plan to "bust the Press." After all, the Union had only a few hundred members in Kingsport as against the thousands in New York, Boston, Chicago, and other large cities in the North. From the point of view of those members it might seem a good thing to reduce the Press's ability to compete against them by raising its labor costs. But where did that leave *him?*

In a flash, Charlie perceived sharply and clearly one of the truths which manages still today to elude the grasp of a great many people, and he simultaneously saw the mythical character of much of what he had heard in Union meetings about "labor solidarity." He saw that a benefit to Pressmen in Boston need not necessarily be a benefit to him down there in Kingsport. If the Union managed to cut down the Press's business, *maybe* the Boston Pressmen would have more work (maybe, too, owing to higher price levels for printing, there would just be less work for everyone). But certainly the Kingsport Pressmen would have less. How that was going to help him, he simply could not see.

"Labor solidarity" is not only an abstraction—it is a *mere* abstraction, a chimera, a myth. There is no more solidarity among wage workers than there is among businessmen or women or Olympic swimmers or any other classifiable human group. Not in an economic sense, anyway. Competition is tough among women for husbands, Olympic swimmers for gold medals, businessmen for profits, and wage-workers for remunerative employment. Charlie was not interested in pursuing this line of thought. "That's for professors," he said. But he knew well enough and immediately that the mere abstraction "labor solidarity," as he saw things at the time, was doing him harm. A practical man living in this world in a moral way has responsibilities which come before such vague talk. "Labor solidarity" was not going to feed, clothe, house, and educate Charlie Heffner's children and grandchildren. He had to rely on the productivity and the prosperity of Kingsport Press and his participation in the work of the Press for that.

Although he did not go back to the Press till the end of August, already in July Charlie had had a bellyfull of the strike. Mind and heart were both full of conviction against it.

For Charlie Heffner it was impossible to keep quiet about something that touched him so sharply and so intimately. He began to criticize the Union and the strike on every possible occasion. Not long after that, Charlie told me, his wife began getting nasty, threatening phone calls, especially when he was away. Charlie collared one of the local Union officers and said: "I don't like this strike, but I'm still striking and I'm being treated as if I'd gone back to work. I'm not going in, but I'm not going to support you any more." According to Charlie, the fellow said: "I don't blame you."

A few days later, though, a move was made to withdraw strike benefits from those who, like Charlie, refused to picket. Charlie threatened to go back to work the minute they quit paying him strike benefits. The benefits continued.

It was no good, however, Charlie said. For him, the strike had lost all meaning, all right, all sense. He could not stay with it much longer. One way or another he had to cut loose from it.

Little by little the basic issue confronting him began to take shape in Charlie's troubled and irritated mind. He had to do something other than the jack-rabbiting around that he had been doing for over five months. He was either going to go back to the Press, get another steady job in town, or leave Kingsport for good.

His wife, Willie Nell, the prettiest girl in Kingsport when Charlie swept her off her feet and still one of the handsomest women in town, figures dominantly in all of Charlie's thoughts. She was suffering, and it was no help to Charlie that she was suffering mainly because he was so continuously upset. Along toward the beginning of August, in the sixth month of the strike, she said to him: "Charlie, should we leave Kingsport, maybe?"

That would mean leaving their charming home, friends, even their oldest child, Barbara Ann, who was married and settled down in Kingsport, too. Willie Nell was seventeen, Charlie twenty-one, when they were married. "We raised each other," Charlie said. Could he take Willie Nell from the town she was born in, from the home she loved, from Barbara Ann, and especially from Barbara Ann's baby, their first grandchild? Barbara Ann tried to be helpful. She said it wouldn't be necessary to separate. She, her husband, and the baby would go wherever Charlie and Willie Nell went.

She helped all right, but not in the way she thought she would. Her offer served to lop off one of the alternatives that Charlie had set. He'd be damned, he said, if he would cause his daughter to move from her home town, where they were all so well settled and content. And that is how three possibilities were reduced to two: either go back to the Press or get another job in town.

The latter possibility was lopped off in roughly the same way. Charlie got a $100-a-week job offer from another Kingsport firm. He thought and thought. The $100 a week would be about half what he made at the Press. At forty-four he had seventeen years of seniority at the Press, while he would be at the bottom of the seniority roster in the new job. The Press had the best profit-sharing plan in the industry—a plan in which he could accumulate more than $50,000 by retirement time. "Why should

I give up all those years—throw them down the drain—and the profit-sharing plan, one of the best things that ever happened to me?" On a hot day, late in August, Charlie arranged his tool box, got in his car, and drove past the pickets.

"They yelled like hell, and are still yelling. But I don't mind. I done my share of that."

Charlie had had a bellyfull. By the time he went back to his job, his confidence in the Union was completely gone. He wouldn't believe anything the Union officials said. On the other hand, his mind was finally cleared of all doubts; he was sure he was doing the right thing.

He has no regrets today about having abandoned the strike. He said to me that he would strike again, if he believed that the Company was going to tamper with his seniority, but he remains sore as a boil about the way in which he believes that the Union "suckered" him.

Charlie Heffner is nobody's man but his own—and Willie Nell's and maybe his young grandchild's, upon whom he dotes. Certainly he is no more a "company man" now than he was before the strike, when he was not at all reluctant to let his feelings be known about conditions in the pressroom. He said to me that in his opinion the Press management and supervisors are more "considerate" now than they were before the strike. It's not that he thought the management ever hard or cruel or insensitive; he reminded me that he would never have favored striking but for the belief that the Company wanted to take away his seniority. As it turned out, he had been misled; the Company was actually disposed to strengthen seniority somewhat. Yet, the fact remains that Charlie *believed* the Company capable of treating its older employees callously. This misapprehension could only have come about as a consequence of a weakness in Charlie's confidence in the Company. Since there was no real basis for the lack of confidence, there must have been a failure of communication somewhere.

Jack Rhoten never wanted to strike at all. He was satisfied with things as they were at the Press, and he saw a solid future for himself there. He stayed out only because he could not bring himself to antagonize his fellows. Charlie Heffner presents a sharp contrast all along the line. Originally against striking when he thought that only wage rates were involved, he turned strongly in favor of striking when he was told—and believed—that the Press wished to take away his seniority. When he learned otherwise, and when he believed that the national Union leadership was interested more in protecting the Northern shops and Union members than in its Kingsport members, he abandoned the strike. He took no pleasure in breaking off with old friends; crossing the picket line the first time was an ordeal. But in his opinion the Union had been guilty of fraudulent misrepresentation. It had broken faith with him, played him for a sucker. Fraud releases a man from any contract. Charlie abandoned only what he thought was a void, fraudulent contract. He had the resolution to pursue his own interests, to face up to his own responsibilities as a husband and a father. He says that he has not for one moment regretted returning to work. I do not know whether Jack Rhoten—or any of the other "bitter-enders," for that matter—can say the same thing about staying out.

And What of the Others?

I have reported my discussions with Jack Rhoten and Charlie Heffner at some length because they seemed to me to define some of the most interesting and revealing features of the strike, from the point of view of the strikers. By the time I began actively to investigate the strike, in January of 1965, it was already almost two years old. By then, the workingmen who began the strike had to strain somewhat in order to remember why they, as individuals, had favored striking in March of 1963, for something much more vital was keeping the strike going than had started it in the first place.

I talked at length with a number of strikers in private interviews, as I had with Rhoten and Heffner, and more briefly with others in groups on the various picketing posts around the Press.

It seemed obvious to me that there had been no sharp motivation among them as of March, 1963. I met not a single one who said that he had been anxious to strike over wages. Of course, one of the *formal* strike issues involved wages, and the workers themselves would all *like* to have had higher wages than the Press was offering. But on the whole they expressed no more feeling on the wage question than one would have expected after examining what Jack Rhoten and Charlie Heffner had to say. Mr. Michael G. Gartner, writing in the *Wall Street Journal* on April 22, 1964, came to a similar conclusion. In an excellent article, he wrote: "Many of the placard-carrying strikers . . . don't seem sure what they're striking about. On a recent rainy day Harvey Light, a bookbinder at the company for seven years before he went on strike, told a questioner at the picket line that 'seniority was the biggest issue,' insisting that 'wages were good.' "

Over eighty-five per cent of the members of each of the five unions bargaining with the Press authorized the strike. This did not mean that all those men and women wanted to or expected to strike. Yet, when the Union leaders actually called a strike they all stayed out. Some, presumably, stayed out because they actively wished to do so; Charlie Heffner represents that category. Others stayed out because they were reluctant to antagonize their fellow Unionists; Jack Rhoten represents that category. Within three months, roughly 200 men and women had abandoned the strike; within six months, about 300; within a year, exactly 398 had gone back in, of the 1740 original strikers.

"This Senseless Strike"

One after another striker told me, in January of 1965, and later, that neither he nor she nor anyone else that he knew expected the strike to last so long. A year earlier, in February, 1964, ten or eleven months after it had all begun, Mr. DeAndrade, in his monthly column in the *American Pressman,* discussed the strike at the Press. Among the thousand or so words that he wrote, three seemed to me remarkable. The three words were: "this senseless strike."

The pickets were sick of the strike. John McLellan was calling it the "mess at the Press." DeAndrade referred to it as a "senseless strike." Hundreds of strikers had returned to work. The workers themselves had never been greatly aroused over the money issues (which, however, as we shall see, the Union officials emphasized greatly). Seniority had mainly stirred them, and that, apparently, was not the real issue they thought it was. Finally, it goes without saying, the Press officials were thoroughly fed up with the strike from the day it was called, and their difficulties increased with each day that the strike went on.

As indicated earlier, there are really two basic questions to ask, not just one. In addition to determining what started the strike, we must determine what kept it going so long. I am able to report that certainly by January of 1965 there was only one unresolved issue keeping the striking and the picketing alive. This issue had nothing whatsoever to do with the original "strike issues," whatever they may have been. By January of 1965 the strikers would have been overpoweringly happy to return to work on the basis of the Company's offer of March, 1963, the offer which they and their unions had originally rejected. What this means is quite clear: it means that the workers and the unions had *lost the strike.*

To lose a strike means that a union has been unable to impose on a company the higher labor costs which it had set as the price of agreement. The company has been able to carry on better without the strikers than they have been able to carry on without their jobs. Without using any kind of force or compulsion, it has been able to find people willing to take the employment it offers at the wages and other working conditions which the strikers and their union have rejected.

Certainly by January of 1965, and probably much earlier, the only obstacle to a return to work by the strikers was the simple fact that jobs were not then available for all of them at the Press. You may ask, after having read the first chapter of this book, "Didn't the strikers and their unions realize that people in Appa-

lachia would flock to the Press whenever jobs were open there?"
I shall reserve comment on that question. We shall be analyzing
and evaluating the unions' strike strategy later. Here we are concentrating on the facts.

By January, 1965, the Press had almost as many employees as
it had when the strike was called. On March 1, 1963, total employment was 2,179. As of January, 1965, it stood at 1,900 (as
of May, 1965, there were 1,983 employed at the Press). Approximately 1,740 went out on strike, leaving 439 who did not
strike. By January of 1965 almost an exactly equal number of
strikers had returned to their jobs, had abandoned the strike as
Charlie Heffner had done. The other 1,100-odd who went to
make up the total of 1,900 employed at the Press in January,
1965, were people the unions and the strikers call "scabs," the
Press calls "new hires," and I, seeking a purely descriptive term,
shall call "striker replacements."

The Press management did not hire "professional strikebreakers"—people who are willing to take jobs temporarily, as a
means of putting pressure on strikers to return to work. Nine
thousand men and women, purely "amateur workers," applied
for jobs at the Press within a few months of the beginning of the
strike. These men and women were seeking permanent jobs.
They would not have confronted the howling mobs which kept
Jack Rhoten out; they would not have suffered the countless
forms of harassment to which striker replacements were and
usually are subjected—but for the promise of permanent employment at the Press, with all the desirable results which such
employment brought with it.

The Press pledged its faith with these men and women. Mr.
William Beneman, vice president and operations manager of the
Press and one of the more impressive men I have met in my life,
has the quiet and collected way about him that comes usually
with an unshakable strength of character. He said to me: "We've
made a commitment to these people, and we've always honored
our commitments. We informed the strikers before we hired the
replacements that the company was going to operate and that if
they did not come in to claim the jobs they had held, we were

going to offer permanent employment to the replacements we hired. I just don't see how we can go back on it and remain a company that people would want to work for or deal with."

There it is. The single reason that the strike goes on today is that the Press is unable to reinstate all the men and women who are still on strike. Of course it is no help that the business of the Kingsport Press has undoubtedly been reduced somewhat by the determined boycotting efforts of the five national unions. All over the country those unions have imposed pressure on Press customers; they have used all the forms of political and economic coercion that they command. Undoubtedly, these tactics have brought some results, have lost the Press some business— *and* therefore reduced the job opportunities of the strikers, the people whom the unions are dedicated to represent. It is a grim situation all around for those people. They were taken out on a strike for which they had little enthusiasm. Now, wishing to abandon it, they cannot. And one of the reasons they cannot is that their unions are reducing the ability of the Press to put them to work.

Even without the boycott losses, however, it is not likely that the Press would be able to provide jobs for all of the strikers who wish to go back to work there. The best estimate is that of the 1,740 original strikers, there are still something like 1,000 who would probably want to return, while the Press has at most not more than 300 or 400 jobs open.

As early as September, 1963, a story in the official Pressmen's Union's magazine, *The American Pressman* (page 18), announced that the "chief stumbling block" to a strike settlement was reinstatement of the strikers. In April of 1964, in the *Wall Street Journal* article already mentioned, Mr. Gartner sensed that the only obstacle to a strike settlement was the question of reinstatement of strikers. A settlement is "stalled," he said, "by seemingly irreconcilable differences over the rights of the workers hired since the strike began. The unions maintain, in effect, these workers should be laid off if the strike is settled to make room for returning strikers. The company adamantly says the new workers are permanent employees."

What was probably true as of September, 1963, and as of April, 1964, when Mr. Gartner wrote, was much more certainly true as of January, 1965. At that time, Mr. McLellan, general counsel of the Pressmen, was conducting negotiations for the unions. From all that I can gather, the only point that prevented ratification by the strikers of the agreement that he had formulated with the Press was the Press offer on reinstatement of the strikers. Press officials have told me that they stretched themselves to the limit—offered to reinstate more men and women than they had jobs for immediately, on the theory that natural expansion would take care of the surplus before too long. Moreover, they said that they had offered to reinstate still more strikers within a fixed period of time and to put the remainder on a preferential hiring list.

But because the Press's best reinstatement offer would leave hundreds of strikers still without employment, or, possibly, without even *hope* of employment at the Press, the workers themselves rejected the strike settlement agreement which Mr. McLellan and the Press negotiators had reached.

The bulk of the unemployment would have been among the bindery workers, the least skilled, perhaps, of the printing trades, and therefore the most likely to be replaced. It is much easier to train a bindery worker than it is to train the others, I am told. Lack of training and experience counts less in the bindery than among the more complicated and difficult printing operations. The reader may want to reflect on this point, especially in evaluating the prudence and common sense of the decision of the five unions to act as a unit, instead of each one's going its own way, bargaining on the basis of its own possibilities and limitations.

4

THE UNIONS' SIDE
OF THE STORY

George L. Berry: An American Original

WITH SAM GOMPERS and John L. Lewis, Major George L. Berry was one of the great originals of American trade unionism. "I appreciate the fact that I am taking up a problem such as no young man of my age has ever had," he said on June 21, 1907, at Brighton Beach, New York. He had just been elected president of the International Printing Pressmen's Union, and he was young—only twenty-four years old.

The Pressmen's Union had 11,000 members at the time, scattered all over the country in precariously established locals, each still viewed with lust by the much older Typographical Union, from which the Pressmen had seceded. With just $23,000 in its treasury, lacking the confidence of printing managements which in those freer days was necessary if a union were peacefully to secure recognition, largely devoid of a firm philosophy and character, the Pressmen's future was something to be made, not a thing assured.

Forty-one years later, on December 5, 1948, while still president of the Pressmen, George Berry died. He had been reelected by acclamation continuously in the intervening years. Eight years after his death his memory was still vivid in the Union. At the end of its convention of 1956, the delegates rose solemnly in tribute. The puny Union of 1907 had become by

1948 one of the most powerful in the printing trades. It had 75,000 members, over $2,000,000 in its treasury, and other substantial assets besides.

To call him an original is to say too little of this extraordinary man. He was born in a log cabin, in Hawkins County, Tennessee, not far from the present site of the Kingsport Press. His father was a man of substance: a captain in the Civil War, a judge, and a legislator. However, George Berry was to benefit only genetically from his father; materially, he was left nothing. While serving as a deputy United States Marshal, Thomas Jefferson Berry was ambushed by moonshiners and killed when his son, George, was only six.

The widowed Mrs. Berry sent George to live with an aunt in Des Moines. That arrangement did not last very long. George soon found himself in a Baptist institution in Aurora, Illinois. That too lasted only a short time. A planter from Mississippi adopted him. Within months, George had had enough of the planter's household. He hit the road. He was nine years old when he struck out for himself.

Details for the next few years are skimpy—someone should do a full biography of George Berry. We know that he went to Jackson, Mississippi. Mr. J. C. Johnson, who gave him his first job, described young George as a "little street urchin without home, or family, or encouragement," and insisted that he did not learn to read or write till he was sixteen. We may doubt this late accession to literacy. For one thing, George's first job, which he held for several years, was as a newsboy with the *Jackson Evening News*. He slept in the pressroom and got up his own meals, but he was also learning to feed the presses and set type— scarcely the environment or the occupation for an illiterate.

Those were the days! Still under sixteen, George left the *News* and hit the road again. Sitting around with men he knew, in later years George Berry was to let one and another story slip out. He worked in a restaurant for a while, as a "pearl-diver"—i.e., dishwasher. Inevitably, he found the Great River and worked for months on one of the stately side-wheelers. Before he was seventeen he volunteered as a private in the Third Mississippi Regiment while the Spanish-American War was going on. The war over, he was out once more looking for work. The job he found was as a feeder in the pressroom of the *St. Louis Globe Demo-crat.* He did some boxing on the side for extra cash. Then he got itchy again.

This time he made a long jump, from St. Louis to the gold fields of Nevada. There, barely turned twenty, he struck it rich; for a while he had three producing mines going at once. He was to be a man of considerable substance ever after.

But he did not stay in mining. He went back to the presses, this time heading still farther west. When he attended the convention at Brighton Beach which elected him president of the Pressmen, he was a delegate from a San Francisco local.

He had already come a long way, by a tortured, strenuous path, but at twenty-four, bursting with energy and ambition, full of great thoughts and long visions, George Berry had really only been tuning up. Now he was ready to go again, not as a mere individual, but as a leader of men. During the next forty years he did a great deal more than build a strong, creative, reliable union. He became one of Tennessee's largest landowners, established and operated a sizable printing business, served on an important mission overseas for President Woodrow Wilson, was a confidant of President Franklin D. Roosevelt, as well as prominent among New Deal architects and administrators, and finally, by appointment, became a United States Senator, though only for one year.

But the great story of George Berry's life, the story which most concerns us here, lies in his trade union career. Self-educated, he had no systematic grasp of political economy. He saw the world through his own eyes, his own experience, and his own logical processes. It is a condition with great defects, but also with great advantages. He could, through ignorance of the harmonizing elements built into a competitive economy, refer to the "anarchists of Wall Street" in objecting to ruggedly individualistic free-enterprisers. On the other hand, he never allowed his New Dealing infatuation with regulatory codes and the control of industry to separate him from ultimate economic truths. Like all New

Dealers, he wanted to take wages and labor costs out of competition. However, as one writer paraphrased Berry's position: "There was no value in setting a $100 rate of pay per week, said Berry, if there was no job, and 'we can't draw out of the business that which is not in it.' "* His speeches and writings are full of appreciation of the problems of the businessmen with whom he dealt. He summed up the theme of his leadership in this way: "We regarded it as an obligation . . . to cooperate with management in an attempt to find a basis of accommodation . . . in order that the industry might continue to print and make profits, so that we might share them."†

When Berry took over as president, the great job before the Pressmen's Union was to convince managements that Union pressmen were worth hiring and that the Pressmen's Union was worth dealing with. George Berry, that is, saw the problem of his union in that light. He wanted no part of terrorist methods of imposing unionization. Man of long vision that he was, he knew with Sam Gompers that the solid future for unions lay with the productive and dependable, not with the thugs, the doctrinaires, and the intransigents. When the Pressmen's Union was first ordered to pay damages for violating a collective agreement, George Berry may have gulped a little, but, though still only twenty-six, he said: "If we expect to advance we must also expect additional responsibilities, and, to be eminently successful, we must meet them squarely."‡ From then on he established and maintained a reputation for carrying out his promises. Businessmen respected him for that and praised him.§ When the Taft-Hartley Act was passed with its rigorous controls upon union conduct, some unions, notably the Pressmen's old enemy, the International Typographical Union, swore they would defy it. George Berry took a different position. He said: "We are not afraid of the Taft-Hartley Bill. . . . We have never taken

---

* Elizabeth Faulkner Baker, *Printers and Technology* (New York: Columbia University Press, 1957), p. 370.
  † *The American Pressman*, Vol. 58, pp. 6–7 (Oct., 1948), quoted in Baker, op. cit., p. 387.
  ‡ Quoted in Baker, op. cit., p. 311.
  § Ibid., pp. 251–55, 276.

nor will we now take the position that we are above the law.
. . . There is an inescapable community of interest between
management . . . and labor . . . [which] is in the interest of
public welfare. . . . It is exceedingly unfortunate for the printing industry of America, of which we are the outstanding and
most important factor, that it is being disturbed because . . .
one of the printing trades unions . . . has attempted to stop
our business on the theory that they are above the law of the
nation."*

No one can study George Berry's life without concluding, as
Miss Baker did in her fine book, that "there is no doubt that
George Berry loved his Union." He had another great love, the
hills of Tennessee, especially around Hawkins County, where
he was born. A chance delay, a nostalgic carriage ride in the
hills, brought to his mind an idea of how the two might fulfill
each other. The carriage driver took him through a great tract
of land which was for sale. It was beautiful, with a small lake,
a hotel, a farm, and plenty of room besides. He saw it immediately as an asset of great potential worth to Pressmen and
their Union. Those were the days when Pressmen frequently
contracted tuberculosis. The air of the Tennessee heights would
be good for them. Healthy Pressmen, too, could come and enjoy
the lovely countryside. The farm would provide food, the hotel
lodging. There would be space, also, for a technical training
school, where Pressmen could build a reputation as the most
valuable and productive components of the printing industry.

George Berry took an option on the land. There have been
many rumors and some scandal about the financing of the operation. The fact is, however, that the place is now almost fully
realized as George Berry first envisioned it. It is called Pressmen's Home, and it is beautiful. Headquarters of the Union as
a whole, the president and other Union officials live there. Pressmen come from all over the country, stay at the hotel, and gain
training at the technical school. It is complete, with swimming
pool and all, though Walter Allen, research director of the Pressmen, told me that the farm is a losing proposition, and that the

* Ibid., pp. 385–87.

operation is not nearly so self-sustaining as George Berry hoped
it would be. But then it must be noted that George Berry is not
now alive to run it.

The story goes that there was a close relationship of long
standing between George Berry and the man who built the
Kingsport Press into a successful operation, Colonel E. W. Palmer. Mr. E. J. Triebe, president of the Press, has told me that
Colonel Palmer deserves high ranking among the great pioneers
of scientific industrial management, that Palmer was one of the
creative breed which saw that careful ordering of production
flow and progressive use of technology were vital to the productivity of industry. Be that as it may, the proximity of the Press
to the Pressmen's Home, Palmer's robust vitality and forward-
looking character, with the progress which they promised for
George Berry's well-loved East Tennessee—all these made it
credible that there was a close relationship between Berry and
Palmer. The precise nature of that relationship is one of the
most fascinating of the themes running through the strike at the
Press.

The Honeymoon Is Over

Among George Berry's many contributions to the Pressmen
certainly not the least was the Pressmen's current general counsel, Mr. John S. McLellan. Still a young man, probably in his
early forties, Mr. McLellan is dark and chunky, drives an expensive car, pilots his own airplane, lives in one of the most
beautiful homes in Kingsport, high on a hill with a marvelous
view, and smokes one cigarette after another. He is keen, tough,
and candid; he knows his way around supremely well; he has a
right to his position among the aristocracy of labor lawyers, the
general counsel of the large, international unions, for he knows
labor law inside out. He knows also the extent to which the cards
in federal labor law are stacked in his favor, and he is not about
to pass up an advantage, even while disarmingly recognizing
that things are what they are. George Berry made John McLellan
his protégé and was proud of him.

McLellan was one of the first people I talked to about the strike. A specialist in labor law myself for almost twenty years, I had heard of McLellan, and we knew many of the same people. There is a cautious kind of free-masonry among lawyers, and there is among them, too, a universal proneness to utilize it, as I did with McLellan. He was as forthright as I had hoped he would be, and I wish here to register my appreciation for the help he gave me in understanding the position taken by the five unions against the Press, especially the position taken by his own union, the Pressmen.

John McLellan told me that in general terms the motivation of the strike was compounded of two independent sources of dissatisfaction with the Press. One, he said, was the dissatisfaction of the workers; the other, the dissatisfaction of the leaders of the large national unions involved. The workers, according to Mr. McLellan, had grievances against the lower level supervision (something, I might add, which is apparently as universal, ineradicable, and inevitable among rank-and-file workers as death and taxes are among human beings generally). The national Union leadership, again as McLellan put it, had taken the position that the Press had been coddled by the previous administrations of the Union.

I asked him to expand on the latter observation. With admirable directness, McLellan told me that the national Union leaders thought that the Press had been coddled long enough. He said that in the view of the current national Union officials, the past relations between the Press and the Union had not been genuine collective-bargaining relationships at all. My notes of our conversation, recorded immediately after our talk, contain the words "company union," and I remember McLellan saying that Pressmen research director Walter Allen and president Anthony J. DeAndrade—the two chief architects of the strike at the Press—were of the opinion that Major Berry and Colonel Palmer had set a pattern of cozy, mutual accommodation which simply had to stop. The Pressmen's Union, according to its current national leaders, was going to have to quit acting like a company union, so far as the Kingsport Press was concerned.

The Press was finally going to have to meet the general standards of the industry as a whole.

When I suggested to Mr. McLellan, on the basis of information I had gathered elsewhere, that wages at the Press were not really out of line with industry standards, everything considered, he declined to argue the point. He observed, quite rightly, that as the Pressmen's lawyer it was not his job to gather and to pore over wage statistics—which can become inordinately complex. He demonstrated his fairness and his respect for Mr. Triebe in a really impressive way. I mentioned that Mr. Triebe had said that the Press was very close to the top industry standards, and that the Union negotiators had failed to take into consideration the Press's handsome profit-sharing plan—which the Press itself calculates as adding about 30 cents an hour, on the average, to its labor costs. Mr. McLellan said that when Triebe said something it was usually pretty close to the truth. He also accepted the possibility that perhaps the Union negotiators had failed to give due weight to the profit-sharing plan.

My general impression from my first talk with Mr. McLellan was that the preoccupation of the unions with "national averages" had had a great deal more to do with the strike than the worker grievances he mentioned. I might add that Mr. McLellan, too, did not think that the workers were aroused to any significant degree over the wage issue. It may be of some significance that he did not mention the seniority issue at all. Perhaps, however, that was merely an oversight; for I failed to raise the question with him.

I thus left John McLellan carrying with me a certain conviction that the strike at the Press had been motivated "from the top," that it was no grass-roots expression of insuppressible worker resentment. I had run into that idea in several places earlier—before I talked to anyone at the Press, and before my talk with McLellan. In the *Wall Street Journal* article to which I have already referred, Mr. Michael G. Gartner said: "The dispute does raise one important question that touches at the heart of labor-management negotiations: to what extent, if at all, should wage scales in other parts of the land, where living costs may be significantly higher or lower, affect contract talks in any particular locality?" Writing in April, 1964, Mr. Gartner came to this conclusion: "It seems certain that the prolonged and acrimonious strike would not have reached its current stage if only local issues had been considered."

I had encountered the same basic idea, in a somewhat different form, from a source much closer to the strike. Mr. Walter F. Barber, an international representative of the International Brotherhood of Bookbinders (one of the striking unions), addressed the Photoengravers' Convention on August 22, 1963, not quite six months after the strike was called. It was a matter of one professional describing to others the technical details of an operation. This is what Mr. Barber told the Photoengravers about the background and strategy of the strike at the Press:

> Although the other printing trades unions throughout the country, through their good negotiations . . . advanced and advanced, we advanced very slowly because of the [lack of?] support of the people in Kingsport, Tennessee. They were still afraid. It was a process of education to show them their rights as an American laborer under the laws of this country. So we did not make the progress and *we got a lot of criticism from a lot of International Presidents because we did not make the progress. There was quite a bit of criticism from the workers and local union officers throughout the country who were doing edition work, the same as Kingsport. There was quite a bit of criticism because we could not do as much in Kingsport as they did, say, in New York, Chicago, Atlanta and any other city where edition work was being printed.* We knew from time to time, that something was going to have to happen. We babied those people there, we educated them very, very slowly. [Emphasis added.]

Mr. Barber went on to tell about the decision made by all five unions to bargain as a unit, and about the trials and tribulations which that decision entailed. The main point of his speech lay, however, in his statement to the effect that the push toward the strike and toward "tough" bargaining with the Press came not from the bottom up, but from the top down. The workers were

more supine than they should have been, so they were being
prodded. The national leaders were stimulated to act, Mr.
Barber said, by complaints from local unions in other areas—
complaints concerning the allegedly low wage standards prevailing among Kingsport Press employees.

No More Sweetheart Contracts

Walter M. Allen, research director of the Pressmen's Union
since 1952, and in earlier days a staff member and organizer of
the United Brotherhood of Carpenters and Joiners, is the kind
of man of whom one hears it said: "He is dedicated to the labor
movement." Mr. Allen is a graduate of Knox College in Illinois
and holds an M.A. awarded by the University of Illinois on the
basis of a dissertation which bears some relevance to the strike
at the Press. Its title is "Bargaining Problems of Industrial
Locals Within a National Craft Union—A Case Study of the
Midwestern Millmen, 1941–1951." Mr. Allen said to me that
one of his most instructive and interesting experiences with the
Carpenters Union involved the problems raised by the competition of unorganized or weakly organized lumber mills against
the tightly organized mills in Chicago and other large mid-
Western cities. His job, he said, had been to cut down the dif-
ferential in labor costs between the two, so that the organized
mills would not be driven out of business and their union employees thrown out of work.

Mr. Allen was a great deal harsher on the Press management
and the strike issues than anyone else I met. "This strike was a
long time coming," he said. He did not think it could have been
headed off. He said that the whole background of relations between the Press and the five unions with which it dealt was
bound sooner or later to break out in a serious strike. According to Mr. Allen, the Kingsport Press had always been anti-
union in the old days—that is, in the twenties and early thirties.
Then, still according to Mr. Allen, Colonel Palmer got the idea
that he would have less trouble getting orders from publishers
if he could pass the plant off as a union shop. So, in order to

gain relief from union-inspired boycotting, Allen said, Palmer invited unions in, even though the people in the area knew nothing about unions and were, if anything, antagonistic to them.

Mr. Allen was blunt. He said in so many words that there was a "sweetheart" relationship, not real collective bargaining, between Colonel Palmer and the unions he had invited in. I might point out that in the trade a "sweetheart contract" is one in which the wages and working conditions are simply those which the employer wishes to put into effect. Such a contract is a mask covering a corrupt relationship. The union involved is usually referred to as a "racket union," operated by men who have no interest in the workers they supposedly represent. They are interested only in the money which the employer turns over to them, either in the form of checked-off dues or some other more or less disguised form of bribery.

I do not think that Mr. Allen intended to accuse his own union of having been as corrupt as that, but he came pretty close. He said: "There were no really opposing forces in the days of Colonel Palmer and Major Berry; there were accommodations. As a result, without the unions really striving to get all they could for their members, Kingsport Press wages lagged seriously. Furthermore, the Press followed a divide and conquer strategy. The unions bargained separately, and each felt itself too weak to come to a flat confrontation with the Press."

Mr. Allen said that the unions did not intend in the 1963 negotiations to try to close the gap entirely between wages at the Kingsport Press and those in comparable book-manufacturing firms. The intention was only to keep the gap from widening. Specifically, he said, the unions had decided to aim at a flat increase in the same absolute amount as had been gained on the average in the printing industry as a whole. That would come to about 10 or 11 cents per hour, or 3 per cent on the basis of journeymen wages throughout the industry. The Press at first offered to sign a three-year contract providing for no increase at all in the first year, an 8-cent-per-hour increase in the second year, and a similar 8-cent increase in the third. After a certain amount of negotiating, said Mr. Allen, the Press raised its offer to 5-8-8. I observed that this move brought the parties pretty close together, but Mr. Allen said: "No, not really. We wanted 10-10-10 across the Board, the Press offer was only for the top-paid people and was to be scaled down so that hundreds of lower-paid people would be getting increases of not more than 2½ cents per hour."

"Even so," I said, "it would seem that there was not so great a gap that it was insurmountable." Here I may add that Mr. McLellan had expressed the opinion to me that perhaps the strike might have been avoided if both parties had been a little more compliant. Mr. Allen, however, said that the strike came because the Press management misjudged the seriousness of the unions and of the employees, underestimated their "determination to see this one through."

Allen said: "Triebe dared us to take these men out on strike. 'These are my people,' he said. Well, we took them out, rubbed his nose in it. We figured that we proved our point by taking the men out solidly and then we went in four days later suggesting a quiet meeting in which we'd settle. We met quietly enough, in a motel dining room. Walter Smith [ex-president of the Press and chairman of the board at the time the strike was called] said: 'Well, you called the meeting, now you can come back or stay out.' We came down to 8-8-8 across the Board, but the Press held firmly at 5-8-8 on a sliding scale, which really meant, on the basis of our demands, only 3½-5½-5½. That difference was too big for us to accept. The strike continued."

There were other serious issues, Mr. Allen said. The unions wanted a strict, rigid seniority system, like the one that prevails on the railroads. They would have been content to relax this demand somewhat, so that the senior qualified man would be entitled to the promotion or shift change or whatever other job plum might have been in issue. An arbitrator would be authorized to settle any case in which the union and the Press management failed to agree on the qualification question, under the union's last proposal. The Press, however, was very much against giving such authority to an outside arbitrator.

As a matter of fact, said Allen, the unions wanted terminal

arbitration on all problems arising under any agreement that might be reached, whereas the Company would agree to go no further than the fragmentary arbitration provisions of the existing agreement.

Then, too, there was a sharp conflict on the hours issue. Most of the industry, Allen said, was on a 37½-hour basis for the day shift, while Kingsport Press stuck tenaciously to a 40-hour day shift (though its second shift was 37½ hours and its third 35 and had been for many years). The unions asked to have the day shift reduced to 38¾ hours in the second year of the contract, in addition to the 8-cent increase for that year. The Press would go to 38¾ hours but only after 40 months, according to Allen— and, at that, he added, it wanted the reduction in hours balanced by a reduction in the wage-increase it was offering.

Mr. Allen said that as serious as the differences were between the parties on wages, hours, and so on, all those were secondary in the opinion of the unions and their members. The primary objective of the fateful 1963 negotiation for the unions, he said, was to see that the unions had a real voice, and a continuing voice, in representing the interests of the workers in the plant. He said: "The plant had become inbred over the years. The nepotism practiced by low-level supervisors had reached an absurd point. Top management knew this and approved it. Bloodlines counted more than ability, also what church you went to counted a lot. If you got a son into a Sunday school class taught by your supervisor you were on the ball."

Mr. Allen expressed the opinion that the Press management had gotten out of touch with its workers, did not appreciate the sentiments that were brewing in them, regarded as still simple hillbillies workers who had become much more complicated and exigent. These are Allen's words: "As Kingsport Press hired more and more union men with its expansion, it had to go to people not in the cozy club, and the new men, better educated, more worldly, not quite so provincial, detested the idea of having to suck up to the supervisors."

I wanted to discover how much of the motivation for the Union's firm stand on wages came from pressure exerted by the

Northern employers and employees, but I had to be cautious about putting the question. I had good reason to be. When I asked Mr. McLellan whether the unions were more concerned to defend the interests of the Northern book manufacturers and workers than to advance those of the Kingsport workers, he almost exploded. He said: "I would have to resign if I thought that the Kingsport workers were only being used as a pawn by the unions!"

I put it this way to Allen: my inquiries among the strikers had turned up no great animosity toward the Press—no particularly strong feelings about working conditions, and almost no feeling at all on the wage issue. Why then, I asked, did the unions push so hard on the wage issue?

Allen repeated at this point that the wage issue was not all that important for the unions, and he emphasized that the main drive was toward getting the unions a genuine voice in the representation of the workers. But he also said this: "If Kingsport Press is allowed to run loose on labor costs, as it has been, then you get a disproportionate amount of production and employment in the lowest wage areas." Allen apparently has a keen sense of harmony and proportion, for he also remarked that "Kingsport Press is making a disproportionate profit margin— much more profit than Plimpton or Riverside [two other book manufacturers]."

Nor Apologies for the Press Contract

Since I was never able to make contact with Mr. Anthony J. DeAndrade, president of the Pressmen's Union and one of the central figures in the strike, it is impossible for me to report directly his feelings about the negotiations. However, sources of insight into Mr. DeAndrade's attitudes are available, quite reliable ones at that.

The first of these is composed of the minutes of the negotiating sessions, recorded by Mr. Homer Clevenger, manager of public relations for the Press.

According to Mr. Clevenger's notes, Mr. Allen, who was leading the negotiations for the Pressmen, said that the Kingsport Press contract was "an embarrassment to the International president [DeAndrade] with other locals around the country." Allen went on to say that the International had been accused of "sweetheart" relations with Kingsport Press; that the Pressmen wished to "get the heat off" Kingsport by starting an hours reduction; that if the 40-hour day shift continued, Kingsport Press would have an unfair position in the industry; and that if the Press reduced hours it would remove criticisms by both the unions and competitive managements.

The Clevenger notes ascribe to Mr. Allen still more direct references to the industrywide aspects. Allen is reported as voicing the Pressmen's concern with keeping any one company from getting a corner on the market; as insisting that the International officials were "not getting competitors off their backs" with what they were asking of the Press; and as complaining that he wanted to get only to the point where he did not have to apologize to competitors of Kingsport Press.

These are further excerpts from the Press's minutes of the negotiations:

> On February 28, 1963, Allen said all the locals in Kingsport are part of internationals and there are many relationships between competing firms, and these have a bearing on the welfare of all union employees.
>
> He said it is contrary to the premise on which unions were formed for a local to think only of itself. He said they should keep their labor costs in line with competitors of their own company.
>
> He said they don't want to lock horns with Kingsport Press to get a contract—but if the Press says nothing more can be done (in meeting the union's demands) then one of us must be forced to our knees. . . . that in light of this the Company ought to reconsider so they (the unions) would not have to be put into a position to call names and take other drastic measures.

There is no reason to believe that Mr. Allen was speaking for himself only. On the contrary, there is every reason to believe that he was speaking for all five unions in general, and for Mr.

Anthony J. DeAndrade, president of the Pressmen, in particular.
Mr. Allen's comments, both to me personally and as recorded in
the Press's minutes of the negotiations, reflected essentially the
same sentiments which Mr. Walter F. Barber of the Bookbinders
had expressed at the Photoengravers' Convention just a few
months later in August, 1963. Official spokesmen of the other
unions said the same thing in one form or another.

One of the five allied unions, the International Typographical
Union, ancient enemy and still more ancient parent of the Pressmen, presented the unions' position in much the same way as
Allen had done in the negotiations and as Barber had before the
Photoengravers. Barely a month after the strike began, a front-
page story in the April 18, 1963, edition of the *ITU Review,*
official organ of the Typographers, sharply and boldly advanced
wages and the problems of industrywide "harmony" or "competition" as the central issues. It said:

> The main issue in the strike is wages, which are some 20 per
> cent below the industry's norm. Kingsport Press' employees
> have averaged, over the past ten years, wage raises of roughly
> 1½ per cent per year as against the industry's average of
> three per cent. Also, no major competitor of the Press is
> still on a 40-hour week for production employees, as the Press
> is. These two elements, coupled with six-day, three-shift opera-
> tion put the Press' competition at an extreme cost disadvan-
> tage. Management, according to union officials in Tennessee,
> has dreams of a near-monopoly in the book publishing field by
> underbidding and freezing out other firms with more realistic
> labor relations.

About a year after the strike began, the allied unions issued
an undated pamphlet entitled "WHY." The foreword to this
pamphlet, in contrast to the theme of the *ITU Review,* said that
"it was past-era management attitudes, more than the inadequate
economic proposals, which precipitated the strike." On the
third (unnumbered) page of the pamphlet, the writer objected
to a statement made by the Press management to the effect that
the strike issues, as the Press saw them, were purely economic,
not personal in nature. The pamphlet said: "Such a conclusion

clearly shows the Company's callous disregard for any moral responsibility to the workers whose only fault was daring to question the fairness of the employer."

The pamphlet then asked this question: "Are workers to be regarded as pawns upon a chessboard, to be moved about at the employer's will or to be replaced as though they were pieces of wood?" The reply by the writer of the pamphlet: "No! We contend there is nothing more personal than this struggle to improve or retain the jobs which workers have held all of their adult lives."

I have presented this statement because it reflects one of the themes constantly encountered among the union officials. When the appropriate time comes—after still more facts about the strike have been disclosed—we are going to have to try to unravel the various causal factors of the strike. The contention that the Press was "callous," with its reinforcing suggestion that the Press sought to move workers around like pawns, is among the more difficult and significant of the charges that we shall have to evaluate. Remember that Mr. Allen had said much the same kind of thing to me in the interview which I have reported a few pages earlier.

Perhaps I should add here that I did not happen to encounter any strong resentment of Press "callousness," or the feeling that the Press had moved them around like pawns, among the rank-and-file strikers. I encountered strong feelings of that kind only in the union literature and in the remarks of the union officials. Of course that may be a consequence simply of the fact that rank-and-file workers are not accustomed to think in such terms or express themselves at that level of abstraction. On the other hand, Charlie Heffner, who had neither talent nor taste for philosophizing about the strike, did express sharp resentment about the way in which his union had, in his opinion, "played him for a sucker."

DeAndrade and the JAYCEES

For years Anthony J. DeAndrade has been a high elected official of the Pressmen's Union, dating back to the days when

George Berry, the Pressmen's old maestro, dominated the Union's personality and coordinated its activities with the same supreme authority that Arturo Toscanini used to command the La Scala orchestra. Finally, in 1959, two other men having served in the post since Berry's death, Mr. DeAndrade was elected president of the Pressmen's Union. Taking over the presidency meant writing in the Union's excellent magazine, *The American Pressman,* the monthly "President's Letter," which George Berry had instituted. It has always been a matter of considerable pride, cherished and vaunted by working Pressmen and their officials, that the Pressmen's Union has a reputation, dating back, as apparently all its reputations do, to George Berry, of being anything but a "strike-happy" union. Many of Mr. DeAndrade's monthly contributions to *The American Pressman* boasted about that reputation.

One of Mr. DeAndrade's monthly articles, however, lamented the more recent events involving his union—events which, whether or not he intended by his reference to them to do so, tended to darken the Union's reputation for avoiding strikes. The article, beginning on page 2 of *The American Pressman* for July, 1963, was mainly an appeal to Pressmen all over the nation for contributions to the Kingsport Press strike fund. Mr. DeAndrade wrote:

> *Do our members believe that the $1.00 per month per member assessment is adequate to meet strike benefit payrolls likely to occur?* [Mr. DeAndrade's emphasis.] Our defense fund is not very old and we have had an up and down experience related to it. With about 58,000 members contributing to the Fund it took close to a year to build a minimum $500,000 before expenditures were allowed. At that time, other than Seattle and Miami newspaper strike situations there were but a few work stoppages and the Fund continued to build up to over $750,000. Then the roof caved in. First there was the Cleveland newspaper shutdown, involving some 300 members, with the extraordinary New York City shutdown following upon its heels which added more than 2,200 on strike benefits. Altogether, and for several weeks, there were more than 2,600 members receiving

$50.00 per week benefits or an outgo of $130,000 per week. . . .
[T]hen the Kingsport strike, which could not have been avoided
honorably, followed. The payment of strike benefits in Kingsport alone now exceeds the income from the $1.00 per month
assessment. We can be grateful that our Defense Fund was created to partially meet our needs but it should be clear to all that
it is not fully adequate.

Mr. DeAndrade went on to emphasize the peculiar importance
of the strike at the Press to Pressmen all over the country. He
repeatedly stated that their interest was direct and immediate
owing to the competitive threat that Kingsport Press posed for
their own employers. He said:

> *Is it possible that our membership has failed to grasp the im-*
> *portance of the Kingsport strike or its relationship to the future*
> *success of each member through his own local?* [Mr. DeAn-
> drade's emphasis.] . . . The Kingsport Press is a major book
> printing plant, in national competition, which consistently has
> been behind its competitors in wages and working condi-
> tions. . . .

On other occasions, Mr. DeAndrade was much more explicit
concerning the competition-motivation for the strike. One such
occasion was a meeting with the members of the Junior Chamber
of Commerce (the "Jaycees") in Kingsport on June 14, 1963,
when the strike violence in Kingsport was at its frenzied peak.
One person in the audience asked Mr. DeAndrade, according to
a report in the *Kingsport Times* for June 14:

> Whether the strike was for the benefit of workers at the Press
> or for the benefit of workers and firms that compete with the
> Press.

According to the story in the *Times,* Mr. DeAndrade's direct
answer to this question was: "No, that isn't so. The workers
here are concerned about the welfare of their fellow craftsmen
in other cities."

If you will read the reply over again, I believe you may find it making more sense recast in this way: "Yes . . . but the workers here are concerned about the welfare of their fellow craftsmen in other cities." For Mr. DeAndrade was obviously saying that the strike turned upon the welfare of the "fellow craftsmen in other cities." He was speaking in terms of the "labor-solidarity" concept which Charlie Heffner had come to think of as a pure but harmful myth.

There is no doubt that in calling the strike Mr. DeAndrade was reacting to the competitive threat which he supposed that the Press was posing for the Northern firms. In the main body of his speech, again according to the *Kingsport Times* for June 14, 1963,

> He spoke frequently of the unions' "major reason" for seek-ing higher wages, shorter hours, and longer vacations in the negotiations surrounding the strike. He said the wages paid at the Press were considerably lower than those paid at New York, Boston and Philadelphia printing firms, although they are higher than most paid in other Kingsport plants.

As a matter of fact, Mr. DeAndrade made it absolutely clear that consideration of the welfare of the Northern firms and workers had motivated him sharply. Still according to the *Kingsport Times,* "Mr. DeAndrade said that 'pressure from the Press' competitors' was a major factor in the unions' demands."

For much the same reason he said that he did not regret that the strike had frustrated the Press's plans for expansion. Some-one in the audience asked him if he thought that halting con-struction of a new plant which the Press was building in Hawkins County was not a high price to pay for striking, in view of the many jobs that would have been created. Mr. DeAndrade re-plied that this creation of new jobs in Kingsport "would cost jobs elsewhere."

The Jaycees, upset by the strike's economic cost and still more deeply afraid that the growing violence would make life an absolute hell in Kingsport, kept probing at Mr. DeAndrade.

They asked him "what part the Kingsport cost of living had played in the unions' arrival at negotiating wage demands." Mr. DeAndrade's answer suggests that they may have caught him off balance with that question. He said "Kingsport's cost of living should be a factor in figuring the union's demands," but that he had "no idea what the cost of living is [in Kingsport] and that it had not been a factor in the negotiations."

There are subtle difficulties involved in resolving questions of causation and motivation in human affairs. Mr. DeAndrade's appearance before the Jaycees in Kingsport presents a tantalizing example. He denied that the strike was motivated more sharply by concern for printing firms and printing tradesmen elsewhere than it was by concern for Kingsport workers themselves. Yet he also said a number of things which cannot be squared with that denial. He said that he had been moved to act by pressure from Press competitors. He said that Pressmen all over the country had a vital interest in the strike at the Press. He said that he did not regret halting the expansion plans of the Kingsport Press because carrying out those plans would cost jobs elsewhere. He said that the cost of living in Kingsport *should* have been a factor in arriving at the unions' demands but that it had not been. Finally, he said in so many words that the Kingsport workers were to benefit from the strike only in the sense that they "are concerned about the welfare of their fellow craftsmen in other cities."

Summing Up

It seems to me that only one conclusion can be derived logically and accurately from Mr. DeAndrade's various comments. When he referred to what motivated him to act, he referred to a fact—that is, the pressure exerted on him by Kingsport competitors. Again, his state of mind concerning the Press's expansion plans was a fact. Finally, his confessed ignorance concerning the cost of living in Kingsport involved a matter of fact. All these were not only facts, but facts known better to Mr. De-

Andrade than to anyone else in the world, for they were facts relating to his own consciousness.

On the other hand, his denial that the strike was designed more for the benefit of workers elsewhere than for the benefit of the Kingsport strikers possessed nothing of the factual quality characteristic of his other statements and admissions. It was an argument, or possibly a theory, but not a fact. It was something easy to say, and very politic to say, in all the circumstances. It would scarcely do to tell men preoccupied with the welfare of Kingsport that their town was being hideously disrupted in order to ease the competitive strain upon high-cost book manufacturers in faraway places. The strikers themselves might have revolted if they had been told that the sacrifices they were making were for the benefit of workers elsewhere. We know how Charlie Heffner reacted when he suspected that the strike was a response to pressure from Kingsport competitors.

The only conclusion that one may logically draw is, to put it in the most cautious form, that Mr. DeAndrade was motivated *primarily*—according to his own statements—by the nationwide or industrywide competitive considerations. This is not to say that the union officials had no interest at all in the men and women employed at Kingsport Press. It is only to say that the direct and immediate interests of those men and women were, at the time, less vividly preoccupying the union leaders than other problems were. The real reason for the strike was not that Charlie Heffner, or Jack Rhoten, or Hugh Reece had one or another criticism to make of how the Press was being run. It was, as Walter Allen, Walter Barber, and Anthony J. DeAndrade put it repeatedly, in many different forms, that the Press's allegedly low labor costs were posing a competitive threat in the industry—that a "disproportionate amount of work" was going to Kingsport.

5

THE COMPANY'S SIDE

Ed Triebe: Soft Heart, Tough Mind

EDWARD J. TRIEBE has spent almost all his working life at the Kingsport Press, this year marking his fortieth with the Company. At one time or another, he has done with hand, heart, and mind every job that there is to be done in a plant which takes raw paper and ink and turns them into a hard-bound book.

His parents were German immigrants of modest condition who raised their son and their two daughters in Queens County, New York. Ed Triebe went to the New York City public schools, spent a year at New York University's School of Engineering, and then went to Annapolis, the U.S. Naval Academy, for three more years. At the Academy he was among other things business manager of its annual, *The Lucky Bag*. In life's strange way, editing *The Lucky Bag* in 1924 started Ed Triebe on the steep path which led to the top of the hill for him, the presidency of Kingsport Press, in 1960.

Putting together a college annual is a ticklish job. Good make-up calls for taste, experience, and a fair knowledge of the printing process. Like most college editors, midshipman Triebe got help from the firm which did the printing, the J. F. Tapley Company. Mr. E. W. Palmer went down from Tapley to Annapolis to give him a hand, and they took to each other immediately. Ed Triebe says today that he has never been as swiftly and as profoundly impressed by any other man. When Palmer offered him a job at Tapley, he took it. Palmer left

Tapley to go to the Kingsport Press, and Ed Triebe followed him in six months, going on the payroll as an executive trainee at $35 per week on January 26, 1926.

Organized in the mid-twenties, Kingsport Press ran in the red till the mid-thirties, when it first began showing a modest profit. The sustained deficits year after year were hard to take, especially since they seemed to trace in part to Palmer's idea that the best way to run a book-manufacturing company was as a fully integrated operation.

Manufacturing a book is a complicated job. In fact, each operation is inordinately complicated: typesetting, proofreading, the gravure work—line cuts and screens—lithography in many forms, the makeready and the printing on the big presses in all their variety, paper handling, no mean job in itself, stitching and binding, making and fixing covers, storage and mailing. Everything needs maintenance at all times and repairs all too often. And that is only the manufacturing end of the business. The commercial end sometimes seems even more hazardous. In commercial printing, as contrasted, say, to newspaper publishing, there is competition for the printing jobs, and it is keen. Cost calculations must be sharp and precise. Contracts are won or lost on differences of a fraction of a penny per copy. It is simpler in every way to conduct a one-operation printing concern. But Colonel Palmer was sure that no matter how unpromising it seemed in the short run, the long run future belonged to the fully integrated book manufacturers. It looks today as though he was right.

In any event, Palmer's policy had a very practical consequence for Ed Triebe. Over the years he became familiar with every aspect of book manufacturing. Ever since 1926, his job at the Press has been—in every sense—his full-time job. He used to spend almost all of his waking hours doing one thing or another at the Press, everywhere in the plant, the composing room, the pressroom, the bindery, even the eerily quiet proofreading room. "Colonel Palmer used to kid me in the old days about the dubious prospects of my next paycheck. I never worried, though, because I never really cared. I was having the time of my life. I wouldn't have traded it for any other."

I was talking one day with one of the Press's young super-intendents, Jim Shelton, a man who is not remarkably self-effacing. He said to me: "There isn't any one around here knows more about these presses than Mr. Triebe does. I don't know how he does it." I heard much the same kind of comment from people in other departments. The main difference was that the rank-and-file workers tended to call him Ed Triebe, rather than Mr. Triebe. And as they did so, there was no evidence of a callow, boastful, or strained familiarity. Walking around the plant in his shirtsleeves, as he always does, Ed Triebe falls easily into conversation with the men running the machines, and when he puts his arm over the shoulders of a Pressman, especially an oldtimer, it seems an entirely natural act. I could not help remarking to him once that he was either one of the best and most affectionate of human beings or one of the biggest "pho-nies" I had ever met. He laughed. I have yet to encounter anyone of Triebe's acquaintance who has expressed anything but respect, and usually fondness *plus* respect, for him—including, as I have already said, the men who are still out on strike after three years.

Ed Triebe has knitted himself as tightly into the life of Kings-port as he has into the operation of the Kingsport Press. He has been the chief officer or has figured centrally in so many civic organizations and activities that it would take a printed page to list them all. And if perchance there happened to be a welfare organization in which Ed Triebe was not active, his wife prob-ably had something to do with it. I have the impression that E. W. Palmer was involved here, too. Mr. Triebe told me that E. W. Palmer had been a man of unlimited energy and ability, practical and visionary, an apostle of scientific management, a pioneer in organizing, rationalizing, and systematizing business management. But that is not what he told me first about Palmer. The first thing he said was, simply, that E. W. Palmer was a great "humanitarian." Since E. W. Palmer was quite obviously the person above all others who shaped Ed Triebe's character, it seems likely that his "humanitarianism" rubbed off, too.

In any event, whether you like it or not, Ed Triebe is a busi-nessman—a profit-seeker, the biggest stockholder of Kingsport Press, its chief executive officer—who is also friendly, universally well liked, as comfortable as an old shoe to be with, *and,* on top of everything else, an incurable "do-gooder." When I objected to his strenuous efforts in favor of fluoridating Kingsport's water supply (on the ground that each person has a right to make up his own mind on such therapeutic issues, except possibly where infectious diseases are involved), Ed Triebe said: "But it's proved that fluoridation reduces cavities."

In my opinion, Ed Triebe does not fit the pattern of the businessman who normally gets into a knock-down, drag-out fight with unions. I asked him how he felt about unions, recognizing as I did so that the question may have been poorly timed, since he was then in the middle of a strike and was having a strenuous time of it convincing important customers that they should continue dealing with the Press in spite of the unions' widespread boycotting campaign. The answer came calmly and candidly: "This company has always been, and I personally have always been, what you might call 'pro-union.' We've gotten along well with unions in the past, and we expect to get along all right in the future. Union leaders and union men can be unreasonable at times, just like any other men, and the unions have been unreasonable, unseeing, and unfair with us in this case. But that doesn't mean that they are inherently bad. It just means that they are human, that they can make mistakes, too, and that there has to be some kind of check on their conduct, just as there is on everyone else's."

Triebe's predecessor in the presidency of the Press, the present chairman of the board, Mr. Walter F. Smith, is a man, incidentally, of much the same attitude. Several years before the strike, he had said in a speech to a business audience:

. . . in all phases of our training programs representatives of the five unions in our plant are always welcome to participate. We have a happy relationship with those unions, and I think I know why. It is a fixed policy with us to give every employee an opportunity to work a six-day week, for, in terms of building a home, buying a car, or sending a youngster to college, that day of time-and-a-half raises the take-home pay more comfortably above the subsistence level. It is a fixed policy with us automatically to give to all unions whatever benefits are granted any one union in negotiation. We meet our people as neighbors in the same town, believing that they are intelligent and fair-minded; and we are determined to do our level best to show them that we in management have moderate intelligence and sincere hearts. Of course, by now we have a tradition of labor-management harmony. When more than 10 per cent of the employees of a company have been with that company for twenty-five years or longer, and when many of those people, having risen through the ranks, hold positions as supervisors and officers of management, history begins to write corporate policy.

Something more of the present flavor of the Kingsport Press management may be gained from listening further to Mr. Smith's management philosophy and practice, for all the present Press officers express largely the same sentiments. Here are additional excerpts from Mr. Smith's speech:

This is why, when we send a man to a campus in Tennessee or elsewhere to take intensive short-course training in some technical specialty, we continue to pay his salary. This is why we give enthusiastic encouragement to the voluntary effort of our employees to teach one another through an organization that they call the Bookcraft Club. . . .

We understand perfectly well that if our industry is to prosper, books in the future must be made quicker, better, and cheaper; the squeeze, or the challenge . . . is upon management to increase its skill. Gone is the day when a book-manufacturing plant could afford to expose itself to a dozen out-of-plant processors or suppliers where the cost of making a book could be skyrocketed through error or lack of responsibility. The book manufacturer of today or tomorrow . . . must streamline his operation to save time, cut costs and give his skilled craftsmen opportunity for working at an honest, relaxed, productive pace.

Our plant, when we completed our expansion program, covered about thirteen acres, yet a system of conveyor belts made the operation snug and sensible. Indeed, those belts did more:

they carried books that our employees once lifted and transported in their arms; and he who relieves even a short backache—or, more explicitly, a succession of short backaches—brightens the day's labors, increases efficiency, and sweetens the toil of the years after fifty. The basic function of automation is too little publicized, and perhaps, at times, too little understood even by management. I can speak only for the Kingsport Press belief that automation must be the servant of skilled labor; to us, the real goal of automation is to permit our employees to work with greater, more thoughtful effectiveness. When, for example, we added teletypesetters to our composing room, we placed journeymen compositors at the keyboards. Others, if they like, may put less skilled operators at such keyboards, at whatever resentment within the ranks of labor its costs them; if we do not respect the skill of our farmers-turned-expert-craftsmen, we are lost.

All that Mr. Smith had thus set down in formal and connected style in his speech Ed Triebe let out in bits and pieces, in the course of the many discussions, short and long, that I have had with him: warm, neighborly interest in the men and women employed at the Press; confidence that the interest and the loyalty were reciprocated; and on the other hand, an active intent to keep the Press striving at the frontiers of printing technology so that it might compete successfully and continue to make profits, in the interests of the workers as well as the stockholders.

Inevitably, I had to ask Ed Triebe why he decided to take a strike, rather than make the concessions sought by the unions—just as I had asked the union people why they struck, rather than take what the Press had offered. Triebe said: "Walter Allen and Mr. DeAndrade have been wrong and misleading and misled about many things, but Allen was right about one thing. For a long time I just did not think that the unions could take our people out. As we came up to the deadline, by about the first of March, I began to realize that there was probably going to be a strike, however unwilling I thought the men and women who worked here might be, and however wrong the strike might be.

But I must say that before then I thought our people had too much sense, that they were too well aware of how deeply their interests were tied in with the Press's, to allow themselves to be dragged out on a strike which they obviously did not want."

I asked: "Then why didn't you give in, when you finally realized that a strike would be called?" What Triebe responded, was in effect that if you want to be soft-hearted, you are compelled to be tough-minded at times, otherwise you can do nothing for anyone. In other words, the offer he had finally made—the 5-8-8—represented the limit to which he felt the Press could go, consistently with his guiding principle. That principle meant being fair to employees, stockholders, and customers of the Press. If by being overly soft with the unions he damaged the interests of the stockholders and the customers of the Press, all would suffer in the long run. And he, as the officer chiefly responsible, had to make the critical decision. It fell to him to decide at what point he was doing the fair thing. He told me that his fear was not that he was offering too little, but that he was offering too much, in terms of the general welfare of the Press owners, its customers, and its employees.

One cannot be fair in a vacuum. There must be standards, guidelines, criteria upon which such judgments are made. What influenced Ed Triebe? What were his guidelines? How could he tell when he had reached the limit of what was fair?

"DeAndrade Neglected His Homework"

Precisely at this point, Triebe brought up a fact which, he said, the unions seemed never to have noticed, and certainly never had mentioned, in their strike propaganda. The unions made a great deal of the competitive threat posed by the Kingsport Press to other book manufacturers. They spoke as though the labor costs at the Press were so far below the industry averages that other firms could not compete with it. But, said Triebe, all that was just not true. As a matter of fact, he pointed out, and demonstrated to me, the Press had in open bidding lost vastly more contracts than it had won, in fact twice as many. Moreover, production and profits were both down sharply at the Press in 1962, the year preceding the strike. (Sales dropped 9 per cent and profits a heavy 38 per cent in 1962.) "I have to keep our production and profits up," he said. "Otherwise I'm not doing my job for anyone—not the employees, not the stockholders, and certainly not the customers we have and would like to have."

I interrupted at this point what looked as though it might turn into a lecture on humanitarian management, because I wanted to confront Mr. Triebe with one of Walter Allen's sharper comments about him. "Did you dare Allen to take the men out?" I asked. He said: "Well, that son-of-a-gun! Did he say that? Of course I didn't! Well, on second thought, I might have. Allen said a good many provoking things during our sessions, and I could have dared him at one point where he was being most threatening—and where he was closing his eyes to all the hard facts Bill Beneman and Cliff Fritschle were presenting."

What facts? "Facts," Triebe said, "which showed that in the first place there was only a small difference between our wage *rates* and the highest rates paid in the industry—facts which showed the gap closing, not opening—facts showing our rates higher than those in any city of comparable size, north or south —facts showing that our people had received wage increases vastly exceeding the rise in the cost of living over the past ten years."

I noticed that when Ed Triebe got worked up, his usually self-effacing, even humble, quietness would be replaced by a grim intensity; his twinkling blue eyes would narrow and become steadier; and his trim, compact frame would gather itself together, much the way a cat's does, when he is ready to leap. Triebe was deadly serious as he said to me:

"There is one thing you have to understand, that everybody has to understand, especially union leaders, about union-management negotiations. That is this: you can't just look at the hourly rate which is being paid if you want to know anything important, such as what people are earning and what the total labor costs per unit of production are. You have to look at all the money a company spends on its workers—*all,* fringe benefits and still more deeply hidden labor costs as well.

"Take our profit-sharing plan. Allen and DeAndrade wouldn't even concede that it was a labor cost at all. But Bill Beneman will demonstrate to you in hard figures that the profit-sharing plan takes 30 cents an hour out of the company till and puts it into the average journeyman's pocket—30 cents every hour, over and above his more than $3.00 per hour straight-time rate, his almost $5.00 an hour overtime rate, and over and above his vacation pay and all other fringe-benefits, too, of which we grant at least our share.

"Consider this, too," Triebe went on. "To give only one example, a simple one, of how careful one has to be in comparing labor costs from one firm to another, take our Christensen-fed presses. We are one of the few book-manufacturers to use the Christensen feed on two-color rotary presses. We have been manning those presses with one pressman and two assistants for a total straight-time hourly labor cost of $9.98 on first shift. Do you know what the total hourly labor cost is on two-color rotaries in New York, the place that Allen and DeAndrade are always throwing up to us? Well, Cliff Fritschle will give you the exact figure, but I can tell you that it is way less than $9.98, which means that our relevant labor costs on two-color rotaries are higher—not lower—than those of our New York competition."

I was to find out later from Fritschle that the New York hourly labor costs on two-color rotaries was $8.25, as against the $9.98 which Kingsport Press paid per hour on its Christensen-fed rotaries. When the roll-fed presses were calculated in, the first-shift average hourly labor costs came to $8.47 at Kingsport Press as against the $8.25 prevailing in New York. The Kingsport Press average for the second shift came to $9.26, as against New York's $8.61. And the Kingsport Press third-shift average came to $9.92 as against New York's $9.61. The average hourly cost for all three shifts on two-color rotaries was $9.18 for Kingsport Press and $8.80 for New York.

"Now," Triebe went on, "if our profit-sharing plan isn't a

labor cost, I'd like to know what it is. You take a look at the facts and figures that Cliff Fritschle patiently demonstrated to Allen and DeAndrade, and if you don't agree that our total labor bill is right up with the top-paying firms, despite our disadvantage in location—far from all the publishers and big customers—and way *above* the labor costs prevailing in any comparable location—I'll eat that book you're going to write."

I told Triebe that I did not intend to make a final judgment on anything so complicated as a comparison of all the labor costs at the Press with those prevailing elsewhere. I would try to uncover and to report the facts and the opinions which I thought were of general interest and of public concern. The reader may draw such inferences and reach such conclusions as he sees fit. As for me, I believe that what the Press offered and what the unions demanded was strictly their own business. Later in this book, I intend to assess the results of the whole affair and to comment on the actual conduct of all parties concerned. But, I repeat, I do not believe that any outsider has either the right or the competence to tell the parties to negotiations what they should demand, what they should offer, or what they should settle for. What I am interested in, and what I think involves the general public interest, is not *what* people go after, but *how* they pursue their objectives.

I did ask Triebe how he would explain DeAndrade's repeated emphasis on the Press's alleged "competitive advantage." Triebe replied: "I honestly think he just did not do his homework."

On Nepotism and Paternalism

I reported to Triebe what Walter Allen had had to say to me about nepotism and paternalism as causative factors in the strike. Triebe said: "I can't believe he was serious. That is really just rabble-rousing demagogy. Of course you have to look out always for all kinds of favoritism, and some is likely to creep in, especially based on blood-relationships, in a community this small. But no management worth its salt is going to encourage it; any management which wants to hold its job has got to run the company aggressively and efficiently, has to keep on its toes. That means getting the best man possible for each job. Actually, we here at the Press have bent over backwards to discourage nepotism in any form. But just as you must discourage nepotism, in the interests of fairness and efficiency, you must also guard against disqualifying perfectly desirable employees merely because they have kin in the firm. That would be unfair to the person involved and to the Press. We cannot rule out a good prospect just because he has a relative in a position of authority."

"My own son was a victim of our policy," Triebe said. "Young Ed grew up here, loved the place, always wanted to work here. But I wouldn't let him apply. Yes, he's here now. But how can I chase him out when he's made such a terrific sacrifice to come and help out when we most needed help, during the early days of the strike? He left a good job, moved back here from where he had been settled down, and took a lot of punishment crossing the picket line. Yes, he's here, and I guess to stay. But if he makes it, he'll have made it on his own."

As for paternalism, Triebe said that the charge was so empty it wasn't worth much of a reply. The Press, he said, just doesn't go in for it. It docs not even have an athletic program, let alone the more elaborate personnel programs and activities which prevail in many firms. "We feel a genuine, friendly interest in our people and will do what we can to help them when they get into deep trouble and ask for our help. But their lives are strictly their own, and that is the way we want it to be."

Triebe reacted similarly to the charge that employees had to adjust their religious affiliations to their supervisors' wishes. "I hope we are a moral crew here," he said, "but we couldn't care less about the religious affiliations of our employees. And we'd better not catch a supervisor doing what Allen said they were doing.

"What may have been sticking in Allen's craw was our stand against letting all grievances go for final settlement to an outside arbitrator. We are aware that many firms have agreed to submit all grievances and some have agreed to submit even wages to such arbitration. But for the life of me I cannot see why such firms should be praised, for they are shirking one of the most essential and vital of management responsibilities, the responsibility for making the decisions on which the future of a firm turns. It bothers me to be condemned for being faithful to my trust. But I take comfort from the fact that all people of good will and sound mind will realize that when we refuse to turn over vital economic decisions affecting the future of *this* company to an *outsider,* who has only a transient and tangential interest in the company, we are being 'good guys,' not 'bad guys.' "

Triebe on the Real Factors
Which Produced the Strike

I must confess that in the course of my meetings with Ed Triebe, I too, despite determined resistance, fell victim to his "charm." "Charm" is not quite the right word; it suggests too much a man who is bent on winning one over, a man who has carefully cultivated the arts associated with Dale Carnegie. Ed Triebe's charm is differently composed. It is made up of other qualities: simplicity, easy friendliness, a quickness to laugh, a kind of a pure openness, a "shining candor." He was never evasive; more important, he was coherent. Everything he had to say hung together; he did not say one thing one time and contradict himself another time.

Toward the end of our talks there was only one aspect of the total situation which troubled and puzzled me. If it were true that Kingsport Press's wage rates and total labor costs were well up with others in the industry and that the employees themselves were reasonably content with their lot at the Press, how, in Triebe's opinion, I wanted to know, were the unions able to take them out on strike, and keep them out?

"As you might guess," Triebe replied, "that's the big one, the question that has cost me some of my most anxious times, and I have given it a great deal of thought." I said to Triebe that I too thought the question a critical one and that I wanted him to reply very carefully, in language that I could quote verbatim, in order to avoid any possibility of error. He was very obliging, and in fact agreed to write out a statement that I could reproduce. Here it is:

THE TRIEBE STATEMENT

It is my opinion that the strike is a result of the following four factors:

1. During the months of bargaining which preceded the strike, the Company did not communicate directly with its employees. Restrictive labor law gave unions control of communication channels; and there were no indications that management's position was being transmitted at the employee level. I believe that, had the Company's position been fully explained to all employees, there would have been no strike.

2. The long smoldering resentments of some of our competitors against the high position of our company, were coupled by present international union leaders to their resentments of the long history of harmonious relations which existed between the Company, its employees, and previous union administrations. These combined resentments were grist for present international leaders, in planning for the capture of what they hoped would be the fruits of successful "economic war" against our company.*

3. The unions wrongly equated the company-employee relationship with paternalism. Because good working conditions were already in effect, they could turn only to economic issues, and highlighted in bargaining only those isolated rates helpful to their cause. They extracted rates from other contracts more notable for reflecting local bargaining conditions than national uniformity. They elected to ignore the Company's position that its wage structure for bona fide total round-the-clock operations, including fringe benefits and excellent working conditions, is the only criterion for comparison. Measured by this yardstick, our company compares more than favorably with the industry. Unable to justify their position through collective bargaining, the unions decided that more demands could be forced on the company only by applying supreme economic pressure —a strike.

* W. A. Allen: *Bargaining Sessions*, January 26, 1963, February 6, 7, 25, 28, 1963. A. J. DeAndrade: *Kingsport Times*, June 13, 1963.

4. Union leaders forced the diverse interests of our five different craft unions into a single, distorted mold. Across the nation, bargaining patterns differ widely even within the same craft, and even more widely between different crafts.

These four factors, in my opinion, motivated the unions to call a strike, and its prolongation rests on a fifth factor.

If the unions measured the risks and obligations they incurred by calling their members out on strike, as carefully as our company measured its risks and obligations to its customers, employees, and stockholders, I believe that the only authentic measurement which both parties could have used are the labor laws governing the rights of individuals and groups. Under these laws, we recognize a union's legal right to strike. Apparently the unions with which we have been dealing do not recognize the equal legal right of a company to operate, and an individual's right to gainful employment.

Bill Beneman: Misjudgment and The Unpredictable, Which Always Happens

One of the men who at the moment seem likely to take over Ed Triebe's job, if he ever leaves it, is William P. Beneman, a great hulk of a man whose calm is that of the sea in those still hours, usually near dawn and sunset, when there is just enough rolling and swelling to remind one of the prodigious fury which it can release in a storm. Present throughout the negotiations with Cliff Fritschle and Homer Clevenger as one of the Press's bargaining team, Beneman was the anchor man. Cost analysis, one of the most critical elements in modern business, has always fascinated him, he told me. He spent more time on that than on anything else in his work at the Press. His role in the negotiations was to relate the unions' ideas and demands to economic reality. It was up to him to determine what the effect of each concession sought from or granted by the Press would be on its total cost structure and thus on its capacity to compete. "I had to help decide whether it would be feasible to meet the demands they made; if not, to explain why not; and in a pinch to say what would be feasible."

Observing Beneman's clear, calm competence and objectivity, I calculated that he might provide me with a disinterested overall view of the affair. His comments, which I believe I have almost verbatim, did not disappoint me. He said:

"Maybe both sides misjudged somewhat. The local union people knew us. They knew that we were not given much to puffing or breast-beating, that we meant what we said during the negotiations. The international officials did not know us as well. They seemed to feel that we would concede more if they threatened a strike, or called one. I myself did not think there would be a strike, till the last minute. Both they and we thought that the strike, once begun, would soon be over. But one thing led to another. Not as many strikers came back as we thought. The unions, despite their propaganda about flexibility and willingness to compromise, stood firm for wage increases which would cripple us, competitively. Time went on, and we started hiring replacements—and found to our surprise that our accelerated training program really worked—that the 6-year apprentice program which the unions insisted upon was vastly too long— that in just a few months green hands could be trained to do a creditable job. As soon as the number of replacements grew to be substantial, of course, a new and even tougher issue was introduced. The unions insisted that they be fired as a condition of any strike settlement, whereas we had committed ourselves to a permanent employment relationship with the replacements, and we do not go back on our commitments."

I asked Beneman: "How do you explain the unions' success in taking the men out? Where do you feel that you had misjudged concerning the strike sentiment of the rank and file workers?" His reply went in substance like this: He had apparently been crediting the employees with more coolness, more self-possession, more common sense, and more resistance to demagogy than they possessed. "This strike has been hell on a lot of people," Beneman said, "but the principal long-run sufferers are the strikers who have been replaced. They let themselves be led down the garden path by union spellbinders who played fast and loose with their lives and fortunes. It's a shame that they emoted rather than thought about what a strike might involve for them. They voted to authorize the strike without serious thought and brought disaster to Kingsport and to themselves in the process."

True to his nature, Bill Beneman preserved his sea-like placidity in saying these things. He had been asked to explain something, and that is all he did. If he was hurt, or moved, angry, or pitying, he kept it to himself. He had been near the storm center, but nothing was showing.

Cliff Fritschle: He Mourns
The Communications Gap

If one man more than any other may be said to have borne the brunt of the strike at the Press, I believe that man to be Clifton E. Fritschle, the Press's vice president for industrial relations. He has taken a beating, and if you look closely, you can see the signs of it now, three years later. He is a quiet, sensitive person, blessed with an attractive personality, a good mind, and tremendous self-control. But he is also cursed with an overgrown talent for suffering, exacerbated by an incurable tendency to look first and last for faults in himself.

I have already mentioned that for many months after the strike began, Fritschle was on the go constantly, and rarely enjoyed a decent night's rest. The violence, the chaos in Kingsport hit almost everyone at one time or another; but Fritschle and his associate, Homer Clevenger, were embroiled persistently—as participant, as witness, as trouble shooter, or as Kingsport Press representative before the world. Clevenger has an ulcer to show for his pains, but that is only a trapping, a suit of woe; Fritschle's wounds are different and less evident. The physical exertions and trials have left no scars on him. He is haunted by his penchant for self-accusation; he cannot help feeling somehow to blame for the whole mess.

Ed Triebe and other members of the executive committee made the ultimate policy decisions for the Press during the negotiations with the unions, and Bill Beneman carried heavy responsibility for the analysis and the information which went into those decisions. But Cliff Fritschle as head of industrial relations and as chief negotiator for the Press carried the ball. He was the architect of the firm's industrial relations. He sat face to face with the union negotiators in more than one hundred bargaining sessions; it was a contest of nerves from beginning to end; and it broke out in a war which rocked Kingsport, did grievous harm to a thousand Kingsport men and women and their families, and came close to ruining the Kingsport Press.

Fritschle's background, character, sensitivity, and professional pride all combined to make the costly strike seem a personal defeat. He was born into one of those big farm families in Olney, Illinois, in 1915. There were eight children in all, with Cliff in the middle. His father, as Cliff described him, was an American Gothic type; a tall man of six feet three inches; stern, just, quiet, and deeply religious. As owner of a 200-acre farm, he was a community leader and contributed more than half of the support of the community's Methodist Church. Cliff called him a stern disciplinarian, a man who rarely raised his voice and who never uttered a curse word in his life. Though the family was better off than most, Cliff says that the last time he received any family money was during his freshman year in high school. Thus he has had a lot of practice, for a long time, in assuming responsibility; his sense of responsibility has been honed consistently from childhood; by now it is excruciatingly acute.

Cliff Fritschle has had a great deal of formal education; in fact, only completion of his doctoral dissertation stands between him and the summit. A candidate for the Ph.D. at Ohio State, he has fulfilled all other requirements.

Having to support himself all the way considerably lengthened this educational process for him. For many years it was a matter of college one year and work the next. Then, too, the five years he spent in the Army in World War II did not hasten the process. Incidentally, his Army record indicates something of his quality. He went in as an enlisted man and was mustered out a lieutenant colonel. His service ranged rather widely—from the ski troops to the South Pacific.

After a year at the Harvard Graduate School of Business Administration, Fritschle worked at General Motors for a time, in its executive training program. From there he went to the faculty of the University of Tennessee, where he soon achieved senior rank as a full professor of industrial management. Concurrently he maintained a consulting practice, and Kingsport Press was one of his clients. In 1957 he accepted the Press's offer to make him director of industrial relations. "They had to make me the offer," he says, "because only I could untangle the mess I had made of their industrial relations." The Press was obviously happy with his contributions to the firm. Within a year he was made an officer of the company, finally in complete control of the industrial relations program which he had designed. It is the kind of thing that ambitious scholars usually dream about but rarely achieve.

I asked Fritschle to comment generally on the negotiations. Here is what he said:

"We went as far as we could to avoid this strike. We couldn't live with ourselves, in fact we were sure that our ambitions for this company would have had to be abandoned, had we made further concessions in an attempt to 'buy labor peace.' The unions are in error when they speak of us as 'adamant' and 'anti-union,' and no one should know that better than they themselves. We made five different economic proposals, each increasingly generous. We were the ones who kept doing the yielding. Remember that these unions filed a charge with the National Labor Relations Board, accusing us of having failed to bargain in good faith. As you know, the Board is extremely tough on employers as far as their bargaining duties are concerned. Its blanket dismissal of all those charges against us, in my opinion, goes far to indicate the distortion in the unions' contention since then.

"And here is a fact about our negotiations which tends to be overlooked," Fritschle continued. "We were having very little trouble during the earlier stages of our negotiations, when we were dealing exclusively with local officials of the unions. With them our only trouble came as a result of their hesitancy to make any final commitment; they said they had to wait for the international officers and representatives before they could take a position. We were practically at the deadline, that is, at the termination date of the existing agreements, before the international people decided to make their appearance. And from then on, the trouble grew and grew. It seemed almost as though they did not wish to come to an agreement, at least not to one that we could accept. The most interesting fact of all, I believe, lay in the reaction of the local bargaining team for the Machinists Union. When the strike was called, all but one of the committee stayed on or returned to work."

A reserved and cautious man who despises emotionalism in any form, Fritschle was nevertheless obviously interested in the implications of the conduct of the members of the Machinists Union. Not all the Machinists returned to their jobs. Yet, in the representation election conducted by the National Labor Relations Board not quite a year after the strike was called, a majority of *all* the Machinists—both those who went back in and those who stayed out—voted against further representation by the International Association of Machinists, and that union thus no longer has representative status at the Press.

Fritschle said to me that the difficult issues were introduced by the staff negotiators of the international unions, not by the local union officials. "For example," he said, "just six days prior to the expiration of the contracts, we asked the local Bindery Union negotiators if a reduced workweek was among their demands. One of the local officers replied: 'Not unless the International comes in here later.' "

"The reason the Machinists acted as they did," Fritschle opined, "was that the international unions were trying to impose a set of contractual conditions which the local men themselves thought were unreasonable. Even so, we had come to a full agreement with the Machinists Union and had an appointment with them for the afternoon before the strike to get it signed. They never showed up. I later learned that they did not show up because the strategists from the other internationals induced them to break the appointment."

I might add here that Mr. Walter F. Barber, international representative of the Bindery Workers, confirmed Fritschle's account. In his August, 1963, speech before the Photoengravers from which I have already quoted certain statements, Mr. Barber had this to say:

> About two o'clock one afternoon, when the strike was already agreed to and was supposed to hit the street the following morning, I got word that one of the unions was having a meeting with management that afternoon at four o'clock. I immediately called a meeting of all the International Representatives that were there on the committee, and we went in to find out what it was all about. We went into a general discussion, and then I asked a question of the chairman, whom we had elected, Walter Eddings [Allen?] of the Pressmen. "Was there anything to the question that one of the unions was fixing us on the contract at four o'clock that afternoon with Kingsport Press?" And it blew almost sky-high. Nobody could believe what they had heard. So Walter Eddings [Allen?] said, "That's the representative of that union, ask him." And I says, "All right, what about it?" He said, "Yes, we are scheduled to sign a contract this afternoon at four o'clock."

The "unity committee" managed to talk the union out of keeping its appointment with the Press, and the strike was on. Barber said:

> So after we got into this union about it, they said, "Well, we won't have the meeting with the company this afternoon and therefore we won't have to sign the contract, we won't have to face them on the issues." So as a result, we did strike the following day. . . .

Remembering my conversation with Walter Allen at Pressmen's Home, I asked Fritschle if it were true that what separated the Press and the unions was not so much the economic issue but rather the Press's refusal to allow the men, through their unions, to participate in the formation and administration of personnel policies. Allen, it will be recalled, said that the economic issues, though important, were secondary. The real issue, he said, was created by the Press's nepotism and paternalism, by its refusal

to let the men have a say through their unions on how their
working lives were to be governed.

"Here is the situation as it existed on March 10, 1963, the
day before the strike was called," Fritschle said. "After more
than one hundred separate bargaining sessions, marked by concession after concession from us, the issues separating the parties
were narrowed to three. Those three were all strictly economic
issues. They had nothing to do with the sort of 'participation'
which Mr. Allen mentioned. The three issues were (1) wage
rates, (2) day shift hours, and (3) the effective date of a liberal-
ized vacation plan with regard to the substance of which we were
in full agreement.

"I believe that I should point out to you," Fritschle added,
"that our proposals as of March 10, 1963, the same offers that
the unions rejected by striking, were not only substantial concessions on our part, but apparently attractive and acceptable to
the men and women who went out on strike. Let me tell you
how I arrive at that conclusion. During the winter of 1964–1965
we had extensive negotiations looking toward a strike settlement.
John McLellan was negotiating for the unions, I for the Press.
The tentative agreement we reached at that time was submitted
to the employees still on strike. I have it from an excellent source
that the agreement was rejected *only* because it did not provide a
certainty of reinstatement for all the men and women still out on
strike. Its economic proposals, in other words, were all acceptable. The significant point of all this is that those economic proposals were the same ones that we had offered the unions on
March 10, 1963, and which they then rejected, without giving
the employees a chance to vote on them.

"The fact is that the issues which brought about this strike
were economic. The unions put before us money demands as the
price of agreement. The price they set was high, too high for us
to pay and still remain competitive. I do not believe they ever
did understand our labor costs."

According to Fritschle, the accusation that the Press's wage
structure was substandard simply departed from the demonstrable facts. "And this was especially so," he said, "in regard to

the comparisons made between bindery wages in New York and Kingsport."

"Kingsport Press rates," he said, "are closely comparable to New York edition binders, and above those paid by competitors in Philadelphia; Binghamton, New York; Brattleboro, Vermont; Baltimore, Maryland; Concord, New Hampshire; and others in the Northeast. With the exception of Atlanta, Kingsport Press leads the South in edition Book Bindery Workers' rates. One union argument throughout pre-strike negotiations and since the strike has been a so-called 'competitive advantage' of Kingsport Press. This argument cannot stand up when the rates of certain Northeastern cities, located near the market place, are *below* those paid in Kingsport—some 650 miles distant from New York, the nation's major publishing center. In addition, some major mid-Western competitors of Kingsport Press, both union and non-union, pay rates below Kingsport Press."

I asked Fritschle what he had to say about the Union contention that the intent was only to keep the gap between Kingsport rates and those prevailing in the industry from growing. "Also," I said, "I'd like to know what you have to say about the Union contention that rates at the Press have increased over the last ten years, on the average, only a little more than one per cent, while those in the industry have been going up at about three per cent annually."

"During the ten-year period just prior to the strike," Fritschle replied, "our wage rates rose *over* 35 per cent. On a cumulative basis, this amounted to approximately 3¼ per cent per year —exclusive of fringe benefits which climbed even more impressively during the period."

Fritschle backed up this and his other statements with the actual figures. He showed me that in the composing room, journeymen basic day shift rates in 1952 were $2.15 per hour, while in 1962 they were $3.00 per hour—a difference of 85 cents per hour or almost 40 per cent over the ten years. The comparable rates in the pressroom were $2.25 per hour in 1952 and $3.10 per hour in 1962—again a difference of 85 cents per hour or a little less than 38 per cent.

As regards the "gap," Fritschle said that the relationships between the rates of different firms are dynamic, not static. He showed me that according to the wage statistics gathered by the Printing Industries of America, Inc., average day shift rates at the Press were 27 cents below the national average in 1950, but that in 1961 average rates on all presses in Kingsport were a little above the national average, while the Kingsport rates on rotary presses have been substantially above the national average since 1959.

"These rates," Fritschle said, "must and do reflect local labor market conditions and the need of particular firms for employees, which in turn is determined by their competitive standing. If the unions were genuinely interested in their Kingsport members, they would be doing their best to promote the competitive standing of the Kingsport Press, not to weaken it."

Fritschle summed up with this observation: "On the basis of the claims made by the unions themselves, the facts show that over the past ten years, *first,* the average annual increase at the Press has been *greater* than the average annual increase in the printing industry, and, *second,* the 'gap,' if any, has been closing."

"Let me explain what I mean about the qualification, 'if any,' " Fritschle said. "Throughout, the figures I've been giving you are basic day shift *rates.* They do not include fringe benefits, or our profit-sharing program, or the shift differentials, which are quite substantial here—and they do not include in any way the effect of premium pay for overtime, which is quite probably more extensive here at the Press than almost anywhere else in the United States. As Mr. Triebe has already said to you, when all those are included, we maintain that the total reward to employees on the Kingsport Press payroll will compare favorably with those anywhere in the printing industry in the United States."

Cliff Fritschle is customarily so quiet, so given to understatement, that this relatively bold contention impressed me no end. It also brought immediately to my mind the question which has dogged me persistently since the first time I looked into the strike at the Press. "If everything you have said is true—and I'm willing to credit it, at least for the sake of the discussion—then," I asked, "how do you explain the unions' success in taking the employees out on strike, and—what's more—keeping them out as solidly as they have?"

I knew the question was going to hurt. The best thinking going on today among industrial relations people tends constantly to center upon the greatest of the human relations problems associated with the growth of modern industry—the problem of welding a large-scale economic entity into a unified production team. No team can do its best unless there is harmony and integration among its various parts. Harmony calls for understanding and sympathy, and the technique aimed at achieving them is called "communications." The job of the professional personnel man or "industrial relations expert" is fundamentally a job of communications. A scholar and an expert in this field himself, Cliff Fritschle understood all too well what I was driving at. I repeat: I knew it was going to hurt, but I had to ask the question.

Obviously haunted by the same question, and given as he is to self-criticism, Cliff Fritschle said: "I failed. My whole effort here over the five years preceding the strike was to convey to the employees our friendly interest, our good faith, our reliability. I thought we had done so. I thought that our people understood and had confidence in Mr. Triebe's management philosophy and practice, which are one and the same thing: be true to management's responsibility to the employees, to the customers, and to the owners of the company. I was confident that our people knew we were doing our best for them, consistent with those other, equal responsibilities. Apparently I did not reach them."

I could not help observing that the best and most laudable efforts do not always succeed. It is a question of what you are up against. The best swimmer in the world, stroking his heart out, will not make it across the English Channel in a bad storm. Certainly he will not make it with his arms and legs tied. As we have seen, Triebe feels that the restrictive legal interpretations of the National Labor Relations Board have made it virtually impossible for the management of a firm to win the loyalty of the employees. The Kingsport Press, respecting the NLRB rulings, entered into no active competition with the unions for the loyalty of its workers. As we have also seen, the mob which gathered at the Press on the day of the strike probably had something to do with inducing uncommitted workers to participate in the strike in the first instance, and the reign of terror imposed on all who returned to work may have kept many out long after they would have preferred to return. Adopting Fritschle's cautious address, I suggested the bare possibility that he was making a mistake in taking so much of the blame for the strike on himself. He was not comforted.

Jim Shelton: "They're Out to Bust the Press"

The pressrooms at Kingsport are not really "rooms" at all; they are enormous, cavernous buildings—like exaggerated airplane hangars. The aisles between the presses are wide enough for six men to walk abreast. Jim Shelton strides those aisles with his elbows out, even when he is alone, as if he is forcing his way through a crowd. He is big, young, handsome, ambitious, aggressive—he is also competent and confident. For years he has been sure that offset printing is the "wave of the future"; he has sung its praises in so many forms, its cost and quality advantages in so many varieties, that the Press management is pretty well sold. At Kingsport, in any event, offset printing is a big thing both at present and in the plans for the future. And Jim Shelton, still only thirty-seven, is superintendent of all offset printing at the Kingsport plant.

There are Hamlets in Kingsport, but Jim Shelton is not one of them. He is Hotspur, with a dash of Prince Hal and another of Owen Glendower. I do not say that he believes he can summon spirits from the vasty deep, but he might try, if he thought it would help him and the Kingsport Press.

Jim Shelton was born in Scott County, Virginia, on June 11, 1928. One of seven children, all sustained by a small farm, he left school when he was sixteen, took a job digging ditches at 50 cents an hour, saved $1,000 in a single year, and then quit to go back to school. But he stayed only a week, couldn't stand the "kid stuff." Turned seventeen, he joined the Army and was stationed in Germany. Within a year he made sergeant. Life in Bavaria, though pleasant, got monotonous. He took almost every kind of training course the Army offered, got himself a high school diploma, set up courses for people who, like himself, had not finished high school back home, but not even all this activity could contain him, especially since all promotions were frozen in his company.

In 1949, still only twenty, Jim left the Army. In April of that year he decided to apply for work at Kingsport Press. "I went in cold," he said. "Everybody always thought he had it made if he got on at the Press, so I sat for hours in the employment office, along with about twenty-five other people. Three were hired that day. I was one."

It took Jim the normal six years to achieve journeyman status, but he became a supervisor in three more years; another three and he was put in charge of all offset printing on the day shift. Eighteen months later, which brings us to September, 1964, he was promoted to superintendent of *all* offset printing.

Jim Shelton apparently has it in the clutches. The job he has done training raw replacements during the strike has been outstanding, according to all reports. The strike has infuriated him, and it has challenged him, and he has risen to the challenge. Although he had withdrawn from membership in the Pressmen's Union before the strike, and although he was in the highest supervisory ranks when the strike began, the strikers apparently regarded him as a "super-scab" because he stayed at his job, and treated him accordingly. They shot up his garage and his car and pestered him twenty-four hours a day with threatening telephone calls. One time they really angered him. It was a Saturday. Jim was home and wondered what his little boy was doing, hammering away at something out on the lawn. He went out to take a look. What the boy had gotten hold of was a string of powerful cherry bombs, twenty-five of them on a single fuse. "I grabbed them. He could have been killed."

Jim was one of the few who thought there would be a strike, quite a while before it was actually called—and that it would be a long one. He said: "I remember just after the strike began, my brother called me and asked me how long I thought it would last. I said: 'Call me in a year, and it'll still be going on, and I still won't be able to tell you how long it will last.' "

Carrying that conviction, Jim decided that it was going to be mighty important to the Press to be able to carry on with replacements for the strikers. The unions, he said, were sure they would bring the Press to its knees because they thought those "hillbillies around Kingsport would never make good pressmen." "They forgot," he says, "that we wuz all hillbillies once, and that what the Press done once it could do again."

Jim Shelton told me that before the strike the offset department was a two-shift operation with four presses and 28 men. Early in 1965, when I talked with him, he said the offset department had 58 men on three shifts, five presses going full blast, and a magnificent new five-color web-fed press just going into operation. Only two strikers had come back, one with six weeks' experience and the other with one year. The remaining 56 were all "greenies"; but according to Jim they were shaping up unbelievably well. "I knew it could be done," he said, "but I never dreamt it could be done so fast. I'll stack up this crew with any average pressman of ten years' experience. We've made production records never dreamt of—records that other companies have trouble believing. These boys don't have to take a back seat to any one. And of course the reason why the strikers went after the supervision the way they did was that they were told that we were the key to training these new men, and also because we were operating presses ourselves."

"Jim," I said, "you've been in the Union, close to the men. You've been right about a lot of things. Tell me, what do you think this strike is all about?"

The great hero in Jim Shelton's life was John F. Kennedy. So far as I could tell, Jim has no "reactionary" inclinations and rather shares the New Dealing sentiments which prevail around Kingsport and the Kingsport Press. His answer was bold and unqualified: "They talk about union-busting *companies*. Well, these unions were out to bust the Kingsport Press, and the men who went out on strike were foolish enough to help them, even though they busted themselves doing it."

6

THE WAR AT THE PRESS

"Economic" Warfare

ACCORDING TO THE PRESS minutes of the negotiations before
the strike, Walter Allen exhorted the Company to yield so that
the unions "would not have to be put into a position to call
names and take other drastic measures. He said that if they
make the decision to strike, they are going to try to win . . .
[and that] things will happen that shouldn't." For a year after
the strike began, the Kingsport newspapers were dominated by
reports of events which should not have occurred, but which did
occur.

Roughly one thousand incidents of violence and vandalism
were reported—some grave, some petty; some tragic, some
funny: none pretty. Festus Maddux, a striker who after two
months went back to his job, was fined on May 10, 1963. His
offense: stopped by pickets on his way to the Press, he was said
to have drawn a gun and yelled: "Where were you when I was
on Normandy beachhead, you damned S.O.B.!" The judge dismissed the charge of carrying a firearm for failure of proof, but
he held Maddux guilty of disorderly conduct and fined him $10.

A little more than two months later, at 1:05 in the morning
of July 14, 1963, the Maddux home was dynamited. According
to the *Kingsport Times-News* of that date, "The dynamite, which
exploded on their carport, shattered their car's windshield, ripped
the ceiling from the carport, ruined three doors and the carport
storage area and mangled their son's bicycle almost beyond rec-

ognition." Mrs. Maddux was cleaning up the debris when the reporters came, too shaken after a sleepless night to do much else. She said: "Our son and a neighbor's boy were sleeping in a tent there in the yard—only a few feet away from where it went off."

"I thought I got away from all that stuff—but it's worse over here than it was over there." Asked to explain what she meant, Mrs. Maddux said: "I escaped from the Russian part of Germany just after the second World War and came over here—I didn't know I was going to get into something like this."

By the time I first visited Kingsport, early in 1965, the violence was mainly a memory. A couple of bomb scares occurred, one involving the Triebe household; and I noted that the pickets, especially during shift changes, were still using threatening and insulting language. Moreover, during all of 1965 I observed that it was standard practice for Press personnel to sweep up tacks and nails from the streets leading to the Press gates. But by then I had to rely mainly on newspaper reports and personal recollections to recapture the violent character of the first year of the strike. Some of the events, though almost two years old, still made vivid stories and a little later I shall recount a few.

By the beginning of 1965 the unions' all-out war against the Press had been refined into political and economic warfare. This is not to suggest that the unions had neglected to use economic and political weapons at first. In this one respect, Mr. Michael G. Gartner's *Wall Street Journal* article of April 22, 1964, gives a slightly misleading impression. Basing his conclusion on an interview with Mr. Walter Allen, Mr. Gartner said: "The Pressmen's Union has switched tactics since the strike started. At first, says Mr. Allen, 'we told locals throughout the U.S. not to accept work that normally would have gone to Kingsport. We wanted to keep the business for Kingsport. . . . After about two months we backed off from this and asked publishers to use their influence on Kingsport to settle or take their business elsewhere.' Now, he says, 'there will never be an end. We'll support the competition any way we know how.' "

Actually the unions used boycotting techniques against the

Press from the beginning of the strike. They tried to prevent trucking companies from making vital pick-ups and deliveries at the Press. And they imposed a secondary boycott against at least one book-manufacturing firm to which a publisher had sent some work after having first contracted for it with the Kingsport Press. Furthermore, as examination of the Allen statement quoted by Gartner will reveal, the unions began very early to ask publishers to quit dealing with Kingsport. We shall see presently that this tactic has come more recently to dominate the unions' whole strategy against the Press. Perhaps it should be called a form of politico-economic warfare, since public agencies are often involved.

Besides the forms of conduct heretofore described, the unions used another, which I shall call, for lack of a better term, purely political. I refer here to the quite obviously strained and artificial charges which the unions filed with the National Labor Relations Board. They charged the Press with "refusal to bargain," notwithstanding that it had engaged in marathon negotiations and made numerous concessions; and with discrimination against the strikers, despite the fact that the Press had clearly offered to reinstate *all* the strikers at the beginning of the strike, and those for whom job vacancies existed, later on. I do not believe that charges may properly be described as "legal" activity when they are obviously trumped up. In my opinion, the unions hoped to get from the NLRB what they failed to win in the market place. However, while it has a quite deserved reputation for being anti-employer in labor disputes, the NLRB thus far has dismissed the unions' charges against the Press. I know of no better way to demonstrate the baseless character of the charges filed by the unions against the Press. A new set of charges relating to post-strike events is at this writing (spring, 1966) awaiting action in the NLRB Washington offices.*

So far as I have been able to discover, and I may add that I have examined the Press's activities as carefully as I have examined the unions' conduct, if not more carefully, the Press and

---

* In June, 1966, the NLRB regional director dismissed the new charges; and as this volume goes to press, has dismissed still another set of charges against Kingsport. The unions probably will appeal.

its management have engaged in no activity even remotely re-
sembling that of the unions. The Press did not engage in any
picketing or mob demonstrations against the strikers and their
unions. It did not make any attempt to discourage anyone from
dealing with the strikers or their unions.

Many strikers found jobs elsewhere during the strike. I have
never heard it even hinted that the Press tried to persuade anyone to refuse to employ a striker or to give him any other type
of aid.

The Press was assaulted in a number of ways. Bombs were
thrown on the premises. Power lines were cut. Accesses were
blocked. I have heard or read of nothing like that happening at
union headquarters. There were a few reports of bombs thrown
at the homes of strikers, and a few instances, such as the one
involving Festus Maddux, of non-strikers or those who returned
to work after a time, having been convicted of one or another
type of disorderly conduct. But there is no indication of Press
encouragement of such conduct.

On the contrary, the dozens of striker replacements or non-
strikers I talked to all said that they were under the strictest
orders from the Press to refrain from getting into any kind of
trouble at all. They were of the opinion that they would lose
their jobs if they engaged in aggressive conduct.

I do not wish to use prejudicial terms, but I believe that there
is no better way to describe the Press's conduct generally than to
call it "defensive." The Press advertised for employees during
the strike, and that infuriated the unions no end. They accused
it of "union-busting" and of inviting violence by this recourse to
"scabs and rats." However, it is as moral and as lawful for a
company to attempt to keep its business going during a strike as
it is for unions to call a strike or for strikers to seek other employment. I do not believe that it is possible to find a moral or
legal *or* rational ground for objecting to the one any more than
to the others.

In the *American Pressman* for November, 1963, on page 37,
Pressman President Anthony J. DeAndrade declared: ". . . an
anti-union plant operated by Scabs and Rats is wholly intolerable

to both union labor and fair management. There is no favorable future for the Kingsport Press except if it settles with the Unions on terms the strikers can accept honorably." I could easily fill many pages of this book with equally inflammatory statements about the Press and its workers by other union leaders. On the other hand, I have searched diligently for signs of similar vituperation by the Press management—but without uncovering a single instance, either oral or in print. In a brief pamphlet describing the strike and its issues, the Press management had this to say: "On March 10, union spokesmen avoided the word 'strike,' preferring instead to use the phrase 'economic warfare against the Kingsport Press.' The phrase was well chosen." The pamphlet concludes with these words: ". . . management has met and will continue to meet with those involved in this dispute whenever there is a glimmer of hope that something useful can be accomplished on any or all of the issues. A dispute clearly exists between the Company and five international unions; but it is economic, not personal, in nature."

We have seen, in Chapter III, that the Press was sharply attacked by the unions for having thus disavowed any personal animosity—sharply attacked, and misrepresented. The unions distorted the Press disclaimer of personal venom into a desire "to move its employees around like pawns."

In any event, the observations from the Press pamphlet which I have just quoted are among the strongest references I have seen to the strike, coming from the Press management. Compared with the union leaders and their publicists, Messrs. Triebe, Fritschle, and Clevenger are simply out of the running when it comes to inflammatory statements and name-calling.

In December of 1965, Anthony J. DeAndrade rose before the AFL-CIO's constitutional convention in San Francisco to talk about the strike at the Press and to solicit the boycotting cooperation of the affiliated unions. He referred to Kingsport Press as "this giant in the printing industry" and said: "We know that this strike cannot be won on the picket lines or in negotiations in Kingsport." However, a year and a half earlier, on June 14, 1963, the *Kingsport News* had reported Mr. DeAndrade as having said to the strikers in Kingsport that "strikes are not won through newspapers but [on?] picket lines." By the end of 1965, apparently, he had decided that neither newspapers nor picket lines, but nationwide boycotts and the use of political pressures were the proper tools for winning strikes. For that was the burden of his remarks before the convention.

Among other things, Mr. DeAndrade informed his audience that "since this strike began the five International Unions have spent up to this moment $7,500,000" in the fight against that "giant," the Kingsport Press. President Walter Reuther of the Auto Workers took the podium a little later to say that "we spent in excess of ten million dollars" in the strike against the Kohler Company. One wonders who the "giants" really are.

Alarums and Excursions

On the same day that Mr. DeAndrade announced that strikes are won on picket lines, not in newspapers, he also told the strikers, according to the *Kingsport News* (June 14, 1963), "to limit their activities to jeering and to avoid violence so no future injunctions would be issued." Again as reported by the *Kingsport News,* Mr. DeAndrade said that the unions "have just begun to fight." The same story quoted him as saying that the unions " 'must now use methods and strategies they were reluctant to use before.' He did not elucidate on the means and strategies."

The day the strike began all accesses to the plant were covered by hundreds of hooting and howling pickets. It took a brave man to go through. That condition persisted till well into June, when Chancellor Jackson Raulston finally issued an injunction limiting the pickets to ten at each of seven entrances to the plant. Each of the five unions was permitted to have two pickets at each of the seven gates. After the pickets were thus limited, crowds of "sympathizers" gathered near the plant, and finally they too were limited—no mob demonstrations were allowed within 100 yards of any of the entrances.

The International Typographical Union's *Review,* on April

18, 1963, declared that "picket-line violence, for a situation in which a firm is trying to produce with scabs, has been minimal." There are those who would disagree—especially the men and women who were jeered and stoned each day, and who, each day, had to have flat tires repaired. But it still may be true that the violence was "minimal," depending of course on what you mean by the term. No one was killed, and I do not believe that anyone was invalided for life.

The picket line violence was not bold and arrogant—at least not as bold and arrogant as that of Mr. Reuther's Auto Workers Union in the strike against the Kohler Company. Yet endless stories could be recounted of how groups of strikers would take out in cars after a striker replacement or a striker who returned to work. They might force him off the road and tell him what an evil person he was, or simply slug him. They did not think that they themselves were in the wrong; they believed their victim to be their assailant.

Doyle Fields, a strapping, good humored young striker replacement, told me that when he came out of the Press the day he applied for work there, he found all the tires flat on his pickup truck. He jacked up the truck and began to remove the tires. As he set down the lugs they would disappear. Little by little a gang of strikers and pickets had surrounded him, and they were stealing the lugs as he removed them. "I picked up one of the wheels," Fields told me, "and waved it around above my head, and I got them to give me room, and then I began putting the lugs in my pockets. It didn't do no good, though. I couldn't buy tires to replace the ones they ruined. The man in the service station wouldn't sell to me 'cause he was for the strikers."

Doyle Fields is a blithe, happy-go-lucky youngster, maybe the only person in Kingsport who got any fun out of the strike and out of the challenge posed by the pickets to a man who wanted to work. For others, the rocks, the insults, the threats were a daily torture.

It was usually no good responding in kind. You were bound to come out on the short end. If you brought charges because a rock came crashing through your windshield, how were you going to establish who threw the rock? According to our criminal laws, *picket lines* are never subject to indictment or conviction. You have to identify a person and prove that *he* committed a crime or misdemeanor. On the other hand, if you took out after somebody in the picket line who, you thought, had thrown the rock, they all saw you, and they would all testify against you. The same people who testified that the man you charged absolutely did not throw the rock, or even that he wasn't present at the time, would swear that you threatened them with a gun—and you would come out paying a fine, as Festus Maddux did.

Homer Clevenger told me about one such instance. As principal observer for the Press, and witness in many cases, Clevenger had a great deal of experience in these matters and got to know the police pretty well. When a policeman arrested a non-striker for gesturing at some pickets, Clevenger questioned him about the incident. The policeman said: "I know he did it, Homer. I was watching him particularly carefully because they were throwing so many rocks at his car." How can you win?

Bad as conditions were at or near the plant, they were much worse at home. The I.T.U. *may* have been right in describing the picket line violence as "minimal." But it would require a far-reaching stretch of the imagination to find the term "minimal" appropriate to describe what went on night after terror-stricken night at the homes of non-strikers and striker replacements.

The violence and vandalism engulfed the city and its environs. Non-strikers and replacements were the principal victims, but the wildness and fury bubbled so recklessly that people with no interest in the strike at all were scalded. For example, the Kingsport newspapers reported: "A Union Street resident who has no connection with Press reported eggs were broken on his car and his garbage cans thrown across the street." Judge Raulston's home was made uninhabitable by a tear gas bomb one night; on another, many of his windows were broken. Merchants who dealt with non-striking employees of the Press were threatened.

Anyone who goes through the files of the Kingsport newspapers for six months or so after the strike began will find them full of reports such as these:

"Press Worker's Residence Shot."

"Striker Bound to Grand Jury."

"Three Charged in Incident at the Press."

"Police were deluged with 80 strike complaints Wednesday and Thursday morning."

"The Crowd on the Bridge—Excitement Crackles as Hour Nears."

"Two Strikers Convicted."

"Striker Gets Lecture Before Cases Dismissed. The judge warned he is getting tired of hearing such cases and said the defendant must have had some reason for being on the scene."

"Beagle Dog Is Wounded in Shooting."

"Rifle Bullet Fired Into Press Water Tower."

"Autos Stoned in Lynn Garden."

"Bomber Hits Again."

"City Police Press Probe of Bombings."

"New Strike Violence Is Reported."

"A tear gas grenade early Sunday morning was thrown through a window of Watson Lithographing Company. . . . Watson's wife is working at the Press."

"KP Striker Posts Bond for Threat."

"Two Press Strikers Fined $35 Each in Fight at Plant."

"Striker Is Bound Over in Alleged Rock Throwing."

"A 19-year-old Damascus, Virginia, youth told police he was forced off the road . . . shortly after . . . applying for a job at Kingsport Press."

"The home of a Kingsport Press employee and a warehouse belonging to the book-making plant were damaged sometime Tuesday night."

"Three Kingsport Press strikers were arrested near the home of a Press worker in Hawkins County, and two more strikers were arrested in downtown Kingsport with 72 'cherry bombs' in possession of one of them early yesterday. . . .

"Deputy Davis said he was watching for a possible incident about 1:30 a.m., and saw a late-model Buick stop before something was thrown into the lawn of John A. Lee's residence. Immediately after the object was thrown, Davis said, the automobile started away at a high rate of speed. Lee is a pressroom supervisor at Press." [The objects were cherry bombs, the same powerful kind that Jim Shelton had found his little boy hammering.]

"Deputy J. B. Davis said he is investigating shootings at the homes of Glen Carroll and Fred Calhoun, both of whom are continuing to work at Press. Davis said a bullet from a high-powered weapon ripped through the garage door and through the front of Carroll's auto. Calhoun's station wagon was shot from the rear, and the slug imbedded in one of the seats."

"Only one night—Easter—has gone by in the last 37 without some violence. City police have gone on 12-hour shifts. The Highway Patrol has added men to its office here. But the creatures of violence have merely moved out into the country. . . . Those who have shot at homes where children sleep, who have thrown explosives into areas where children play, and who have shown a complete disregard for the property of others have flaunted [flouted?] all reasoning." (From a *Kingsport News* editorial of April 17, 1963.)

"Four Persons Hurt in Area Violence."

"Warrants Are Issued for Five [Union Members]."

"Strike Shootings Reported in Area: Violence Increases."

"A 'Molotov Cocktail'—a bottle filled with gasoline and some type of fuse attached—was hurled through a garage window about 3:30 a.m. Saturday at the residence of James E. Sherfey [a guard at the Press]."

"Violence, Vandalism Erupt Again in Strike; 100 Incidents Reported."

". . . one woman worker was cut on the shoulder this morning when her car window was broken by a bottle."

"Two cases of acid-throwing and one 'bomb' were reported."

"Officers said their efforts toward crowd control have been hampered by the presence of children who, they say, are being used as 'shields' by strikers."

"Police said children have been throwing rocks and firecrackers during the demonstrations."

"It is believed by police that much of the violence is organized and well planned.

"They cited as example an incident this morning when a large group of strikers suddenly began to yell and wave their arms. Rocks were thrown from the crowd and officers were unable to see who actually was throwing the rocks." (*Kingsport Times,* June 6, 1963.)

"Rocks, steel ball bearings and marbles have struck many cars taking workers to and from the plant. Police said several windshields, side windows, bumpers and doors were broken or dented."

"Police Busy Checking Out Phone Threats."

"Capt. Jim Broyles investigated a shooting incident at Kingsport Press. Broyles reported several bullet holes in a ventilator on the Press roof."

"Explosion Shatters Recent Calm." (August 12, 1963.)— "After a few weeks of silence and relative calm, violence broke out in Kingsport again Saturday morning. The home of Mrs. Wilburn Carter, [wife of] a Kingsport Press employee, was rocked by an explosion early Saturday morning. The explosion caused a hole in her front yard and shattered a picture window and several bordering windows on the front of the home. It seems to follow a pattern of several explosions of homes in the recent past. It always is a passing car between 12 and 3 a.m. Saturday mornings. The bomber always makes a getaway. . . . Mrs. Carter refused to let the *Times-News* staff take any photographs and refused to say anything about the blast. [She said:]

"I think these skunks are getting too much publicity and that it is encouraging them to do more."

"Explosion Rips Lawn of Press Supervisor."

"Blast Rocks Striker's Home."

"The Hawkins County Sheriff's Department reported three cars were sprayed with red paint in the Rogersville area Friday night. The autos belonged to employees of the Kingsport Press."

"Ambulance Stops at Picket Line. The driver of an ambulance called to pick up a patient on the premises of Kingsport Press refused to cross the picket line Tuesday, witnesses and police reported."

"Three Bound in Assault Case Here. A Kingsport Press striker and two companions were bound over to Sullivan

County's Grand Jury yesterday . . . on charges of feloniously assaulting a Clinchfield Railroad Co. employee. . . . Harwood testified that the four men attacked and beat him for several minutes . . . before a 15-year-old boy helped break up the affair. . . . Harwood said that he is a special agent for the railroad, responsible for all the company's equipment. He added that this includes protecting switch engines that regularly cross Press picket lines."

"A service building at strike-troubled Kingsport Press, Inc., was damaged early this morning by an explosion."

"Cherry Bombs Thrown at Home."

"Police Told of Two Strike Incidents."

"A local grocer was threatened for 'selling groceries to people working at the Press.' Two houses were struck with thrown objects . . . and four boys threw a bottle at a group of pickets on Clinchfield Street."

The foregoing resumé of newspaper reports from May to September, 1963, is as brief as I could make it, consistent with my intention to record with some accuracy the nature of life in Kingsport during the first six months of the strike. I have the feeling that the picture thus presented is inadequate. My talks with people actually victimized during those months has left me with an impression of dread and anxiety that I am afraid is not even remotely conveyed by newspaper headlines and stories. The problem is to bring home to the reader jaded by the horrors of war and of television that the vandalism, the violence, and the assaults thus recorded all have as their victims real, living, breathing human beings who were accustomed and habituated far more to the gentle arts of peace than to the smoke and fury of war. Many of the victims were women, others were small men assaulted by big bullies. The uncertainty created a grueling life by itself. One never knew what was going to happen, or when. Several people have said to me grimly that they went without solid sleep for weeks, that life was "hell."

George Hawkins, Ralph McCoy, and Homer Clevenger— middle-rank executives at the Press—spent a great deal of their

time during the first six months of the strike as "observers."
None of these three is inclined to exaggeration; I have personally
observed that they are on good terms with the strikers, who did
not expect them to go out and who do not call them "scabs."
Clevenger, Hawkins, and McCoy (yes, he is one of the McCoys
of the classic feud) have spent hours recounting the pity, the
terror, and the humor associated with the strike—for they, like
most people in the area, have a broad and strong humorous
streak. I can only repeat to the reader, after listening to them
and talking to a number of victims that the newspaper headlines
and stories which I have reproduced tend to understate, not to
exaggerate, what went on in Kingsport during the months following the unions' declaration of "economic" war against the
Press.

The Unions Speak
On the Violence in Kingsport

On April 21, 1963, not quite six weeks after the strike began,
the five allied unions issued a formal statement on the strike
events which had occurred. The statement was built around the
assumption that the unions and the strikers were being blamed
for the reign of terror. This was apparently a well-founded assumption; most people in town did seem to believe that the
unionists were the aggressors, even though upon occasion a
striker might be a victim.

Signed for the "Allied Kingsport Press Unions" by Mr. Carl F.
King as Chairman and Mr. R. W. Ayers as Secretary-Treasurer,
the "Open Letter to the Citizens of Kingsport and Vicinity" advanced several arguments. *First,* that the Kingsport newspapers
were exaggerating the violence; *second,* that the unions were doing their best to keep it down; *third,* that Kingsport Press was
really responsible for the strike; *fourth,* that the guilt of the Press
was being overlooked; and *fifth,* that the Press was "fomenting
tension, resentment and emotional reactions."

I believe that the reader will be interested in seeing the full text of the "Open Letter," and I am therefore reproducing it here, just as it appeared in the *Kingsport Times-News* on April 21, 1963:

AN OPEN LETTER TO THE
CITIZENS OF KINGSPORT AND VICINITY

Stories, pictures and editorials appearing in newspapers and on radio and television, either by the prominence given such news or by editorial comment, have inferred [sic] that all acts of violence or nuisance are chargeable to the strikers at the Kingsport Press. This we regard as an over simplification of the situation, misleading and a distortion of the facts.

We have noted that usual and common law-breaking or violent acts, or "hot-rodding" on city streets, highways, or rural roads seem to escape the attention or concern of the news media or are given little prominence. Now, however, every unlawful act, and many actions which would ordinarily not be noticed, receive careful scrutiny and dissection for any possible relationship to the strike. Further, no matter how ordinary or trivial, such acts are blown up as other examples of "violence." If one such occurrence happens in a 24 hour period, it is given headline treatment and reviewed and repeated in such a fashion as to appear to be a continuous flow of events. This hardly appears to be objective or "neutral" reporting, nor does such contribute to maintaining some calm during this emotionally charged strike situation. It is difficult enough without the news media adding fuel to the flames.

It is obviously true that some unlawful acts have occurred. Some have been committed by strikers. This, however, should not be interpreted to mean that the Unions involved or the vast majority of the membership should be blamed. The Unions through their officials have repeatedly endeavored by private and public statements to discourage and oppose acts of violence not only on moral grounds but as being contrary to the best interests of winning the strike. We believe that the Unions have succeeded through these and other actions in keeping violence at a minimum. It should be obvious to any unbiased or knowledgeable person that no organization, union or law enforcing agency, can keep a watch on several hundred persons 24 hours a day to prevent all of them from following their own consciences on ways and means of showing displeasure at strike-breaking activities.

It should be stated, too, that many unlawful acts were undoubtedly provoked by inflammatory acts of individuals and made more probable by the overall strike breaking program of the Kingsport Press. Apparently the program of the Company which directly affects the future of hundreds of workers and their families and which seems to disregard the contribution that these workers have made to the Company and the individual equities held by long service workers, is intended to destroy the personal pride and independence of the workers involved. Such action and such results carry no legal penalties but surely the Community can see that the Company has failed in its moral obligations to its employees and to the Community. If the Company had been willing to continue bargaining, or agreed to arbitration, or had not insisted on operating its plant, wouldn't this all be back to normal by now?

We believe that it is time again for the average citizen to evaluate the facts surrounding the strike at the Kingsport Press and if there is blame that it be leveled at the proper persons or party. We ask therefore that each citizen review the following questions and answers.

Wherein does responsibility for this strike lie?

It must be realized that the strike is not solely the weapon of labor. When management adopts an unreasonable attitude and then refuses mediation or arbitration proposals can it be said that the unions have gone out on strike or would it be more accurate to say that the company forced the workers to go out? Is this then a strike or is it really a lockout? In the opinion of local union leaders the strike should not have happened, and would not have happened if the Company had been willing to bargain in good faith within the framework of the industry pattern of settlements of economic matters or the established and common working conditions in a union plant, or had allowed an arbitrator to determine the merits of points of difference. True the unions struck, but the company forced the situation to the point that as honorable people union members had no other choice.

Which party has shown a willingness to negotiate a settlement?

All of the five unions, individually and collectively, have

asked for and, of necessity, insisted upon meetings with Company representatives, expressing willingness to meet any time or place. The Company, when it reluctantly meets, shows no interest in a settlement except on its pre-strike terms and has apparently tied the settlement of non-economic matters to the unions' willingness to accept their so-called economic package.

Which party has created and fomented tension, resentment and emotional reactions?

Instead of trying to settle its differences with its employees who had demonstrated their complete disapproval and rejection of the company's inadequate proposals, first by strike vote and later by strike action, the Company has attempted to operate its plant. In so doing Company officials have used a variety of tactics to try to weaken the Unions support:

(1) Urging union members to disown their membership obligations. (2) Attempting to discredit union leadership, both local and of the International Unions. (3) Advertising for new workers in out of city or state areas. (4) Refusing to pay earned and due vacation payments. (5) Relying upon legal maneuvers and delays to thwart or restrict normal union activities. (6) Hiring workers previously discharged or with doubtful qualifications. (Space prevents us from continuing this list.) Despite all of this provocation union leaders have continuously used every means to keep members on their best behavior and have done so in the face of Company activities designed to disturb and agitate the workers.

Why is it that the workers who were quite recently claimed as "our people" and praised as being the most competent and reliable workers in the printing industry, are now to be condemned, classed as criminals, and scoffed at as unneeded or undesirable?

In attempting to discredit its workers who have devoted, in most cases, their entire work lives to the Press, at less than the going wages for the industry minus other normal working conditions, the Company is discrediting itself. Those on strike are still the same honest, hardworking, moral people who have helped build the Kingsport Press into the giant of its industry.

The Unions involved in the Kingsport Press strike have and will continue to meet their responsibilities so far as conduct and activities are concerned. A strike in this country is not a crime, but a protected and guaranteed right in a free society. Others have responsibilities, too. This includes individual citizens who create or pass on unfounded rumors. It includes the Company and it includes the press and other news media. Those reporting the news, we think, could be a little less headline hungry, more careful about what truly constitutes acts of violence, a little more careful about emphasis placed upon such often totally unconfirmed happenings, and more appreciative of how well mannered and controlled the situation is under very trying circumstances.

Political Sanctions and Embargoes

Seven months after the strike began, the Allied Kingsport Press Unions issued a pamphlet entitled "Facts vs. Fallacies." Sharply and well written, the pamphlet set forth six propositions which it called "fallacies," and under each it presented an analysis which it headed "The Facts." These were the six "fallacies":

1. The responsibility for the strike at the Kingsport Press lies squarely upon the shoulders of the Unions.
2. The strike was engineered and promoted by the International Union representatives and officers in order to get more business for competing plants [of] the Kingsport Press up North and East.
3. The Unions are now trying to put the Kingsport Press out of business.
4. Union leaders have encouraged and incited violence.
5. The Unions have demanded unreasonable and impossible improvements from the Kingsport Press.
6. The Unions, because the Company has succeeded in operating despite the strike, have lost the strike.

The pamphlet proceeded after stating each of these fallacies to develop a general denial. At one point or another in this book each of the first five denials has been presented exactly as it was done in "Facts vs. Fallacies," or in closely similar form, hence there seems little point in reproducing those five denials here.

Suffice it to say that the thrust of each was to shift the blame and the responsibility from the unions to the Kingsport Press.

The pamphlet's analysis of the sixth "fallacy," however, introduces new matter which is both germane at this point and serviceable to advance our story of the strike. With respect to the question whether the unions were losing the strike, the pamphlet had this, among other things, to say:

> Considering the cost so far to both sides, to the community, to the company's customers, and any others, and no matter what the end result of this dispute, it will never be quite correct to say that one side or the other has *won* the fight. However, one thing needs to be made irrevocably clear, it is not the Unions who are losing this strike and certainly the International Unions will not abandon the courageous Kingsport Press strikers, nor will the labor movement, if this dispute goes on seven more months or seven years. The operation of *non-union* plants is always a menace to union conditions but an *anti-union* plant operated by Scabs and Rats is wholly intolerable to both union labor and fair management. *There is no favorable future for the Kingsport Press except if it settles with the Unions on terms the strikers can accept honorably.* [All italics in the original.]

The grim tone of those concluding sentences reflects the grimness with which the allied unions proceeded to exert secondary pressures. Much of the Press's production is composed of textbooks and is purchased by the public school systems of the United States. The unions went directly to the publishers, asking them to have their books manufactured elsewhere. When publishers did not respond favorably, the unions blacklisted *them*. The *Typographical Journal* for December 1964 (page 262), for example, identifies eighteen well known publishers, together with lists of their titles printed by the Kingsport Press. The listing follows this resolution of the International Typographical Union:

> That this organization instruct its officers to advise all its affiliates in detail of the names of these unfair publishers and the titles of books being produced at the Kingsport Press so that all union members will refuse to purchase such books and urge

local unions to protest to school boards against the purchase of scab-produced textbooks. . . .

The Field Enterprises Educational Corporation has been one of the major targets of the unions' attack on customers of the Kingsport Press. Field Enterprises publishes the popular *World Book Encyclopedia,* and Kingsport Press manufactures a part of the volumes. Despite sustained siege by the unions, Field has stayed with the Press. However, the unions keep trying. In October, 1965, *The Specialty Worker,* a publication of the Pressmen's Union, hit on another scheme to embarrass Field and thus Kingsport Press. It suggested to its members that they look up the local *World Book* salesman, invite him to their homes, "act like they are really interested in purchasing a set. . . . Then drop the bomb! Tell the salesman (or lady) that you wish you could buy the encyclopedia but you can't do this because you know it's been printed at the Kingsport Press and you just couldn't buy such a product."

Field Enterprises has explained its loyalty to the Kingsport Press as a matter of moral obligation. *The Specialty Worker,* however, accused it of immorality "in the use of scabs and strikebreakers in printing its books." Yet here is how *The Specialty Worker* explained its own motivation in advocating the little skit it had conceived:

> Whether you win any Oscars for your acting ability is unimportant. If you do this job, however, you will know you have really been a help in making this boycott effective by wasting the salesman's time. If your brother and sister union members are doing the same thing, when will these salesmen find a bona fide customer?

The unions have had some success with their boycotting campaign. According to a release from the office of Mr. John Connolly, President of the International Brotherhood of Bookbinders, the Encyclopaedia Britannica, Inc., has agreed to take its work out of the Kingsport Press and to send it to the Plimpton Press in LaPorte, Indiana. When I talked to the people in Kingsport

about this, they shook their heads. Homer Clevenger told me
that the pay scales are lower all around at Plimpton Press in La
Porte than they are at Kingsport Press.

The unions' successes have apparently been outweighed by
their failures. Production and profits at the Press in 1965 ap-
proximated those in the year preceding the strike. Perhaps this is
why Anthony J. DeAndrade sounded grimmer than ever as he
submitted the following resolution to the AFL-CIO convention
in San Francisco in December, 1965. Among the "whereas"
clauses, two especially are interesting:

> Whereas, the present substandard operation of this plant is
> having a depressing effect upon the wages and working condi-
> tions in an important, mainly-unionized industry, and losing
> this strike would be a serious blow not only to the printing in-
> dustry but to all union industry in the United States and Canada
> and would seriously reflect against the strength and solidarity of
> the labor movement, and . . .
>
> Whereas, several publishers have agreed to remove their
> books from Kingsport, many others have substantially reduced
> the amount of work scheduled for Kingsport, and it is becom-
> ing apparent that all such publishers would be responsive to a
> full-scale boycott against Kingsport Press books; therefore, be it
> RESOLVED: That this convention go on record pledging
> continuing and added support to (1) the boycott of books be-
> ing produced by scabs and strikebreakers at the Kingsport Press,
> (2) objections to the use of public funds to purchase school
> textbooks and encyclopedia produced under substandard and
> anti-social conditions, since such funds are obtained in large
> part from the tax dollars of union labor, (3) the censuring of
> the publishers who continue to do business with the Kingsport
> Press over the protestations of union labor, and (4) condemn-
> ing the union-busting tactics of the Kingsport Press; and be it
> further
> RESOLVED: That the affiliates of this body be supplied
> with the names and addresses of the unfair publishers and the
> titles [and be] urged to take all necessary steps to fully imple-
> ment this boycott and all other programs instituted to halt the
> purchase of these unfair books until the proper conclusion of
> this most important labor dispute.

Mr. DeAndrade expressed great confidence in the power of the AFL-CIO to bring the Press to terms. He said: "We come before this Convention still having complete faith in the strength of the American Labor Movement and firm in our belief that no employer who is engaged in a program against the standards of Organized Labor, in a program of union-busting, can hope to succeed against an effective boycott program of our great labor movement, and we have put our efforts and our money behind this faith."

Mr. DeAndrade said to the AFL-CIO delegates that he had some successes to report in the boycotting campaign addressed to boards of education—but many more failures. His worst failures, he said, were with the boards of education of the nation's two largest cities, Chicago and New York. "But we have not given up in New York City," he said. "The labor movement is incensed in New York City. When I advised President Meany of this, he was quite concerned. We have demanded—the labor people in New York—have demanded a public hearing before the Board of Education and the public hearing has been granted. . . . Now, I say in New York City we are strong; we are numerically strong. We have just proven that. And of course, the mayor of the city of New York appoints the members of the Board of Education. I am sure that the gentleman coming into the office of mayor of New York City on January 1 never would have won if it hadn't been for the backing of labor. I am sure the individual members of labor and officers of this Federation will be able to assist us with the mayor in this campaign by having the Board of Education reverse the defeat they just gave us."

Mr. Walter Reuther rose to tell of his great political victory against the Kohler Company, and to lend moral support to Mr. DeAndrade's resolution. He said: ". . . this struggle is not the struggle of the five unions. It is a struggle of the entire labor movement, because what is involved here is the ability of an anti-labor firm to defy five unions, tear up the whole concept of free collective bargaining, and then peddle their products in communities where the labor movement has great influence in terms of the political process. I believe that the American labor move-

ment cannot afford to have this company defy the labor movement in this kind of a situation and get away with it. . . .

"The labor movement," Mr. Reuther continued, "if we join
ranks with it, is capable of bringing to bear upon this problem
our total leverage. If we do that, this company will be compelled
to sit down and bargain in good faith. When we have done that,
there will be other companies who will flirt with this idea that
they can defy organized labor. . . . When they look at the
Kohler situation, and when they look at the Kingsport situation,
they will say to themselves over their cocktails: 'It doesn't pay.
We had better sit down and bargain in good faith as the law of
the land requires.' "

Perhaps I should add here, for the benefit of the unwary, that
so far as the facts of this case are concerned—and so far, too, as
the law of the land is concerned—there is no evidence that the
Kingsport Press has been guilty of a refusal to bargain in good
faith. So far, at any rate, the Press has been guilty only of refusing to make all the concessions demanded by the five unions in
1963.

The Contest Before
The New York Board of Education

One of the most dramatic and symbolic events of the strike
was precipitated by the unions' demand that the New York City
Board of Education prevent the use in the City's public schools
of textbooks manufactured by the Kingsport Press. In conjunc-
tion with this demand the unions placed in *The New York Times*
of March 15, 1965 (p. 27), the ad reproduced on pages 126 and
127 of this volume.

The Board examined carefully the contentions of the unions
and, after deciding that the union's demand lacked merit, refused to boycott the Kingsport Press.* Undoubtedly, the Board

---

* Later, by a bare majority, the Board reversed its stand, but a local
court immediately enjoined its boycotting resolution on the ground that
it was illegally discriminatory. On October 27, 1966, the injunction was
made permanent.

was much impressed by the Press's defense against the union charges. For that reason, and also because it will add much to our understanding of the issues involved in the strike, I am reproducing here the Press's answer:

THE KINGSPORT PRESS STATEMENT TO THE NEW YORK CITY BOARD OF EDUCATION

Whether or not two of the five unions which originally struck Kingsport Press are still "on strike" is a debatable question. Both the International Association of Machinists and the International Typographical Union have failed to maintain their majority status in subsequent National Labor Relations Board elections.

The long strike continues because the Company cannot fire those employed since March 11, 1963—despite repeated pressures by the unions—and because the unions' leadership refused to accept the Company's offers to settle at a time when poststrike employment would have had practically no effect on the job opportunities of strikers.

Recent attempts to settle the strike have collapsed over the rights of current working employees—not over the offers (economic and non-economic) of the Company made even before the strike, and still outstanding.

The unions' current chief negotiator recently stated that the Company's wage and other offers are entirely satisfactory, *in spite of the fact* that they are the pre-strike offers which the unions could have had without a strike which inflicted hardships on themselves, the strikers, and the Company.

The Company's position on arbitration of the issues is set forth on page 12 of "Kingsport Press and the Strike." The Company has, however, called upon all levels of the Federal Mediation and Conciliation Service—including the Honorable William Simkin—as well as enlisting the aid of one of the nations foremost private mediators.

If by "conditions at Kingsport Press" the unions mean wages, we would point out that our basic rates—even without our profit sharing and other benefits not usually found in this industry—are favorably comparable with those paid in New York City, and we would point out that there have been three wage

WE <u>DARE</u> THE NEW YORK CITY BOARD OF EDUCATION

TO TAKE THIS TEST:

Yes No

1. Is the Board really anti-union? ☐ ☐

2. Should the Board subsidize strike-break-ing operations of a book-printing plant in another State? ☐ ☐

3. Should a kind of competition which harms one industry—and tries—thousands of New York's major indus-tries employing thousands upon thousands of our citizens? ☐ ☐

4. Should the Board ignore the objections upon thousands of New York City's Central Labor Coun-cil's over one million dollars used to purchase of New York one million tax dollars meant to want their tax books? ☐ ☐

5. Should the Board force the children of these scab-produced books to read these one million books? ☐ ☐

6. In spending tax funds, doesn't the Board of Education have a social responsibility to enforce minimal social and economic standards? ☐ ☐

7. Is the Board remaining "neutral" in a labor dispute when tax dollars ultimately reach the anti-union party to the dispute? ☐ ☐

THAT A "YES" ANSWER TO ...QUESTIONS INDICTS THE CITY OF BEING

Book publishers and school officials are actually encouraging and financing Kingsport Press' fight against its long-service, skilled employees.

If this keeps up, it will be the ruination of New York City's book-printing industry—and will cause the loss of thousands of jobs in the city.

THEN WHERE WILL THE BOARD OF EDUCATION GET THE TAX DOLLARS TO KEEP ON BUYING THESE SCAB-PRODUCED PRODUCTS?

WHAT WE'RE ASKING

We believe in justice.

So we've been compelled to ask, in public, some most embarrassing questions of the Board of Education.

We've had to do this because, in private, the Board ignores our pleas.

Acting as a public agency, the Board has been using our tax dollars to buy scab-pro-duced books from publishers doing business with Kingsport Press.

This works against the best interests of workers who pay taxes.

It also works against the printing manu-facturers in New York City—who also pay taxes to support education and other civic services.

FOR...

AN EXPLANATION

Two years ago — on March 11, 1963 — more than 1,700 long-service, skilled printing trades workers found it necessary to strike the nation's largest book manufacturer: The Kingsport Press, Inc., of Kingsport, Tennessee.

The strike by these members of five highly-respected AFL-CIO unions continues today.

Why?

Because management stubbornly refuses to listen to reasonable and proper union proposals . . . we believe management is afraid to submit the issues to an impartial arbitrator.

We charge that Kingsport Press fears just one thing:

JUSTICE.

The strike has worked great hardships on the workers and their families. We in the labor movement are aware of their great sacrifice.

We are also aware of one other thing:

Conditions at Kingsport Press represent a serious competitive threat to decent printing manufacturers and their employees throughout the nation.

Questions:

Who is particularly vulnerable to these low-wage, strike-breaking operations at Kingsport Press?

Answer:

The book printing industry of New York City and its surrounding area. For years, New York's book-printing industry has been hard-pressed by competition from low-wage, anti-union printers.

Just look at these figures:

Two out of three production employees at Kingsport Press are strike-breakers, hired since the strike at the base rate of $1.26 an hour—one penny more than the Federal minimum wage!

We charge that Kingsport Press wants to wring the neck of the New York book-printing industry.

How?

By insisting that the unskilled strike-breakers, hired during the past two years, are permanent replacements for the highly-trained workers who went out on strike to protect their rights as human beings.

The strikers have refused to relinquish their jobs—or those of their fellow members—to these untrained workers brought in off the streets.

How can Kingsport Press keep going?

Because textbook publishers and encyclopedia publishers have continued to send some of their printing orders to Kingsport Press.

And public officials—like the Board of Education of the City of New York—have continued to buy these products.

In other words, Kingsport Press is being rewarded for being anti-union.

So for New York City's more than one million union members and their families—and for more than 15 million unionists across the nation—it is morally and personally repugnant to have school officials use our tax money to buy scab-produced books.

We plead with the Board of Education:

- Require that textbooks and encyclopedia furnished to our schools be printed under minimum economic and social standards.

- Make sure the books which are purchased by the Board are not produced under conditions which damage the book-printing industry of New York— and the citizens who live here.

For our part, we of organized labor pledge:

- We will do everything in our power to cooperate with the Board in so important an undertaking.

A "NO" ANSWER TO EACH OF THE ABOVE QUESTIONS MEANS THAT THE BOARD IS CONCERNED WITH HUMAN DIGNITY . . . WITH RESPECT FOR MEN AND WOMEN WHO EARN A LIVING AND WHOSE TAXES SUPPORT OUR SCHOOL SYSTEM. FOR THE SAKE OF JUSTICE, WE URGE THE BOARD: VOTE "NO."

New York City Central Labor Council, AFL-CIO

386 Park Ave. South, N. Y. C.

Harry Van Arsdale, Jr., President

Allied Printing Trades Council of New York State

27 Union Square, N. Y. C.

Joseph Hellman, President

Reproduction of the unions' ad in the *New York Times*

increases put into effect at the Kingsport Press since the strike began two years ago.

If by "conditions" the unions mean the physical surroundings in which our employees work, we would point out that we constantly strive to improve our plant, and do in fact provide the best equipment and physical facilities; we would point with pride to our safety record, and we invite anyone associated with the New York School System to visit our plant—at our expense—to inspect our operation and interview any of our employees.

On the other hand, if by "conditions" the unions mean a management which spends more money for research and development than practically any other book manufacturer, is willing to risk capital on the latest concepts of modern technology, and is dedicated to providing publishers with the country's best facilities for manufacturing books, then we might agree that Kingsport Press presents a competitive threat to other printers wherever located. We invite you to contact any publishers to receive their opinions of the Kingsport Press's contribution to the industry and on any of the "conditions" to be found at our plant.

The question "Who is particularly vulnerable to these low-wage, strikebreaking operations at Kingsport Press?" is not only inflammatory, but contradictory in its very construction. "Strikebreaker" is defined in the *New Standard Dictionary* as follows: "A person who conducts an agency for the purpose of supplying, usually, skilled workmen to take the places of strikers where a strike is impending or declared."

The unions themselves in their official strike publication, on April 11, 1963, had this to say regarding strikebreakers: "How many skilled workers can be found, in all these cities combined, who would want to work at the Press during a strike? We cannot believe there will be many takers unless the Company is offering *strikebreakers' wages* (*usually double*) *plus expenses.*" (Emphasis added.)

In modern industrial jargon, strikebreaker means a highly paid professional who works only until the strike is over.

Now the unions charge the Kingsport Press with "low-wage, strikebreaking operations."

None of the above descriptions typify the Kingsport Press's

operation. Our employment procedures, practices, and wage progressions have not been changed to accommodate a strike situation.

Those employed since the strike are local people, selected from some 9,000 applicants, who expressed an interest in making the graphic arts industry their lifetime vocation. Many of these people gave up other employment to enter the printing trade.

In reference to the unions' allegations concerning the New York book printing industry's being hard pressed by competition from low-wage, anti-union printers, the following facts are presented:

1. In the last three quarters of 1962, the year before the strike, Kingsport Press lost, on price, 66% of the jobs on which it bid on a competitive basis.

2. In the face of such keen price competition, Kingsport Press's sales dropped 9% and its profits fell 38% during 1962.

3. Some of these jobs were lost to firms located in New York City and the surrounding area.

4. Some of these lost jobs went to union firms, others to non-union firms.

Of all the statements made in the March 15, 1965 *New York Times* advertisement, "Two out of three production employees at Kingsport Press are strikebreakers, hired since the strike at the base rate of $1.26 an hour—one penny more than the Federal minimum wage!" qualifies as the most clever (and most insidious) to be found.

The facts are:

1. Of 1,464 production employees currently at work, only 59 are receiving $1.26 per hour.

2. Of the 59 receiving $1.26, 37 are among the 864 persons employed in the Bindery.

3. Ironically, it is the unions themselves who are largely responsible for holding the beginning KP rate to $1.26. But for a fluke in negotiations, this rate would now be $1.35, $1.465, and $1.59 on the three shifts respectively.

4. According to Printing Industries of America, the starting rate for men and women edition bindery employees in New York City is $1.25 per hour—the minimum under both the

Federal Fair Labor Standards Act and the New York minimum wage law. (This figure—as well as all New York figures used herein and in the outline—was verified on March 16, 1965, by Mr. Mathew Kelly, chief negotiator for New York Bindery Employers, New York City.)

5. According to Printing Industries of America, new, unskilled male employees, hired on or after 9-29-62, receive $1.97 per hour after 24 months' employment, while new, unskilled female employees receive $1.50 per hour after 24 months.

6. At Kingsport Press, new, unskilled employees (both male and female) automatically progress to $1.885 per hour on day shift, $2.06 on second, and $2.19 on third after 24 months.

7. Of the 864 Bindery employees at Kingsport Press, approximately one third are presently receiving, or will progress to, the $1.885-$2.06-$2.19 (three shifts respectively) level, and the other two thirds are receiving, or will progress to, rates ranging up to a $3.215-$3.51-$3.745 (three shifts respectively) level.

In regard to the statements made under the heading of "HOW?" Kingsport Press makes these observations:

1. We recognize and honor the unions' right to strike.

2. We ask only that they respect our right to operate our plant and the right of each individual to work if he so chooses.

3. All we ask is to be allowed to compete on the basis of price, quality, and service.

4. Kingsport Press has not been "rewarded" by any publisher. Once a publisher has satisfied himself of the integrity of Kingsport Press, neither that publisher nor Kingsport Press should suffer from discrimination. Price, quality, and service should be the sole criteria.

5. Kingsport Press is not involved in a "fight" against "its long-service" employees or anyone else. The unions, and only the unions, have used such terms as "fight," "warfare," "brings them to their knees," etc.

6. To allege that Kingsport Press could take "thousands of jobs" away from New York City is utterly preposterous.

We too believe in justice. Kingsport Press is not a foreigner to the State nor the City of New York. Over 15% of the outstanding shares of company stock are recorded at New York addresses—concentrated primarily in New York City. We maintain a well-staffed office in New York City and are therefore taxpayers to the City and the State. We contribute funds to the charitable and cultural organizations of the City.

In their "plea" to the Board, the unions imply that Kingsport Press operates with working conditions and wage rates below "minimum economic and social standards." The data herewith submitted, our reputation among publishers and industry groups, and our standing in the community, prove these union implications to be false.

The unions emotionally state also that Kingsport Press constitutes a threat to the printing industry of New York. Even before Kingsport Press was launched, the recognition and recording of New York City's problem was the subject of a scholarly dissertation including commentaries by employers and union leaders of that area.

The majority of the texts required by this city's huge educational system are produced in plants located in many states, some union and some non-union; and some of the products originate in foreign countries. If the posing of a "threat" to the city's industry is accurate, the "threat" is most assuredly national and international in scope, and not focused in the Kingsport Press.

The unions' plea for "neutrality" is in fact an appeal to the Board to join with the unions in their unjustifiable attack on the Kingsport Press. We submit that to remain neutral in this dispute, purchasers of school books should neither add to nor take away from their past criteria for selecting educational materials.

We, at Kingsport Press, believe that we have been vindictively chosen as a target because the unions—for reasons known best to themselves—have directed their own actions along a course which has proven to be unwise.

7

OF "SCABS AND RATS"— AND STRIKERS

"Nowhere Is Cruelty More Abhorred"

POWERFUL UNIONS and an able management were arrayed against each other in the strike at the Press. Allen, Barber, De-Andrade, and McLellan smote mightily; Beneman, Clevenger, Fritschle, and Triebe were formidable in defense and counter-attack.

Stories about strikes have a tendency to stop after thus depicting and concentrating upon the union-management conflict. When they do, they stop too soon, perhaps much too soon. For there is another level of action, another confrontation, in strikes; one which is at times both more interesting in human terms and more significant in social terms than the union-management conflict. I speak of the clash between the working people involved: the strikers, on the one hand, and those who are called "scabs and rats" on the other.

The strike at the Press has had more than its share of interest at this level. It split families in almost every conceivable way. In one, the father chose to continue working and broke off all contact with a son who picketed to the bitter end. In another family, the positions were reversed: son returned and father stayed out. In a third, son returned but maintained normal relations and customary mutual regard with striking father. Brothers and sisters opposed each other; some became enemies, others maintained affectionate relations. Certain husbands have been escorting their wives for years now up to the Press, leaving them to cross the street and to enter the plant gates alone, while they, the husbands, joined their fellow-strikers on the picket line. In one prolific family, a striking uncle carries on a bitter feud with a "scab" nephew while maintaining a parental affection for his own son-in-law, who happens to be "scabbing" in another company.

There is material here for comedy. Like all slices of life, however, the strike at the Press provides material for tragedy, too. The violence recounted briefly in the last chapter disintegrated the Kingsport community; the cruel assaults brought deep misery to many persons. The sympathy, the understanding, the mutual respect which are necessary if human beings are to live together peacefully dissolved in a dreadful solution of enmity and spite.

Men do not make war upon each other in the way that animals do, instinctively and impersonally. Men have reasons for their wars, and personal hate to spur them to atrocity.

Strangely, though, war's passions cool when men see, and really *feel,* that their adversaries are men, too, men just like themselves. During World War II, American movies cast German and Japanese soldiers as vicious animals. Movies of the War made in recent years deal much more sympathetically with our erstwhile enemies; they are now our friends and stout allies.

A firm grasp of the common humanity may never serve to eliminate wars between nations, because governments, loaded with their own interests and their own defects, intervene between people. But it is possible that the destructive civil strife which prevails between strikers and non-strikers may be transformed into the creative rivalry which rules relations between grocer and grocer, shoemaker and shoemaker, auto manufacturer and auto manufacturer—if those involved and society as a whole come to the conclusion that the participants on both sides are all human beings, all children of God, with much in common; and therefore that there is no occasion for obliterating between them the rights and respect which hold society together.

Lord Bryce said of America: "Nowhere is cruelty more abhorred." Possibly we have changed since Lord Bryce surveyed this land and this people. But kindness and mutual regard are still essential features of the American dream. It will do no harm to try to develop them, and thus learn, and learn to prize, the deeper inward meaning of that most seminal and profound of national objectives, domestic tranquility.

Claude E. Smith:
"The Strike Was a Big Mistake"

Claude Smith is a man who shoots out swift arrows of astounding candor when the talk gets serious. They are astounding because much of what he has to say falls into the stylized pattern of the professionals of the "labor movement," with all its glittering generalities and clichés. He is himself a kind of professional. He has been president of Pressmen's Local Union 336 for more than ten years, covering all union pressmen in Kingsport and vicinity. More than that, he makes no secret of his great passion, which he describes as "intellect"; and of his great pride, which is his library. He has read widely; his conversation reflects that. How well he has read, I cannot tell; but I gather that much of it has been in what may be called the "literature of revolt and social criticism."

And yet, after having dutifully given voice to all the usual complaints which professional unionists express against business management, Claude Smith is capable of turning the sharp edge of criticism against himself, his fellow unionists, and even his international union leadership.

During our talks, he described the strike issues much as Walter Allen had done, indeed using almost the same words in many places: the management was callously old fashioned, "paternalistic," unwilling to keep up with modern trends in labor relations, inept in the selection of supervisors, unwilling to give the employees, and especially their unions, a share in the determination of working conditions, wallowing in nepotism, and so on. Upgrading and promotions were what chiefly aroused the men,

Smith said. But he contended, too, as Allen had, that Kingsport Press enjoyed a heavy competitive advantage all across the board —its wages were lower than those paid by its competitors, day shift hours longer, vacations less generous, utilization of manpower more rigorous, promotions and upgrading less fair and generous. Like Allen and DeAndrade, Smith agreed that the Press profit-sharing plan was generous; but again like them he was unwilling to concede that it was properly included in any calculation of the Press's labor costs. Still echoing his union superiors, Smith summed up with this statement: "We wanted to keep the margin between Kingsport Press and its competitors from growing still greater—we were not trying to erase it."

But from there on out he parted company. Claude Smith has lived in and around Kingsport for more than thirty years. Since 1942, his only civilian employment has been with the Press (he was in the Army for a little less than two years). He has been a journeyman pressman since 1947. He said: "You could never get our people excited about wages or hours; the seniority issue— making seniority the basis of upgrading and promotions—is what they got aroused by." I had not as yet known when I talked with Smith, that he was the union official who had initialled an agreement on seniority with Clifton Fritschle three weeks before the strike was called, and I have not had an opportunity since then to ask him to explain his emphasis upon seniority as a basic strike issue in the light of his pre-strike agreement with Fritschle.

But perhaps it is unnecessary to ask him about that. For Claude Smith is willing to admit now that it was all a big mistake. He said that the strike was, at least, very badly timed. He observed that Kingsport is surrounded by an "underdeveloped area" and that unemployment was exceptionally heavy at the time the strike was called. He said: "I wish we had given that more thought. The men are going through their life's savings. Many are deeply in debt, though the grocers and other tradesmen are going along pretty well. The Hardship Fund helps, but if things continue this way, more and more are going to lose their homes. The strike was a big mistake. I wish we had never called it."

Making mistakes is easy, and shifting the blame is both characteristic and easy. Owning up manfully, as Claude Smith did, is harder, especially when the mistake brings disaster. But Claude E. Smith has had a tough enough time of it in life to make him, for all his diminutive physique, quite a man, anyway.

He was born in Stonega, Virginia, a mining camp, in December 1914, and he has no memory of any home prior to the John Tarleton Home for Orphans, in Knoxville, where he was raised. Claude does not bemoan his childhood condition. Far from it. His mercurial smile lights his face as he refers to Miss Lea Fletcher, the superintendent of the Home. "She showered all the kindness on us that her limited budget permitted. She taught us well, gave us a fine background. We got a two-week vacation every year in the Smokies. She took us into town every Sunday."

Yet, there is in Claude Smith's psyche a shadowed zone, where old wounds from his orphanage days are hidden. He told me that he thought people were laughing at him when they saw him march in ranks with the other orphans. He determined then, he said, that people would never laugh at him when he grew up. He would make something of himself, and he would start by studying, and he has been doing it ever since.

Life was rough for him when he left the Home, at sixteen. He shined shoes for a while, washed cars, worked in a restaurant. At first he could not afford a room, so he curled up in a barber's chair at night, or slept in one of the cars he washed. The restaurant job paid enough for him to rent a room, and thus to sleep in a bed for the first time after leaving the orphanage.

Then, in 1934, age nineteen, he found a real job, in the Card & Label Printing Plant in Rogersville, thirty miles from Kingsport. And he married Emma Evelyn Price. In two years, Claude and Emma had two children—Robert Aaron, born in 1935, and now a graduate of East Tennessee State University; and Peggy Ann, born in 1936, also a graduate of East Tennessee State, in nursing. Both children are married, and have given Claude and Emma six grandchildren.

Claude left Rogersville after eight years there, to take a job as assistant pressman at the Kingsport Press. In the years since then he has made his presence felt in the community. Besides his leadership of the local Pressmen, he is prominent in the affairs of his church. Baptized a Presbyterian, Claude is now a member of the Church of Christ; but more than just a member, he is active in all its affairs. He fills in frequently for the minister and lectures to the congregation.

Claude Smith is quick to laugh and quick to grow serious; he has pride almost to the chip-on-the-shoulder point; he enjoys talking and does it well; there is an earthy realism in him, half cynical, that makes him see things close-up in agonizing sharpness, indeed out of proportion, and far-off things fuzzily or not at all. He has been a pillar of the Kingsport community for years. People listen to him when he talks. I don't think he needs to worry about their laughing at him, for even if they do, which I doubt, it is probably nothing more than the crackling of thorns under a pot.

Hugh W. Reece: "The Scabs Were Not Brought Up Right"

Every Northerner who goes down South (except possibly those who march in "Civil Rights" demonstrations) probably gets the same feeling: these people are too gentle, too friendly, too polite—they must be hypocrites. I have often felt that way, and, sad to say, I have often left the South confirmed in that conclusion. But not as far as Hugh Reece is concerned.

Not even when Reece's calm and smiling amiability gave way, and he revealed a repellent capacity for scorn and loathing. The reader will remember Hugh Reece as one of the characters introduced in the first chapter of this book. He is the journeyman bindery worker, still out, who mourned the social disintegration brought about by the prolongation of the strike.

With Jack Rhoten, Hugh was inclined to think that the strike might have come to a swift conclusion if the strikers had been able to maintain absolutely unbroken ranks. "If everyone had stayed out, the Company wouldn't have gotten the idea that it could continue to operate, and it would have been more inclined to give in. And it wouldn't have had to give in very far, either, because the unions only wanted to prove that they *could* take the men out. It would all have been over in days, except that some of the biggest strike agitators went back in right away. Now look where we're at." That was Jack Rhoten talking, but it might as well have been Hugh Reece, for he expressed essentially the same ideas.

With such ideas, it is not strange that he should have harsh feelings about the people who went back to work shortly after the strike began. However, unlike Jack Rhoten, Hugh carries in him a bitter resentment against all who have taken jobs at the Press since the strike began.

I am not in a position to report verbatim Hugh's thoughts concerning those people; the discussion grew too warm and interesting for note-taking. As soon as Hugh left, however, I set down the substance of his arguments, along with a few quotes I managed to capture. They were fresh in my mind, and I am confident that I have them correctly.

Hugh insisted that there is not much to choose between a "scab" and a "rat." As used in Kingsport, the term "rat" refers to union men who have abandoned the strike. A "scab" is a man who has taken the employment which a striker has left. Hugh held that the strike-defectors, the "rats," must be considered traitors. "I don't hate them" he protested, "but we were all so close. Take my brother-in-law. We married sisters. He dragged me up to the gate, and he went in. He betrayed me. It wouldn't be so bad if he had come up to me and said straight out that he felt he had to go in. But he was always real strong for the strike. He had us all believing he was with us, and then he doublecrossed us. In fact, I believe a majority of the people who went back in were strong for the strike."

Hugh's position is that once you go out on strike, the only honorable course is to stay out till there is a settlement. He is proud, he said, that no one has ever tried to induce him to go back. He thinks this an indication that people regard him as a man of principle. I asked him to expand on that. He said:

when a man goes out on strike he makes a firm promise to his fellow-strikers that he will stick it out until an agreement is reached which the majority are willing to accept; there is a solemn pact under oath when a strike is called, and a man of character must abide by his pacts. I asked: what about a man who resigns *before* a strike is called, on the ground that striking would be against the best interests of all? Hugh was firm: it is not right or moral to resign from any organization in an emergency situation, any more than it is right to refuse to fight for your country.

"Maybe," he yielded, "it would be different if a man resigned from the union at a time when there were no big issues at all, no bargaining going on or anything like that." But after the briefest of pauses he drew back this concession and charged even further forward. "No. A man has got a duty to join the union in any organized shop; otherwise, he's a 'free rider,' taking the benefits of union organization without doing the manly thing—sharing the burdens and costs."

"They know they're wrong," Hugh said, echoing something Jack Rhoten had said to me earlier. Jack had said: "You can't respect those people, and they know it. That's why they cross the street to avoid encounters with strikers, and why they put their eyes down, won't look you in the eye." I was reminded by this of something that Vilfredo Pareto had said in his massive work, *The Mind and Society:* ". . . as regards the 'strike-breaker,' the 'scab,' . . . he has, as a class, very little spirit. He is not inspired by any lofty ideal, he is almost ashamed of what he is doing, and does it with as little talk as possible."* I was also reminded of something much more immediate. A little earlier that day I had been talking in the plant with Hal Newman. He told me that he, his wife, and one brother had agreed two weeks before the strike was called that they would continue working. They went together to their father, also employed at the Press, and strong for the strike. They said to him that they thought a strike would be senseless; that the Press was too good an employer to deserve a strike; that striking the Press would be both a disloyal and a foolish act; that the men didn't know what they

---

* IV, 1514 et seq.

were striking over; that they'd never gain back what they would lose in striking. Hal Newman said that his father remained unconvinced, but that he respected his children's right to make up their own minds—and that relations among them have not been changed by the strike.

Pareto was a great scholar, a pioneer, a professional sociologist. Jack Rhoten and Hugh Reece may be amateur sociologists. I am no sociologist at all, but a lawyer. I reserve judgment on their reading of the character of strike-defectors and striker replacements. The ones I have met in Kingsport and elsewhere do not conform very well to their descriptions.

"You've told me about your feelings toward the defectors," I said to Hugh. "Now tell me what you think about the 'new hires,' the 'replacements,' the people you call 'scabs.' What's their character, in your scheme of things?"

"It all goes back to the parents," Hugh said. "My son wouldn't take a striker's job—I hope he wouldn't, anyway. (I have to allow for the kids, who don't know any better.) We consider a scab to be stealing—stealing our jobs. I think that the people who have been there so long, who have built the place, are entitled to protection—to have their jobs protected against such thieves—because they have given a heck of a lot of their lives in building it. A man who will steal hasn't been brought up right and is immoral."

Seeking to draw him out, I argued the point with Hugh. I said that there is no way known to the law in which the usual relationship between employer and employee can be stretched into job-ownership by the employee. Workers take their pay day by day, week by week, year by year. Yes, they make a contribution to the company. But they insist upon pay for their contribution right along. They do not agree to forgo their pay when the company loses money, as its owners and stockholders do. So they do not build up the kind of equity in a firm that both law and morality accord to the owners. Workers want a contract of employment, which assures them a fixed rate of pay regardless of the company's profit position.

Thus they are in the same position as others who agree to

furnish supplies to the company. Suppose, I said, that the Mead
Paper Company, which has been supplying the Press with paper
for forty years, should raise its price to a level which the Press
refused to pay. If another company offered to supply the Press
with paper at the old price, and the Press then began doing
business with the other company, would Hugh say that there
had been any theft? Remember, I said, Mead had been doing
business with the Press for forty years. It was a long relationship, an intimate one, with many problems shared, a great deal
of close cooperation, many ups-and-downs together, and all that.
But did Hugh feel that Mead *owned* the Press's paper account?
Does any supplier *own* the right to fill any buyer's needs? Workers supply labor. They withdraw it at will, and nobody can
stop them. Often, during a strike, it happens that a striker finds
a job which he prefers over the one he has vacated. Has the
company the right to force him to come back? "Of course not,"
Hugh said. Or again: John Doe goes to work at the Press on
Monday for the first time; a strike is called on Tuesday; he joins
it, leaving his job. Does he *own* the job he left? How does he
acquire so strong a title, so soon?

I have been searching a long time for a way to justify Hugh
Reece's position. I have been searching equally long for flaws in
the reasoning and the analogies presented in the preceding
paragraphs. I must report that I searched as vainly in Hugh
Reece's mind as I have elsewhere. He protested the reasoning,
said that the analogies were "different cases." But he failed to
produce a moral or a legal argument in rebuttal or refutation. He
produced only protests and succeeded in only one thing: he remained as strongly convinced of the moral depravity of "scabs
and rats" after our talk as he had been before.

The strikers apparently feel that the strength of their emo-
tions gives them a one-sided set of rights against their employer.
They reserve the right to leave their jobs whenever they wish;
they reserve the right to strike whenever they wish. The incon-
veniences, even the catastrophic problems, which they may
create for employers in thus exercising *their* rights, however,
create no kind of moral claim against them. They have only

rights, not duties, in the premises. The employer must sit there when his employees call a strike against him. On pain of being regarded as thieves or "scabs" (who, of course, are beyond the pale of human respect, and therefore have "coming to them" anything they get), others must not take the employment spurned by the strikers—no matter how badly they need work or how foolish the strike may seem to them. In short, production must cease till the strikers decide that it should be resumed. If production is resumed before the strikers decide to return, any violence which occurs in the interim is the responsibility of the employer and of the "scabs and rats"—not of the men who actually hurl the stones and bombs, or spread the tacks, or make life hell in a thousand ways for a whole community.

It is emotionalism and prejudice run wild. It is a convenient philosophy for thugs and scoundrels. I cannot see it, though, as the seriously held conviction of such decent and civilized people as Claude Smith, Jack Rhoten, Walter Allen, and Hugh Reece.

Thus I had the feeling toward the end of our discussion, that Hugh Reece was being a lawyer rather than stating his own conviction; that he was defending a position to which he was perforce committed, not articulating what he truly believed. He would not admit that, of course. But in a last effort to get through to his own opinions, I said: "Hugh, if all rights belong to the strikers, and none to the company or the defectors or replacements, as you say you believe, then what kind of responsibility do unions and their members have when it comes to calling a strike?" In substance, he replied: the responsibility is a lot heavier than we all thought. "We all know now that you can't call a strike lightly; that you've got to give it a lot of thought; and strike only when you absolutely must."

Fred Campbell Calhoun:
He Thinks Hard Before He Acts

Fred Calhoun, linotype machinist and local official of the International Typographical Union, went out on strike but returned to his job after two weeks, having resigned from the Union the day before he returned to work. He says that he never approved the strike; that as a member of the Typographical Union's local negotiating team he dissented from the position taken by the International; and that he considered the Press's offer fair and reasonable.

He struck, he said, only out of a sense of duty as a union member, and with the hope of a speedy settlement. As the days went by and the unions showed no sign of willingness to accept the concessions offered by the Press, but instead grew more and more vehement, he concluded that it would be a long drawn out affair. He had wanted no part of a short strike; he was certainly not going to rot away in a long one. He called up his chapel chairman (chief shop steward) to resign from the Union and to announce his decision to return to work. The chairman said: "Ancel Carmack is going back tomorrow; maybe you ought to wait till the next day."

Born in Kingsport in 1929, and still well under forty, Fred Calhoun is one of the more deliberate and deliberative men I have known. He thinks long and hard before voicing an opinion on any serious question. You can almost "see" his mind working. The answers, while slow in coming, are straight and firm. He breaks up questions and answers into their logical components, and looks at them piece by piece. As a result, he is rarely flustered, almost never confused. He makes an occasional mistake in analysis, but when he does it is easy to spot and isolate, and he recognizes it himself with grace and candor.

An only child, Fred Calhoun has apparently always been precociously sober and responsible. Perhaps because his father, a construction worker, was a heavy drinker, Fred is a rigorous teetotaler; he is against drinking, not only for himself, but for everyone else as well. He married young, when he was only eighteen. Still only thirty-seven, his daughter, Elaine, is eighteen; and his two sons, David and Gregory, are seventeen and ten, respectively.

Fred was apparently born for community responsibility. At eighteen he was superintendent of a small country school, and musical director as well, a post he still holds. He has been a lay leader of the Grange Hall Church Community for years, is chairman of its Education Committee, and has chaired its Committee

of Visitation and Evangelism. Before the strike he had always
held positions of comparable responsibility in the Kingsport
Press chapel of the Typographical Union. He was chapel chairman for one term, an active member of the Negotiating Committee, and a member of the Grievance Committee (a not so
active job, he said, because grievances were few and rarely
reached the level of his Committee).

It is almost twenty years now since Fred Calhoun started
working at the Press, in 1947. He joined the I.T.U. shortly after
he got on the Press payroll. People in the composing room were
never much interested in the I.T.U., he said. It was hard to get
them to join, infinitely harder to get them to be active. Fred
said: "I was never really absorbed by union matters myself. I
was interested in the welfare of the Kingsport Press composing
room, but I couldn't care less about the national problems of the
Union. They seemed to me to have no bearing on our problems
or interests here, though I suppose they were important to the
national Union leaders. My active role was really forced on me
by the general lack of interest in the Union among the workers.
I feel that if an organization is worth belonging to it is worth
one's active interest. But the strike was brought on by national
problems of the Union, not by local problems, which were
not at all serious. I wanted no part of it at any time."

I asked Fred whether he had feelings of guilt or shame in
abandoning the Union during the strike. He said: "It's been a
real trial, but not in that way. I've had a lot of trouble with the
strikers, most of it with men who were the biggest backsliders as
Union men before the strike, men that I had to work for in the
Union because they were too lazy to take on any responsibility.
In fact, the man who has given me the most trouble was not even
a Union member before the strike. Probably he joined the
Union because its strike benefits are so high—more than $70.00
a week. There's been a lot of baiting, and the hard thing is to
keep from reacting violently. What got to me most was accusations. Things said to me about my family, low remarks about my
church activity. Somehow they went all over me. Shootin' the
back of my car, that didn't worry me too much.

"I regret leaving the Union," Fred continued. "But the regret isn't strong and it has nothing to do with any guilt feelings. Every man has to decide these things for himself. Nobody, inside or outside a union, can do a man's thinking for him. I have to make my own decisions, and I want to make them myself, and I want to leave others to do the same. That's why I'm in favor of the Right-to-Work Laws and why I think it would be terrible to repeal 14 (b) of the Taft-Hartley Act. I thought that way when I was in the Union, too. Men have got a right to make their own decisions about these things. I've always thought those people were wrong who said that everybody should have to join a union where the shop had one."

I asked Fred how he felt about the local prohibitions on the sale of hard liquor. He said he was strongly in favor of them. "How can you square that with your stand on the right and freedom of every man to make his own decisions? Why shouldn't I have the right to buy liquor openly here, instead of having to sneak around?"

"Well, you're right," Fred said. "I could say that liquor is different, harmful; but I know that freedom means free to do things that might hurt yourself. But I don't favor prohibition in order to limit the freedom of adults. It's the children I'm thinking about. It's the responsibility of adults to bring up children right, and prohibiting the sale of hard liquor is necessary to keep kids from developing bad habits before they're fully responsible."

I observed at that point that if the object is to control children, then the thing to do is to have age limits on liquor sales, not general prohibition. Fred agreed as a matter of logic and reason, but I am not sure that he is out campaigning for repeal of the anti-liquor laws prevailing in and around Kingsport.

Jack Darris Salyer: Actions Speak Louder Than Words

Jack Salyer was asleep when he heard the window shatter in his dining room. He jumped out of bed, saw a heavy fog-like mist rising and spreading from the dining room floor, and as he ran out of the back bedroom, his eyes began to sting—tear gas! He ran back to get his wife up, but she already had the kids out of bed and was hustling them out the back door. They were on their feet and moving, but still asleep. Young Barry, weaving around, bumped into the refrigerator and got a bloody nose.

There were no other personal injuries, but the house was a mess. Floors and walls had to be refinished, the furniture had to be cleaned with special chemicals. It took ten weeks before the family could move back in. For months afterward, said Jack, you could still smell the tear gas during a heavy rain.

Jack made two telephone calls as soon as he had the kids out of the house and had gathered his wits. One was to the police, the other to Clifton Fritschle. The police came promptly, but they weren't equipped to go in to get the canisters, so the tear gas kept spreading through the house. Cliff Fritschle had been asleep, but he moved fast as soon as Salyer explained the situation, called the State Police, and they came equipped with gas masks and removed the canisters.

Jack had to borrow clothes to get to work. He said: "I wouldn't miss showing up for work that morning if I had to crawl in, nekkid."

"I was expecting something, but I didn't think it was going to be that bad." He was expecting something because he had just gone back to his job at the Press, after staying out on strike for about three weeks. He had gone back on the morning of April 2, and the tear gas was thrown less than twenty-four hours later, at 2 A.M., the morning of April 3. I suppose that is why they call picket lines "observation posts."

Jack Salyer is six feet tall, and thin, weighing maybe 150 pounds. He is a lively fellow, full of fun, quick to joke, and generally high spirited. The fifth of nine children, he comes from a very poor family. His father was killed in a mine accident in Lecture County, near Harlan, Kentucky, when Jack was only nine. That was in 1939. The family moved from Kentucky to Kingsport, and Jack went to the Kingsport public schools till 1947, when he was seventeen. He had to quit then, at the end of his third year in high school, because the family needed money.

He got on with the Jones Wholesale Grocery and worked there as a stock boy till 1949, when he went into the Army. "I stayed in the Army," Jack said, "for three years, three months, and seventeen days, till February 3, 1953."

Jack started working at the Press in March, 1953. By 1960 he was a journeyman maintenance mechanic, a highly responsible, well-paid position. He joined the Machinists Union in 1956 and was active in its affairs: a delegate in 1958 and 1959, vice president of Local 1694 in 1960, and a shop steward when the strike was called.

Jack said that his position made it possible for him to understand the sentiment among the Machinists pretty well. Of the 44 Machinists members, no more than four or five wanted to strike, and they had strictly "personal" reasons. The worst "strike agitator," Jack said, had been a strong "company man" till just two weeks before the strike. He changed when he heard that he was not going to get a foreman's job that he had been angling for. "This man," Jack said, "had a way with him, a golden tongue. He had our local president by the ear and influenced him."

Of the 44 Union members, only 24 participated in the "strike-sanction" vote, and 20 voted in favor of authorizing the Union to call a strike. Jack said he had circulated a petition a couple of days before the strike. He wanted to have a regular strike vote, with all members voting. But he could get only six of the ten signatures required for such a vote. "The others wouldn't sign because they were afraid to create hard feelings. If you were just talking about it, none of them were for a strike. But they wouldn't sign the petition."

Jack said that the lack of strike sentiment was demonstrated by the more or less swift return to work of almost all the more active members of the Machinists local. They understood the situation better. Only the more ignorant and uninformed have stayed out, he said.

"I was always against the strike, but when everybody else went out, I wasn't going to be the only one to come in. I told the bindery superintendent that when one man came back in I'd come too. I wouldn't be the first, but I'd be the second. I almost was. Two came back on one day, April 1. I came back the next day. The day after that our house was gassed."

Going back was hard. "The picket line was tough. Four or five hundred people out there, rocks a-flyin'. But I always figured I'd have to pay my own bills. No one else would pay them. I had a pregnant wife and kids to support. I wanted to support them myself. The best way I knew how to do that was to go back to work at the Press. I wasn't about to lose my house, so I just had to go through the line."

Jack said it has been rough ever since. They've broken windows in his house seven times, with steel ballbearings, an inch in diameter. "They come in pretty hard at times. One went all the way through and broke a vase on the other side of the room. Once they threw a sack full of house bricks. It missed the window, landed up on the roof, sounded like a herd of elephants."

During the spring of 1965, they were still spreading tacks and nails. Jack said he had to inspect his driveway every morning and often picked up a handful of nails. The kids checked the driveway every night before he came home from work. No one ever bothered his wife or children while he was away, but on Halloween night, 1963, a bunch of kids stood off on a hill looking down at his house, screaming obscenities and making foul gestures.

Jack seems to have real difficulty understanding how the strikers can be so "mean." "I just can't see how they can act the way they're acting, some of them. They didn't feel any differently than I did. I've averaged over $10,000 for the last five years. I can't complain about that kind of pay or about the way I'm treated personally. I've been here for twelve years and never anything out of the way has ever been said to me. And I've never seen anybody else treated anything but well. I've never seen the company mistreat anyone or deny anybody a chance to get ahead. Of course they can't let people run machines who can't do it, who aren't qualified, but they sure give him every chance.

"Everybody knows these things, deep down. Some of my old friends won't have anything to do with me, but they're all wrong and all mixed up. They're false friends. I'm getting along right now better with some of the strikers than I was before the strike and before I came back—at least when they are alone, not with other strikers. They wish they had never struck, but they still can't force themselves by that picket line. I know a boy who actually applied for his job back but couldn't bring himself to cross the street. That boy tells me he'll never join another union. He feels he's made a serious mistake, but he's got nothing against anyone in or out of the plant, except the International. They should have never called the strike, and they could have settled it long ago, if they wanted to."

I asked Jack what he thought about the strikers' theory that defectors and striker replacements were evil people, nothing better than thieves and not entitled to the decent respect of mankind. Jack said: "That's a lot of talk. They say scabs is bad people. But no scab threw the tear gas into my house, and no scab has been breaking my windows and putting nails in my driveway. Decency is how you act, not how you talk."

Ruth Burdine: No Right to Be Rowdy

Ruth Burdine, age "over twenty-one," and four times a grandmother, is a vivacious, handsome, vigorous woman. She had been working as a proofreader at the Press for almost ten years when the strike began. Although she did not return to work till the strike had been going on for two weeks, the lapse had nothing to do with the strike. She had fallen off a chair while washing windows in her home and broken her shoulder. As soon as she was able, she returned to her job.

It was quite a shock. "The girls were acting so unladylike. They had a right to strike, and I had a right to work. I never weakened for an instant, though the nasty things they said— calling me 'Granny Burdine' was nothing—disgusted me and made me more than ever convinced that I was doing the right thing. I've never been sorry I came to work during the strike. I can't quit work with my husband in the condition he is in.

I've built a new life now around my work. The company has a marvelous profit-sharing plan providing for our retirement. The strikers lost the sympathy of Kingsport by their rowdy conduct, violence and name-calling. They'd have done better if they acted like ladies and gentlemen."

Ruth Dougherty was a general office worker and a skilled stenographer when, at twenty-one, Anderson Burdine convinced her that she should marry him. She took to marriage, motherhood, and home-making as if nature had designed her for them. "My life was built around my two sons, my husband, and my home," she said. She could not understand how being a housewife might be considered boring. Making her home attractive for her men and involvement with the P.T.A., the Garden Club, and the activities of the First Baptist Church—these were the things which filled her life, and she found them good.

Then, in 1952, when her first-born, Doyle, was sixteen, and Arlan twelve, tragedy struck the Burdine household. Anderson Burdine, supervisor in the Press bindery at the time, a strong and able man, one of the best liked and most competent men employed at the Press, suffered a paralyzing stroke. He was unable to move, unable even to speak.

Weeks and months went by, and Anderson showed little improvement. "There were a lot of adjustments to make," Ruth quietly said. The boys were at an age when they especially needed their parents. Anderson Burdine's speech impediment made it impossible for him to counsel the boys. "It was all up to me. I had to be mother and father." Ruth never wielded the stick as the boys grew up—"only a teeny-weeny one when they were teeny-weenies." Instead she reasoned with them, "talked to them, explained to them when I wanted them to do something."

The boys turned out well. Ruth said: "They took our trouble like soldiers and are the better for it. Of course Arlan resented it some when Doyle tried to be a father over him in my absence." Today, Doyle is a popular and well-known figure in business circles in Kingsport. He was named Kingsport's "Man of the Year" by the Jaycees in 1965, and he has been chairman of the board of directors of Kingsport's Boys' Club and president of the Junior Chamber of Commerce. Arlan, a graduate of East Tennessee State University and of the Naval Officers Training School, is an ensign in the Navy.

Two years after Anderson was stricken, it became apparent that the new condition of the Burdine family had to be regarded as permanent. If the boys were to get through college, as Ruth was determined that they should, she was going to have to give up her life as a housewife. She had to find a job. The Press management had shown in countless ways that it would do everything it could to help. Ruth asked for a job and got it. Within a year, after having brushed up her English grammar, spelling, and so on, she became a proofreader. She has shown me around the Press's cheerful, attractive proofreading rooms with much the same proprietary pride as I suspect she would have had I visited with her at home.

The family fortunes, having taken one turn for the better, went ahead to another. While his speech remained (and remains) impaired and the paralysis continued to grip most of his body Anderson improved to the point where he could use his right arm with confidence and competence. The Press found a job that he could do, and gave it to him, in 1955, and he has worked steadily at it since then.

"How could I forsake the Press?" Ruth wanted to know. Though some proofreaders were members of the Typographical Union before the strike was called, she had never been asked to join till after the strike. When asked, she said: "No, thank you." "I had no reason to join, then, or ever. I had never given the Union a moment's thought. It had never done anything for me. There was never anything I wanted from it. I've only had trouble from the unions and the strike. They had my phone ringing all night, till I just took it off the hook when I went to sleep. They heckle me at the picket line. One time they threw a lot of eggs into my car, all over the windshield and the dashboard. It was a hot day and they made a real mess. But the eggs weren't rotten, anyway."

David Earl Draper:
He Found the Job He Wanted

Davey Draper is small and slight, gentle and soft spoken. He likes gardening and fishing, but what he enjoys most is just sitting out in the quiet country, and it doesn't make much difference to him whether or not he has company. But you must not mistake his character. His folks did once, when they moved from Bristol, Virginia, to Chattanooga over Davey's objections. Davey was only a high school student at the time, but he was sweet on a Bristol girl, Linda Lou, and he intended to marry her. When the family moved to Chattanooga, he stayed behind. Two years later, in 1960, he married Linda Lou while home on leave from the Navy.

The pickets mistook him, too, during the strike at the Press. Davey had wanted for a long time to get a job at the Press; he had heard most of his life that it was the best place in the area to make a working career. He was a handy fellow in a number of trades, carpentry and plumbing included, and thought there should be a place for him at the Press. He first applied on March 1, 1963, ten days before the strike was called. Nothing doing, the Press said at the time; but his background and experience looked good and his application stayed in the active file. On March 27, the Press asked him if he was still interested in working there, in view of the strike. Davey was a little uneasy, but he wanted the job, and took it.

"The picketing was hot and heavy. I parked my car on Roller Street the first day, instead of in the parking lot, so I had to walk through the howling pickets. There was a lot of noise, but no violence. Then I had to walk back through the line, to drive uptown for my physical. Four pickets followed me to my car, and told me not to come back. These four weren't bad, but the ones across the street were foul."

Day after day the pickets kept following Davey, talking harder to him each time. A week after he began working at the Press, two men accosted him in Bristol. It was 6:15 A.M. and Davey was standing on a corner, waiting for his ride. One asked where he was headed. "I told him I was going to work. When they asked me—'where?'—I told them, 'Kingsport Press.' "

"Don't you know a strike is going on there?"

"Yes."

"We don't want you to go back in there any more. The Union has turned us loose to keep you out any way we have to."

"I need the work, I like the work, and I'm going to work," Davey said.

"Then they asked me what my name was. I told them I'd just as soon not tell them. Then they said, 'We haven't been sitting out here since 5 A.M. for nothing.' I told 'em I still wasn't going to tell 'em what my name was. So then they said they'd find out. About that time my ride drove up. My driver got out and they talked to him the same way. He said: 'I'm going in today but I don't know whether I'll go in Monday.' They drove off and we drove off." Nothing more happened that morning.

A few days later a blue Chevy followed Davey and his driver all the way to Bristol from Kingsport. Davey got out to walk to his truck. The men in the Chevy jumped out and blocked him. Davey pushed his way into the truck, but the window on the driver's side was open, and one of the men jumped up on the running board and struck Davey twice in the jaw. Under instructions from the Press management to avoid all fights, Davey put his truck in gear and pulled away so swiftly that the fellow tumbled off the running board. The gang chased him in the Chevy for a while, but he lost them. Later, Davey was to testify against his assailant. Despite the latter's denial, the judge believed Davey and sentenced the aggressor to seven days in jail. The unions had him out on bond within four hours of the sentencing.

Davey has had no more such experiences. He says that he has never had any doubt that taking work at the Press was the right thing to do. "They can and probably will call me a scab for the rest of my life, but it don't matter. I must provide for my family, and I don't know of any better way to do it than working for the Press. I feel that as long as you do your day's work the

Press will go all the way with you—pay, advancement, and everything else."

He feels no remorse, no guilty conscience, stoutly resists any suggestion that he has been a wrong-doer. "I've never done any harm to anyone in my life, unless it's evil for a man to live his life his own way, the way he wants to live it himself."

Joe H. Martin and the Manly Art

Joe Martin is twenty-eight years old, just about the same age as Dave Draper, but the resemblance slows down there. Joe is a powerful fellow, close to six feet tall and 180 pounds of beefy muscle, as against Dave's five-feet-six and 135 pounds. Unlike Davey, Joe has had no hand-to-hand encounters with the strikers. They have confined themselves mainly to shooting up his house, late at night, with "punkin' balls" and big ball bearings, hurled with sling shots.

Joe Martin had one other thing in common with Dave Draper —a long-nourished desire to get a job at the Press. Even while stationed with the Army in Iceland, the longest, dullest year he ever spent, Joe says he used to think about getting on at the Press. His father and mother and two older sisters had worked at the Press before the strike, and it was a commonplace in the Martin family that Press was the best place in town to work for.

The strike brought Joe his chance. James Martin, Joe's older brother, had gone out on strike against the Blue Ridge Glass plant after working there for ten years, even though he had been on the verge of a foremanship at the time. The strike cost him his job and a year of idleness. When he got a job later at the Holston Glass Company, Jim settled down industriously and became a superintendent. "Jim told me," Joe said, "that if he didn't have the job he has, he'd have gone through the Press picket line."

In the middle of March, 1963, Joe got talking to Ralph Mc-Coy, a Press executive, at a funeral, and asked him if it was true that the Press was telling the strikers that it was going to start hiring replacements. Ralph McCoy said it was true, and Joe said: "If those people don't want to work at the Press, I do; and I'm willing to cross the picket line." McCoy said that Joe's application would be given serious consideration. It was. Joe said proudly that he was either the first or the second man to be hired during the strike.

Crossing the picket line was wild, Joe said: "Pu-lenty of name-calling. You name it, they called it." There was never a dull moment in his job, for he was a truckdriver and had to cross and re-cross picket lines many times each day. In the early days it was hard because the Press was short of truckdrivers, and Joe had to do by himself—largely after sleepless nights—the work normally done by three or even four truckdrivers. "I had 'em throw eggs, rocks, and everything imaginable at me. They used to gang up, before the injunction, three or four hundred of 'em out thar'—throwin' eggs, rocks, what have you. First time, comin' by the warehouse, I had my window down and they threw an egg that splattered all over me. After that I kept the window up, though I didn't like to because if one of those rocks had hit it, the glass would have cut my haid off."

Joe is big and tough. His hands look as if they could tear a man apart. They kept clenching as he recounted his experiences when walking or driving through the picket lines. "They are still saying rotten, filthy things to me at one picket post, which I can't avoid—men and women, too—filthy things about my wife. It makes my blood jump but I know that if I give in there'll be real trouble. If it wasn't for hurting the Press and myself, I'd jump out and let them have it, but that's probably what they want. So I just take it. I've taken two years of it, and I can take two more. In the less than two years I've been here I've made nearly $13,000, while they've been picketing, and I'm providing for my boy and my wife."

The strikers have provided Joe with some occasion for relief, however. Maybe without it, he would have exploded by now. The relief may be measured in terms of what he has left of three boxes of shotgun shells which he bought shortly after going to work at the Press. There were 25 shells in each box, he said, and there are only six left. "So," he said, "I must have shot 69 or 70 times the first three months of the strike."

"Many a night," Joe said, "I sat up with the bottom window of the storm door up and my shotgun in my lap. One pesty fellow would pull his car up, aiming the headlights right at the house. One night he yelled out: 'Why don't you shoot, Joe?' I said: 'One more time, Ernie, and I'll blow those headlights out.' He never came back."

But others did, night after night, shooting up the front of his house. Joe reported it to the police. They always came quickly, when he called, but they said they couldn't keep a man stationed constantly at his house; for the same kind of thing was going on all over town. Joe said he intended to defend himself, his family, and his house; he was going to load his rifle and "get" the vandals. The police officer said he had every right to defend himself. "But he told me," Joe said, "that I shouldn't use a rifle because the bullets might ricochet and hurt innocent people. He said I should use a shotgun and punkin' balls." (They are extra large pellets.)

After a while, Joe took to stationing himself across the road from his house, on the tin roof of a welding shop. That gave him a better line of fire. A car would show up in the small hours of the morning about every other day, stop in front of Joe's house and fire at it. Joe would return the fire from the welding shop. "There was very few times I would miss," he said. But the cars kept coming back. After a while, Joe took turns standing watch on the welding shop roof with another striker replacement. Staying up all night, every night, was getting to be too much for him after working long hours every day. The assaults came to a climax, and to an end, one morning toward the end of June, 1963. "My friend, Eugene Pyle, and I were standing watch together that night. A black four-door Corvair with four men in it drove slowly up to the front of my house, stopped, and someone shot a big ballbearing through the glass on my storm door. Pyle and I stood up on the top of the shop. He fired twice, I fired three times. We blew the glass out of the left side and the rear of the Corvair. They took off as fast as they could, and they was only one head showing. We jumped down, ran across the street, over the broken glass, got in my car, and drove all over looking for that car, but never did we see a black Corvair.

"I was up all night that night, like I had been for most of three months. It was a lousy, lousy way to live. I was a mess, our life was a mess. But I had to stick it out."

Doyle D. Fields: Out of This Nettle, Danger

Anybody interested in exploring the comic possibilities of the strike at the Press would be well advised to consult Mr. Doyle D. Fields. Doyle's mother came from a family of nineteen children, which endowed him with a passel of aunts and uncles, and they, with their own voluminous offspring, all seemed to be involved in the strike, on one side or another, or in the middle, or somewhere.

Doyle Fields was born May 1, 1941, in Scott County, Virginia. The family has a farm, but the cash crop came from father's job at the Tennessee Eastman. When his father died in 1961 Doyle had to think seriously about work. He had older brothers and sisters, but they were not inclined to help mother along, and the burden fell to Doyle, who, for all his Great Dane buffoonery has a sober and responsible side to him.

Doyle got work first in a grocery store, then digging ditches, and then, for a year, in the Virginia Forestry Service. There was always someone in the family, somewhere, working at the Press; several cousins—later to become bitter-end strikers—had told him it was a great place to work. But by the time Doyle got around to thinking seriously about applying for work there, the strike was on, and he wasn't quite sure he should apply, "what with aunts and uncles and cousins all carrying on about the strike." What finally decided him, he said, was that one of his aunts told him he didn't have the nerve to cross the picket line.

"Let's go out thar to Press for a job," he said to a friend and to one of his cousins. Early on Monday, April 15, 1963, Doyle picked up his friend and his cousin, and they all drove in his mother's pickup truck along the Ridge Road from Fort Blackmore to Gate City, Virginia, and thence to Kingsport. On the way, they picked up a friend who said he too wouldn't mind getting a job at the Press. So all four went on together.

When they arrived at the main gate, Doyle said, there must have been more than a hundred pickets, and each seemed to have a separate threat to make. One of the four, according to Doyle, said: "Let's not drive through, let's park and walk through, and see what they will do. Let's see if they're as rough as they are letting on."

"We parked the truck," Doyle said, "got out, and as we approached, the pickets kept threatening us, but they backed out of the way, let us pass and didn't do anything to us. I didn't hardly think they would do anything; if I did I'd probably have backed out. I guess it was foolish. Maybe we should have driven through."

When he came out, Doyle found all the tires flat on his truck. What really got to him, though, he says, was the conduct of one of his aunts, who just happened to come on the scene. She drove up and said angrily: "Doyle, what in the world did you want to come down and go in there fer? You knowed they wuz out for a good cause." Doyle was having too much trouble with the strikers all around him to pay much attention to what his aunt was doing and saying, even though she was on him worse than the strikers. He doubts that his aunt ever did find out what the strike was all about, and he remembers with glee that a police officer came along and dragged her off his back.

Doyle was harassed plenty after that, mainly, it seems, by members of the family. But I believe that he might have been the only man in Kingsport who got any fun out of the strike— or maybe it was just his family. Aunts, uncles, cousins, all jumped on him. He had two uncles on the picket line who were employed elsewhere than the Press, who in fact never were on the Press payroll. They were picketing because their sons were on strike. Those uncles made a point of calling the police whenever Doyle crossed the picket line, announcing that Doyle should be searched because he was sure to be carrying a gun.

"Then there's Uncle Horton," Doyle said, "who takes care of

the family burial plot, in the purtiest graveyard in the county, not braggin', at the foot of High Nob in Scott County, Virginia. Uncle Horton mowed around the graves of all the family, except my father's—just because I'm scabbin'. It seems unChristian. Uncle Horton's been specially mean. It's hard for me to understand it. His daughter married a scab, and Uncle Horton isn't holding it against *him*."

There are a lot of things like that going on, and Doyle finds them comic and interesting. "One female striker—she warn't no better than I was—told me that I ought to go back to the hills. Funny thing, that ol' gal's husband is working here at the Press right now."

Doyle has his mature, serious, and sensible side, and may turn out to be a pillar of society when he reaches full maturity. He says there is just nothing in the area to compare with a job at the Press—the pay, the future, the working conditions, the foremen, the cleanliness. "I don't understand these strikers. They're stupid, crazy. They had it made and just walked out and left it. You'd have to shoot me to get me to strike against the Press.

"The strikers used to say, 'You scabs are only going to be in there for a few days, cleaning up and getting things ready for us. We'll be back, and you'll be out.' Now, after two years, they aren't saying things like that any more.

"They hurt themselves by striking, and they hurt themselves more by being mean and nasty and threatening and violent. If they'd talked nice to people, maybe not so many would have come in. A lot came in just to show they weren't going to be scared away. That's my opinion about it."

It would be interesting to confront Vilfredo Pareto with Doyle Fields.

Pencia Millsap: Fantine

"Pencie," as everyone calls her, has two young daughters to raise, a disappointing marriage has brought her to the point where she is "through with men," though she is still only a girl herself, and so she will stick with the Press no matter what the strikers do.

Pencie was born in Edenton, North Carolina, in 1939, and was graduated from high school there, in 1957. She has a Carolina drawl as thick as molasses, and as sweet, and would like to revisit Edenton. "It's just a small colonial town, right on the coast, old, but pretty, and has a lot of old plantations. I've chopped peanuts, picked cotton, handed tobacco and tied it, hoed potatoes, and dug 'em too. I say I only want to *visit* Edenton, not stay there. I like it here in Kingsport and intend to stay. I like production; the more I get out, the more I want to. And the pay is real good, even without overtime. I intend to put my girls through college, or whatever else they want to do. Some day they'll be giving me grandchildren." Pencie is just 26 now, but she's looking ahead.

Pencie will have stories to tell her grandchildren about the strike. Maybe she will tell them about a free haircut she got one morning. It was a lovely May morning, a little misty, and Pencie wished she had some time to enjoy it. But her little girls had fussed worse than usual about her leaving them to go to work, and she was late, afraid to miss her ride, so she was hustling right along to meet her driver at the appointed place on the old Bristol Highway.

"This car, a red and white Pontiac, pulled over and followed me, asked me if I wanted a ride. I said no, and the driver pulled away, but he stopped again and asked me where I worked. I said 'Holston Ordinance' (that's the only other place I could think of —my husband worked there). Then three girls got out of the car. They grabbed me. Two held me and one started cutting my hair. I just put up my hands to cover my hair and started hollerin'. You wouldn't believe me, but a car went right by. One girl said I was taking other people's jobs and was I going to quit. I said, 'No, I have to support my kids.' Then my ride came and they ran off. I wasn't scared, and I might have been a little angry. But I don't hold a grudge, and anyway I was going to get a haircut. I needed one."

Her job at the Press has revitalized Pencie. She feels confident that she can raise the kids by herself. Dawn is now seven, Patricia five. They still don't like her working, and that makes her a little sad. But she is full of plans. She is going to buy a house out in Bloomingdale, five miles from Kingsport. The schools are good there. All she needs is a steady job at decent pay to make the important things possible. She has that kind of a job at the Press, and she will do whatever is necessary, confront anything she has to, in order to keep it.

Richard L. Lamaster: In Kingsport to Stay

It is quite a way from Franklin County, Pennsylvania, to Kingsport, Tennessee, and a saxophone seems an unlikely connecting link. Yet if Richard Lamaster had not been a talented "sax man" he would not have been in the Army Band, stationed in Fort Jackson, South Carolina; would not have met Nancy Lee Hodges, a teacher in the Kingsport public schools, and would not today be in Kingsport, working at the Press.

Instead, he would probably be working the family farm back in Franklin County, for that is what he had been looking forward to after his two years in the Army; it is what he did in the six years between his graduation from high school, in 1954, and his induction in 1960. The farm was of a fair size. There were 10,000 chickens and as many as 1,800 eggs a day to gather. Dick had the major responsibility for its operation. Of the five children, three girls and two boys, three were college graduates. Dick's brother is an electrical engineer, with no interest in farming. Dick himself would probably have done well in college, too. His high school grades were generally good, and he did outstanding work in mathematics. But someone had to take over the farm work, and somehow it fell to Dick. His parents were happy that way, and he didn't mind it.

Meeting Nancy Lee changed all that. He couldn't get her out of his mind even though he left South Carolina for overseas Army duty shortly after meeting her. His band, a unit in the 8th Infantry Division, traveled all over Europe, and Dick enjoyed the sights. But he kept writing to Nancy Lee. Never much of a letter writer, he was mildly astonished to find it no chore. The habit took hold. He kept it up even after he was mustered out and found himself back on the farm in the spring of 1962. Letter writing all by itself is no way to conduct a love affair, though. Pretty soon, Dick was traveling weekends down to Kingsport. During the holiday season of 1962, Dick and Nancy Lee were engaged.

The elder Lamasters left it to him to decide whether or not the family should carry on with the farm. Undecided for a while, marriage made up his mind for him. He and Nancy were married in January, 1963, and Dick decided to continue farming through the year. He wound up at the farm after harvest in November of 1963 and went down to Kingsport to join Nancy Lee, who had gone back to continue her teaching at Kingsport's Washington Elementary School.

Dick applied for work to only one Kingsport firm—the Press. He had known about the strike ever since it began. All he had heard convinced him that the Press was a good place to work, and that it would provide him with the opportunity to make himself a good future. He was vaguely troubled by the prospect of crossing a picket line every day to get to work, but he had never been exposed to any kind of union indoctrination, and the thought never entered his mind that he might be doing something wrong.

"I can't agree that I 'stole' any one's job. The work was there to be done. The strikers had left their jobs. They were free to come back and take them. The company was looking for workers, offering the best pay in town and what looked to me like the best future. I was looking for something like that. I don't understand how I can be called a thief, or how it can be said that I did anything sneaky. Everything was out in plain sight and above board.

"The way I feel, I'm doing the company a job, and the company is paying me. Whatever they say out there on the picket line just goes in one ear and out the other. I don't pay any attention to them. I've gotten a few telephone calls in the evening, but they don't say anything, and I just hang up."

Jim Shelton is Dick's boss and thinks a lot of him. He selected Dick for special training shortly after the latter had come to work; sent him along with four others to Rhode Island, where the company's new, impressive web-fed offset press was being built. "Mainly what I have to do with Dick Lamaster," Jim Shelton said, "is to keep him from trying to move too fast. We take him along gradually and soundly, and he'll be one of the best men around here in just a few years."

Dick Lamaster still carries around him a character aura somewhat different from that which emanates from the hill people in and around Kingsport. He was born and raised and spent most of his life on a farm, but it was farther north, out of the Bible Belt. The Lamaster children had quite a bit of education; it was not an affluent family, but poverty, real poverty, was something they only heard about. All were musically inclined and talented. "If the Lamaster kids weren't there," Dick said, "half the local American Legion Band was missing." They were actively involved in the 4 H's too, exhibiting their own work, usually with emphasis on the Baby Beef Club. In fact, Dick's oldest sister, Betty, had raised a Grand Champion Hereford. Dick himself made the National F.F.A. (Future Farmers of America) Band.

His father, Jacob Russell Lamaster, was a stern enough disciplinarian, Dick says, and a serious church-goer. But the family as a whole was not religion oriented in its daily life, and fairly liberal in general. "No bible-spouting around the house," in Dick's phrase. "My church-going used to be pretty spotty, but I've grown regular since I've been living in Kingsport. Nancy Lee is quite religious, and some is rubbing off on me, I guess."

Almost thirty now, Dick Lamaster is set on settling down in Kingsport and making a career at the Press. "Nancy Lee and I have a regular social life, mainly among her friends, but we go out to eat a lot since she's teaching." He has some contact with strikers. He buys gas at a station run by strikers, and his next-door neighbor has a son on strike. "The son visits his father often, but there's never a conflict or embarrassment between us, and we see each other often."

Nancy Lee is going to continue working for a while longer.

But Dick is looking forward to the day when that will not be necessary, when they will be able to settle down in a home of their own, and raise their family. "Before too long," Dick says, "I'll be a full-fledged pressman, and I hope to be on a web press, making at least $4.00 an hour, straight time. With $10,000 or more a year, we can have pretty much every thing we want in a material way. I intend to give the Press all I've got, and I expect it'll be like casting bread upon the waters."

8

THE RESPONSIBILITY FOR THE "PRESS MESS"

Gloomy Pickets and a Haunted Management

HERE ARE SOME NOTES I jotted down on Saturday, March 20, 1965, the day on which everything about the strike seemed to me to touch bottom:

It snowed heavy wet flakes all the dark morning; the afternoon cleared a bit, so that the sky grew pale, but the sinking sun was still only a ghost behind the sickly overcast. The afternoon has grown colder right along, and every damp spot is now freezing, the snow piles are getting crisp, icicles are growing from the bottoms of the parked cars. . . . It's a raw cold, twenty-five degrees according to the bank thermometer, and the pickets, four at some gates, six or eight at others, huddle around salamanders, arms stretching down, scrubbing their palms, stomping now and then. I stand near by, curious to hear what they might be talking about. But they aren't talking. They are gloomy, withdrawn, a spiritless crew. These men are breathing, waiting for time to pass, but they aren't doing much more; right now they aren't doing *anything* more. Their jobs have been filled. Many of the strikers, more than four hundred, have gone back to the Press. Others have taken work elsewhere or set themselves up in little businesses. Some of the bitter-end strikers have working wives. A large number have dug into the Press profit-sharing fund. Some are getting a little extra money from picketing in the place of strikers who have found other work; sometimes, I hear, picket and worker share what they make. Others get along on the strike benefits alone, eked out by grants from the allied unions' Hardship Fund. A few spend the better part of the day in Carpenters' Hall, strike headquarters, where there is usually a card game or two going, and always a bull session. The Hall is dark and stale, but comforting because everybody there is in the same boat; the solidarity of nothingness is a species of "labor solidarity," too. They don't discuss the strike among themselves, and not with me, either, unless I bring it up. They've come out with the short straw. . . . The unions keep trying to induce the Press to get rid of the "new hires," so that the strikers can get "their" jobs back. The Company considers itself committed to the replacements. The only real hope now appears to lie in the Press's plans for expansion, with the additional employment expansion will bring. But the unions keep exerting pressures, some of which, if effective, will prevent expansion, perhaps even cause a cutback in employment at the Press. The boys at Carpenters' Hall wonder how the various possibilities will affect them. The unions have new unfair practice charges filed against the Press. Maybe those will induce the Press management to give in. The National Labor Relations Board is on "labor's" side. Managements can never be sure that they'll win if the Board decides to take a case. Maybe the boycotts will take hold. If they do, the Press will have to think twice about its "commitment" to the "scabs." . . .

In the plant, later this afternoon, I see Triebe, Fritschle, and Clevenger working away, as usual. It's warm in the plant, it's always *too* warm. Maybe that's why all the executives, from the president down, work in their shirtsleeves. If I complain about it and compare conditions inside with those outside on the picket line, Homer Clevenger will tell me that the office girls moan when the temperature falls much below eighty degrees. Same story everywhere. It was a mistake to let women into the business world; now we can't do without them there any more than we can anywhere else. . . . But Triebe, Fritschle, and Clevenger are busy, and harassed, and grim. It was never easy to achieve success in the competitive commercial printing game. Making profits while a strike is going on, as the Press is doing, takes the extreme effort of the best of men. But what haunts these men is not the competition. They are haunted by the noncompetitive and anticompetitive threats of destruction which the unions are attempting to unleash. Refuting the unions' unfair practice charges is something that has very little to do with running a book-manufacturing plant, but if they are not refuted it may become difficult to keep the business going at all. Hence, a prodigious amount of work has to be done—the pre-strike events reviewed; the bargaining re-examined; dates, names, and places carefully checked; long consultations with the Press lawyer; two years of strike events examined bit by bit, piece by piece. Complying with the NLRB rules is like trying to keep one's footing on a swiftly disintegrating icepack, in a wild sea. One false step and you are lost. . . . The Press cannot hope to survive, either, if the unions are successful in their nationwide boycott efforts. The Press's biggest customers are the most widely known and prestigious publishers, and they are run by men who are sensitive to "public opinion." The unions know this, and spare no effort to induce the publishers to believe that the Press is evil, reactionary, anti-union, backward—an anachronistic "sweatshop," drowning in "paternalism," shot through with "nepotism." These charges, too, must be met and refuted. The burden falls mainly on Cliff Fritschle. He is incapable of replying in kind. He avoids emotionalism because he despises it and because he believes that in the long run it is better to be objective and dispassionate. So he concentrates on the facts, calls no names, refuses to involve himself in emotional generalities. He and the other Press officers must travel a great deal, personally presenting rebuttals to the unions' charges. Often a detailed memorandum is required. In Chicago and New York, the Press officers had almost as rough a time of it before the boards of education as they would have had in court. It is always the same. The unions charge and charge and charge, without respect for courtesy or fact. The Press officers calmly and with restraint point out the errors in the charges. Thus far the Press method has been effective. Notwithstanding union boasts, the boycotting has been largely ineffective; most boards of education have refused to participate. However, with their keen appreciation of the power of political pressure, the unions keep at it. The burden on the Press management is heavy and relentless. . . . But these men are fighting for two things, honor and survival. They could easily settle everything—in a minute. All they would have to do is fire the replacements and reinstate the strikers. The burdens would vanish immediately. The unions would withdraw the unfair practice charges and—with great pleasure—disband the picket lines (and quit paying strike benefits). They would lift the embargoes and the boycotting. Thus the Press would have its survival guaranteed. But Ed Triebe and his associates are not interested in survival at any price. They showed by taking the strike in the first place that they would not "buy labor peace." And now they will not buy survival when the price is honor.

Who Started It?

The allied unions have on numerous occasions emphasized that it would be wrong to place the responsibility for the strike exclusively on them. In a certain sense, their contention is sound. It always takes at least two to make a fight, or an assault, or a robbery. Had the Press given in to the union demands, there would have been no strike. But while that is true, we must ask ourselves how relevant, how important, that truth is.

I am reminded of the old socialist contention that "property is the cause of crime." I suppose that if there were no property rights, there could be no "theft." And if no one had a right in the inviolability of his own person, the idea of "assault" would not mean very much. But private property and personal inviolability are implicit in the idea of civil order. What is mine, including my own person, belongs to me; and if you take it from me, you are a thief. And if thievery and assault are common, and commonly accepted, the condition is not society at all, but chaos and anarchy. So I agree that, in a sense, "property is the cause of theft," but only in the same sense that civilized order is the cause of crime.

Where civilization and order are the basic values, however, it becomes irrelevant to speak of property as the cause of crime. The relevant observation, when a theft or an assault occurs in a civilized social order, is that the crime has been caused by a lack of respect in the wrongdoer for the rights of others.

In the same way, and for the same reasons, we must insist that nothwithstanding their denials, the unions must bear the responsibility of calling the strike. Even though the strike would not have been called had the Press yielded to their demands, the fact remains that the choice of positive action was exercised by the unions and their members, not by the Press. The Press most certainly did not lock out its employees. It did not want a strike. When the management decided to try to carry on after the strike was called, it announced the decision first to the strikers, and offered them employment completely without prejudice to their pre-existing standing.

It is necessary to remind ourselves here that the Press did not fling a callous and degrading ultimatum at the unions and the strikers. It did not make a mock offer, one of no substance, and say: "There it is; take it or leave it." We can agree that such conduct would have been provocative. But there was no such conduct. On the contrary, the Press offers were progressively substantial. The unions could have accepted them without "losing face." As Clifton Fritschle has pointed out, the 5–8–8 offer amounted to more than a 7 per cent increase over the three-year life of the contract, and there were other concessions, too.

In allocating responsibility for calling the strike exclusively to the unions, I do not wish to be understood as accusing the unions of having done something wrong or evil. The unions had a right to call a strike, just as each of us has a right to break off economic relationships which we consider disadvantageous. We may regret what we have done; I don't suppose there is a person alive who has no regrets of that kind. But those regrets are only the necessary consequence of the right to make mistakes which men insist upon, and must have, if they are to be free.

So, I emphasize, the unions committed no *wrong* in calling the strike at the Press—even though it turned out to be a big mistake. They too have a right to make mistakes.

The right to make mistakes is one thing. Shifting the burdens of one's mistakes to someone else is another. We all do that, too; and so, if we are understanding and sympathetic, we do not take a holier-than-thou stance when we see someone else doing it. But if we are to survive and prosper in a world in which fools come out on the short end, we must try to keep our wits about us. We may sympathize with the unions for having made a mistake, even for being evasive about it; but we must still insist that, if the strike was a mistake, the unions made it. They were not forced to call the strike, and they *could* have called it off at any moment of any day from March 11, 1963, onward. I am convinced from all the evidence that the Press would have been overjoyed had the strike never been called, and that it would have been only slightly less joyful had the strike been called off on March 12, 1963. I do not see how it is possible to say that and to say at the same time that the Press in effect "locked out" the employees, as the unions have said. In consequence I am constrained to conclude that the unions have certainly been misleading and quite possibly have also been mendacious in insisting that the strike was a lockout.

The Violence

As to the conditions of terror which prevailed in Kingsport for months after the strike was called, it would not be wise, I believe, for the people of this country to abandon the old, civilized principle that individual acts of violence are always the responsibility, basically, of the person who acts, the thug or bully or sneak who raises his fist, hurls a stone, or shoots a gun. Shifting responsibility from persons to groups serves only to dilute it and thus to hasten its entire disappearance. Ultimately, therefore, I believe that the burden of guilt must be placed on the persons who acted badly, not on the unions to which they belonged, or on the Press, if they happened to be working for the Press when they engaged in unlawful conduct.

But the union leaders must share the guilt. While recognizing in their "Open Letter" that some strikers had committed unlawful acts, the allied unions said: "This, however, should not be interpreted to mean that the Unions involved or the vast majority of the membership should be blamed. . . . It should be obvious . . . that no organization, union or law enforcing agency, can keep a watch on several hundred persons 24 hours a day to prevent all of them from following their own consciences on ways and means of showing displeasure at strikebreaking activities."

If the reader will reflect carefully on that statement, he will observe, I believe, that for all its apparent regret for the violence that had occurred, the statement was more likely to promote than to discourage violent reprisals against the company and the non-strikers. The statement does not say that it is wrong and evil for strikers to assault non-strikers. On the contrary, it implies that the assaults were, after all, meritorious. For we do not talk about "following our consciences" when we wish to make reference to evil conduct. Conscience is supposed to indicate the path of virtue. Covering the acts of sneaks and bullies with the mantle of "conscience" meant that whatever they may have intended, the unions were condoning, even encouraging, such "means of showing displeasure at strikebreaking activities."

There is no evidence that the Union leadership instructed or commanded the sneaks and bullies to assault David Draper or to bomb Festus Maddux's house, or to make the massed picket line a tunnel of fear and provocation. But we do know that the unions planned and conducted the strike activities in general and conceived and executed the general strategies. Mass picket lines and mob demonstrations do not form themselves spontaneously. Union leaders call mass meetings in order to build up "morale and solidarity"—but the people come out of the meetings angry and resentful. Union leaders exhort their members to turn out in crowds—but people in frenzied masses lose the inhibitions which tend to control the solitary person; they feel themselves infinitely strong and beyond reproach, especially when they in the crowd confront only one person or a few at a time.

According to the *Kingsport Times* (June 6, 1963), the police believed that "much of the violence is organized and well planned. They cited as example an incident this morning when a large group of strikers suddenly began to yell and wave their arms. Rocks were thrown from the crowd and officers were unable to see who actually was throwing the rocks."

Such incidents do not necessarily indicate that union leaders were at work, giving detailed instructions on the spot. When a crowd is worked up and the mass man replaces the person, small stratagems of that kind may be conceived and executed "on the spur of the moment." The mildest and meekest person in the crowd might have said: "Now! Let's all shout and wave our arms; that way no one will be able to see anyone throw things." Yet the fact remains that mass picket lines and frenzied resentment, the conditions in which such conduct is possible or even probable, are planned and organized by union leaders, as they were during the strike at the Press. Moreover, union leaders know that bad things will happen. Walter Allen warned of them during the negotiations.

I have been told by numerous persons who were there that during mass meetings Walter Allen and Anthony J. DeAndrade both displayed considerable demagogic ability. Having spent several hours with Walter Allen, I find that hard to believe. He was pleasant, civilized, and companionable with me; in fact, I came away thinking him somewhat shy and retiring. Nevertheless, his speeches and those of DeAndrade were reportedly more rabble-rousing in character than DeAndrade's well known and often quoted statement in the *American Pressman* for November, 1963 (p. 37): ". . . an *anti-union* plant operated by Scabs and Rats is wholly intolerable to both union labor and fair management."

On Friday, June 14, 1963, the *Kingsport News* reported that nine hundred strikers had attended a rally the day before. The purpose was "to adapt activities to comply with a court injunction." Judge Jackson Raulston had only a week earlier supplemented his first injunction, limiting the picketing, with another limiting mass demonstrations. According to the *Kingsport News,* the strikers were told "to limit their activities to jeering and to avoid violence so no future injunctions would be issued." The instructor may have meant well, but instructing people to jeer—which is what he in effect did—is no way to avoid provocation and to reduce violence.

There is a story in the *AFL-CIO News* of June 1, 1963, which sheds further light on the role played by the allied unions in the strike at the Press. The *AFL-CIO News* proudly announced that the picketing was carefully planned and supervised by the allied unions. In fact, the unions had established a two-way radio scheme of communications, so that "union staff representatives [could] keep in continuous contact with the picket lines through thirteen patrol cars equipped with receivers."

If people are indoctrinated with the idea that crossing a picket line to enter a struck plant ranks among the lowest and most pernicious forms of conduct, they are likely to visit reprisals upon those who engage in such conduct, especially when they think they can get away with it. Sometimes their blind indoctrination carries them to ridiculous lengths. John McLellan told me that as he was entering the Press one day during the strike, to negotiate a strike-settlement agreement, the pickets jeered at him, called him a "scab." McLellan walked over to the pickets and said: "No, I'm not looking to go on the Press payroll. I'm here trying to get you off our payroll and on to the Press's, and we'll sure be glad to make the transfer." I myself was called a "scab," and often much worse things, each time I entered the plant. No such hazard marred my visits to the allied unions' strike headquarters.

I do not see how it is possible to absolve the unions of all responsibility for the bulk of the violence which disrupted Kingsport.

The Press's Conduct

In deference to critics of my previous books, I have tried my best to find some conduct by the Press officers which I might indignantly deplore and condemn. For, apparently, the fanatic insistence that management must always be culpable or that at least they must share some part of the guilt when things go wrong in labor relations, can be placated in no other way.

With trepidation, I must unhappily report that in regard to the strike at the Press—as in regard to the Kohler strike—I have been unable to uncover any management conduct to deplore.* On the contrary, I have found in the Kingsport Press, as I did in the Kohler Company, a management which comported itself consistently according to high standards of dignity, legality, and morality.

I have looked at any number of pamphlets, news reports, memoranda, and journalistic analyses relating to the strike at the Press. I have spent many days in the company of Messrs. Triebe, Beneman, Fritschle, and Clevenger. I have inspected with care every management statement I have been able to find. A fair cross section of my researches is presented in this book. It is all the same. The name-calling, the distortions of fact, the weak and contradictory arguments, the rabble-rousing—all these characterize only the statements emanating from the unions. They are absent from the management side.

The unions charged the Press with creating and fomenting "tension, resentment and emotional reactions." They said that the Press disregarded the contribution of its employees, "the individual equities held by long service workers," intending thereby "to destroy the personal pride and independence of the workers involved."

With respect to these charges, the first thing that must be observed is that they refer to no words or acts of the Press. The Press has always prided itself on its long-term employees, has always spoken with warmth of its workers. The reader need only recall the words of Mr. Smith, the chairman of the board, quoted earlier, in Chapter V.

Viewed objectively, the unions' charges must be interpreted as fresh examples of their capacity to distort reality, to heap guilt

* See *The Kohler Strike* (Chicago: Regnery, 1961).

and abuse upon the Press for words, acts, and attitudes which should more properly have been associated with themselves and the strikers. For—to repeat—it was not the Press which broke off relations.

We must lash ourselves to the mast of reality in the hurricane of evasion and distortion which the union propagandists have set loose. Persuaded by their union leaders to do so, the Press employees left their jobs; *they* abandoned the Press; *they* broke off the continuity of their service.

The Press management does not wear its heart on its sleeve; it does not run around moaning about the disloyalty and the betrayal which it suffered from employees who had been given an opportunity to lift themselves out of the poverty which surrounds Kingsport. At most, the Press officers shake their heads, indicate sorrow, and ask themselves searching questions about what they might have done to keep the employees from having made so disastrous a mistake.

The union charges of inhumanity and immorality are without foundation in fact or actual conduct. But they are built upon a premise—the premise that the Press was responsible for everything that happened when it refused to give in, and when it decided to keep operating after the strike was called.

This premise has cropped up time and again. Let us now examine it with care.

Is there any sense in the proposition that a business firm commits a wrong in declining to yield the concessions insisted upon by a union? Wages and conditions of employment in a free country are a matter of agreement between the person who offers and the person who seeks employment. If the employer offers less than the seeker will accept, there will be no employment contract between them. If the seeker insists upon more than the employer is willing to pay, then again there will be no employment contract between them. Neither party has the right or the authority to compel the other to enter into a contract of employment on unacceptable terms.

This is not only the law of the land, not only a dictate of morality. It is an absolute requirement in a free society. Thus the

Press committed no greater wrong in refusing to grant the concessions sought by the unions than the unions did in insisting upon those concessions. The National Labor Relations Act goes very far in granting unions special privileges denied to every one else. But it falls far short of the position taken by the unions in the strike at the Press. It expressly declares that neither union nor employer is required to make any concessions in collective bargaining.

Consider the other aspect of the union premise: that the Press was guilty of fomenting violence in undertaking to keep the plant operating after the strike was called. Each of us has a right when we are dissatisfied with an existing economic relationship to abandon it and try another. We may limit this right by contract, for example, by agreeing to deal only with one supplier for a fixed term of months or years; or, again, as many employers do, by accepting the seniority principle and reserving the right to discharge only for some good cause. But in the absence of such voluntary qualifications, we retain the right to look elsewhere when an existing arrangement becomes unsatisfactory and certainly when it breaks down.

By and large these general principles apply in labor relations as they do in other aspects of society. They apply universally because to depart from them would be to create conditions which the vast majority of the people would not tolerate. Moral dictates, they are imbedded in our institutions and our customs, as well as in our law. They are what distinguish America from Soviet Russia. In Russia you must purchase mostly from one supplier of goods, the State; and you must work for only one supplier of employment, again the State. In America, you may change whenever you wish.

I have said this before, but it bears repeating: to say that you may change, that you may break off relations at will, is not to say that you will necessarily be happy with the change you have made. Abandoning one supplier, you may find the next even less satisfactory. In that case, you will have committed an error. But then you may take some comfort from the fact that in jail, or in Russia, you would not have been permitted to make such an error. As indicated earlier, freedom involves the freedom, too, to err.

Thus men are free to go on strike when they wish. They are free during the strike to seek and to accept other employment. Unions are further free in the course of strikes to seek aid and comfort and support from other unions. The allied unions in the strike at the Press availed themselves of all these freedoms, and more. They have had probably more than a million dollars in financial aid from other unions and cooperation from some publishers who have withdrawn their patronage from the Kingsport Press. Many of the strikers have taken jobs elsewhere, some permanently.

On the other hand, we know that when the Press decided to continue to operate, it offered jobs first to the strikers. It went out to the free market, offering jobs to "new hires" only after the strikers declined them. In thus acting, the Press did nothing wrong. It merely exercised the freedom which distinguishes this country from Russia; the same freedom which the unions and the strikers exercised.

Wrongs were committed and mistakes were made during the strike. But not by the Press management. The unions and the strikers committed wrongs in distorting the truth, misrepresenting the Press's conduct, raising hell in Kingsport, and then trying to shift the blame to the Press. They made a tragic mistake in calling the strike in the first place and a still more profoundly tragic mistake in continuing it. No one in his right mind, thinking calmly, can possibly conclude that it would be a good thing for companies to give in always to union demands or automatically to shut up shop whenever a strike is called. The main product would be even more stupidity and arrogance among union leaders than we are plagued with today.

Again: This Senseless Strike

I have before me as I write, two large printed schedules of Pressman's wage rates which Mr. Walter Allen kindly supplied when I visited him at Pressman's Home, in Tennessee. These schedules indicate first-shift wage rates for cylinder Pressmen in cities of over 50,000. Kingsport, today a city of less than 40,000, is not included in the schedules. Furthermore, we must bear in mind that pure wage rates are no definitive indication of the total rewards accruing to employees. Working conditions, the local cost-of-living, fringe benefits, and other factors are relevant, difficult to measure as they may be.

Bearing in mind these qualifications, let us briefly survey the relationship between the Kingsport Press wage rates, which averaged $3.11 per hour on the day shift in 1962, and those prevailing in the larger cities carried on Mr. Allen's schedules. Certain cities and areas immediately stand out. For example, in and around San Francisco, Detroit, and New York, the pure wage rates were substantially higher than those in Kingsport. Of course, total labor costs, as we have seen in Chapter V, may in Kingsport exceed even the New York and San Francisco levels. But that is another question. What seems very interesting to me here is that pure wage rates were higher in Kingsport as of January 1, 1963 (the date of Mr. Allen's compilation) than they were in Bay City, Michigan; Brockton, Massachusetts; Cedar Rapids, Iowa; Columbia, South Carolina; Galveston, Texas; Huntington, West Virginia; Johnstown, Pennsylvania; Lawrence, Massachusetts; Lima and Lorain, Ohio; Manchester, New Hampshire; Muncie, Indiana; Pensacola, Florida; Pittsfield, Massachusetts; Port Arthur, Texas; Pueblo, Colorado; Raleigh, North Carolina; Reading, Pennsylvania; Rock Island, Illinois; Saginaw, Michigan; Sioux City, Iowa; Sioux Falls, South Dakota; Springfield, Missouri; Terre Haute, Indiana; Troy, New York; Waco, Texas; Waterloo, Iowa; and Wilkes-Barre and York, Pennsylvania.

There were a good many other cities, all larger than Kingsport, with lower wage rates, some much lower. The range was wide. Union pressmen in Waterloo, Iowa, were being paid $2.35 per hour, while those in San Francisco were getting $3.96 per hour. However, San Francisco has, I believe, the highest cost of living in the United States, with the possible exception of Honolulu. Moreover, Pressmen there do not have the profit-sharing fund that Kingsport employees do. Finally, day shift hours and overtime are so limited that the weekly pay of a San Francisco Pressman is only $138.61. I know as a fact that many Pressmen in Kingsport earned more than $138 a week before the strike was called.

I present these wage figures not because I believe it is any business of mine—or of yours, gentle reader—to tell the Press what it should have given or the unions what they should have demanded—but merely to exclude the possibility that the Kingsport Press was running a sweat shop, far below national standards. Thus, again the facts are with the Press management, and against the union propagandists. It is perfectly clear from the Pressmen's own figures that the Kingsport Press had nothing to be ashamed of even in terms of pure wage rates, let alone total labor costs. That is what the Press management has been saying all along, and it is apparently the truth.

While an outsider has no business telling people how they should dispose of their lives and property, he is nevertheless in a position to judge, on the basis of objective standards, whether the disposition has in its own terms been successful or unsuccessful, stupid or intelligent. Observed in that light, the outsider must agree with Anthony J. DeAndrade, president of the International Pressmen's Union, in calling the strike at the Press a "senseless strike"; with Claude Smith, president of the local Pressmen's Union, in calling it a "big mistake"; and with John S. McLellan, general counsel of the International Pressmen, in calling the whole affair the "Press mess." Hindsight establishes that the strike should never have been called in the first place, and that the longer it went on the stupider it became.

Not only hindsight, though. Appalachia's poverty and Kingsport's affluence, smack in the middle of extensive unemployment, should have been obvious to all. It should have been obvious, anyway, to Press employees and to their union leaders, who pride themselves upon their economic sophistication. It was never a secret, at least it should not have been a secret, that a job at the Press was a very desirable thing. As reported in the first chapter of this book, news that Press was hiring had about the same effect on the hill people around Kingsport as a mating call has on stags during the mating season. People came running.

Again, Mr. DeAndrade's confession of ignorance concerning the cost of living in Kingsport, which he agreed was relevant, is significant. He should have known that the cost of living in Kingsport is materially lower than the cost of living, say, in New York or San Francisco. He should have known that $3.11 an hour, forty hours a week, and plenty of overtime, in Kingsport, stack up mighty well with $3.96 an hour, thirty-five hours a week, and no overtime, in San Francisco.

He should have known, above all else, that people in the hills around Kingsport were not comparing $3.11 with $3.96. *They were comparing it with zero.*

I say he should have known those things, not because I set the rules for union leadership, but because I believe that union leaders have very little else to commend their services—very little other than the undertaking to be a bit more intelligent and a bit more sophisticated about conditions on the labor market than the people they undertake to "represent." Moreover, that is the basis upon which union leaders sell themselves to workers. Union leaders do not say to workers: join up and we'll see to it that you will wind up out of a job. They say: join up and you will enjoy the benefits of an organization which can do better for you than you can do for yourselves.

Who Was Trying to Bust Whom?

As time wore on, after March 11, it became more and more apparent that the Press was serious about its last offer, that it was not going to budge from 5–8–8. It was back in production on a small scale by the end of March, 1963, and its employment rolls were increasing all the time. By the middle of April, 1963, there was enough activity in the plant to induce the unions, if they were really concerned with serving their members, to consider calling off the strike. Had they done so, the employees would have had a good raise; infinitely more important, they would have had their jobs, for there would have been little or no problem in reinstating all the strikers who wished to return to work at that time.

Instead, the unions heightened their campaign against the Press. They insisted that the Press could not operate. The vituperation became more frenzied; the picket lines more belligerent; the mob demonstrations uglier; the propaganda more demagogic. One heard from numerous union sources the same refrain: "It is not the unions who are losing this strike."

Somewhere along in June, 1963, the unions reached the point of no return. Before that time, they could have settled the strike with no lasting harm to the community and to their members. Jobs were available for almost all of them. The unions have vaunted their reasonableness, while excoriating the Press for its "union-busting" adamancy. Nevertheless, it was Mr. DeAndrade who, on June 13, 1963, dramatically compelled the strikers to burn their bridges behind them. The scene was the Kingsport Civic Auditorium. Nine hundred strikers had gathered. According to the *Kingsport News* of June 14, 1963,

> On DeAndrade's request, union members arose en masse, raised their right hands and pledged not to return to work until the Press accepts the union contract, particularly the clause that all striking employees will return to their jobs in the same seniority as when the strike started. They also pledged not to return until all newly hired workers leave. . . . DeAndrade said he told a federal mediator the strike will not end until all employees are returned with seniority rating equal to when they left and new workers fired.

Unconditional surrender ultimatums are great luxuries even for the victorious side, even for the supremely powerful. Coming from apparent losers, an unconditional surrender ultimatum is downright stupid.

With this pledge, the strikers doomed themselves. The reader may believe that there was no other way out for them; that the strikers could never have brought themselves to work with the "new hires." It is true that unions have been striving for a long time to establish that strikers and union men generally will not work with "scabs" and non-union men. But that is mere union propaganda. The fact is that union and non-union men work together all over this country. It is also a fact that strikers and "scabs" have managed on numerous occasions to patch up their differences and to work together. There may be resentment, but a certain amount of friction and resentment are to be found in all human relationships. The union myth that "scabs" are "bad people" soon dissolves when strikers learn that "scabs" are people, too, much as other people are. For the union myth very much resembles the mythology of some white supremacists, who have always insisted that black men and white men cannot work together. I have seen black men and white men working together in real amity; I have seen strikers and "scabs" working together in equal amity—in Kingsport and elsewhere.

The dramatic oath of June 13 did not emerge spontaneously from the 900 assembled strikers. Mr. DeAndrade brought them to their feet, he got them to raise their right hands, he recited the pledge and induced them to repeat it after him. The big question, the one that quite possibly we shall never be able to answer satisfactorily, is: Why did DeAndrade thus lead the strikers to destruction? Why did he insist, with defeat looming plainly before him, on unconditional surrender when it was still possible for him to protect his men from the worst consequences of the mistaken decision to strike?

Possibly the union leaders themselves are unable to answer these questions fully. Still, unless we are content to leave this story of the strike at the Press a cryptic fragment, we must seek an explanation, and I am going to do so.

Jim Shelton has a blessed immunity. He is not sicklied over with the pale cast of thought, does not plague himself with thinking too much upon the event. He said, surely and confidently, the reader will remember, that the unions "were out to bust the Press."

There are points in favor of Shelton's theory; it explains a few otherwise inexplicable facts: the distorted and misleading character of the union propaganda, the disregard of the cost of living in Kingsport, the refusal to admit that the Press wage rates were high and that its total labor costs were among the highest in the industry, the rock-headed refusal of the union leaders to recognize their mistakes and to cut their losses in June 1963.

Still, I cannot believe that Jim Shelton was right. It made no sense for the union leaders to put the Press out of business, or even to wish to do so. Union leaders want to gain members, not lose them. The union leaders involved in the strike at the Press are not malicious devils stirred by a motiveless malignity. They are decent men. Destroying the jobs, almost the lives, of two thousand people would constitute an evil of which I do not believe them capable. Furthermore, I think that if the international unions had intended to destroy the Press, John McLellan would have got wind of it, and he would not have tolerated it. He is a Kingsport native and resident, tutored by that flexible, far-seeing, humane union leader, George L. Berry. Mr. Berry died long before the strike at the Press was called. Yet if Walter Allen's statements are to be credited, George Berry's relationship with the Press had much to do with the motivation of the strike. I believe that Mr. Berry's presence must be reckoned with also because he left a representative—John McLellan. I am convinced that Mr. McLellan would at least have resigned if the unions' object had been to bankrupt the Press, and I am fairly confident that he would have opposed the unions even more vigorously. He is neither a knave, a fool, nor a doctrinaire.

The Villain in the Piece

Webster's Unabridged defines a "doctrinaire" as "one who would put into effect a political or economic system based on abstract doctrines or theories, without regard for practical difficulties."

My opinion is that the union leaders in the strike at the Press were doctrinaires, mesmerized by the old union goal, half political, half economic, all destructive, of "taking wages out of competition." Let it be said at the outset that there is nothing wrong in being a doctrinaire; in fact, scholars and theorists probably can make no special contribution to society without being rigorous and doctrinaire. But men who run governments, businesses, or trade unions assume the responsibility of being practical representatives of the persons and the personal interests which have been entrusted to them. They have chosen to operate in the practical world; they have sought, usually aggressively, the authority to lead people. This means they must know *how* to compose differences—to compromise—and *when*. We have the right to insist that our leaders be practical, prudent, responsible; they carry our lives and fortunes in their hands. We want them to have ideas, but we want their ideas to serve our practical ends, not destroy them.

As we have seen, the top unionists in the strike at the Press disavowed any doctrinaire intention to reduce the competitive threat posed by Kingsport Press to higher-cost book-manu-facturers. The disavowal cannot be taken seriously. The idea that the Press was a competitive threat is insuppressibly evident in too many of the things that too many of the union leaders had to say about the strike.

Furthermore, "taking wages out of competition" dominates the whole literature of the "labor movement." It looms large especially in the history of the printing trades unions. I have referred several times to Elizabeth Faulkner Baker's excellent book, *Printers and Technology*. The curious reader will find in that book alone enough first hand evidence of this objective in the printing trades to convince him that it would not be strange to find it figuring largely in the strike at the Press.

For example, the 1940 convention of the Pressmen's Union passed a resolution condemning competition in the printing industry. According to Miss Baker, a caucus in the convention "accused some publishers of stirring competition among the International's own locals by having their printing done where production and labor costs were lower. The resolution was, therefore, that in negotiating local contracts organizers and International representatives should strive to increase the number of men per press and reduce the number of apprentices." (Baker, p. 375).

The reader will no doubt recall Walter Allen's concern with "a disproportionate amount of work going to lower-paying firms." In voicing such concern, Allen was only reflecting a preoccupation common in the "labor movement," especially among its more studious components. On the other hand, the pure politicians of the "labor movement," the acting, elected heads of the trade unions, find it politically expedient to "take wages out of competition." In doing so, they are relieved of the complaints, and of the potential defections, of union members employed in high-cost firms. The reader will recall here the remarks of the Bindery Workers' representative, Mr. Walter Barber, and of Mr. DeAndrade before the members of the Kingsport Junior Chamber of Commerce.

Naturally, union leaders will disavow any such motivation when a strike has gone badly, as the strike at the Press did. They may be doctrinaire, they may even be stupidly so. But the responsibilities of prudent leadership rise up to haunt them, however agile they may be in the attempt to escape. A thousand men are out of work in Kingsport. Mr. DeAndrade lives not far away, in Pressmen's Home. It would be dangerous in a number of ways for him to admit straightforwardly that those thousand men are unemployed because he and Walter Allen, possibly for various reasons, had decided that the time had come to reduce the competitive threat posed by the Kingsport Press to the higher-cost, less efficient book manufacturers in distant parts of the country.

At a certain point, too, the dangers of antitrust prosecution must be considered. The antitrust laws of the United States are in such a state of confusion that no one can be sure of the precise danger point. Yet it is always there, and the Supreme Court of the United States has recently emphasized the peril inherent in union attempts to eliminate competition between business firms. In June of 1965, the Court handed down a decision outlining its views concerning the legality of combinations between unions and businesses to eliminate competition from low-cost firms. Speaking for the Court, Mr. Justice White said:

. . . we think a union forfeits its exemption from the anti-trust laws when it is clearly shown that it has agreed with one set of employers to impose a certain wage scale on other bargaining units.*

Mr. Justice White said that "a legitimate aim of any national labor organization is to obtain uniformity of labor standards and that a consequence of such union activity may be to eliminate competition based on differences in such standards." He went on to say, however, that "there is nothing in the labor policy indicating that the union and the employers in one bargaining unit are free to bargain about the wages, hours and working conditions of other bargaining units or to attempt to settle these matters for the entire industry."†

Mr. Justice White concluded with a practical observation that seems intimately relevant to the strike at the Press. He said:

The union's obligations to its members would seem best served if the union retained the ability to respond to each bargaining situation as the individual circumstances might warrant, without being strait-jacketed by some prior agreement with the favored employers.‡

It would have been well for everyone concerned in the strike at the Press if the unions had—all and each—taken to heart the sage counsel implicit in Mr. Justice White's remarks. Had they done so, there would have been no "Press Mess," no gloomy pickets, no haunted management, and no deep community wounds.

I do not believe that the unions violated the antitrust laws in striking the Press. The required evidence of a clear agreement between the unions and other book-manufacturers does not exist, at least not to my knowledge. But it is clear that each of the five unions relinquished its freedom of action; differently circumstanced as they were, they decided to act as a unit. Their propa-

* United Mine Workers *v.* Pennington, 381 U.S., pp. 657, 665.
† Ibid., p. 666.
‡ Ibid.

gandists made much of this unity, boasted and bragged about it as though it amounted to a second coming. As a practical matter, what it accomplished was long-run, perhaps permanent, unemployment for hundreds of bindery workers. That was the result of their Union's having given up its "ability to respond to each bargaining situation as the individual circumstances might warrant."

Again, had the union leaders not developed a fixation on "industrywide standards," they would have been better able to adjust themselves to the local bargaining pattern in Kingsport. Perhaps they would have had time to do their homework, and have been clearsighted enough to see, after studying the facts and figures, that wages in particular and labor costs in general were already pretty high at the Kingsport Press. They might even have taken a look at the local labor market, which is what any competent union leader should do before he calls a strike.

The strike thus appears to analyze out as a dreary, perhaps even a tragic, monument to a pernicious theory. Edward Triebe told me that he and Walter Allen had argued the theory. Allen had said that the unions were aiming ultimately at establishing identical labor costs in all book-manufacturing plants. Triebe asked, "What, then, will happen to competition?" Allen took the position that the only proper place for competition is in the management of the firms. Triebe says he could only shake his head in wonder at such naiveté.

It *is* a naive view. Practically all the costs of production, taking industry as a whole, reduce themselves directly or indirectly to labor costs. Rents and interest represent only a tiny fraction. Profits are not costs at all, but what remain, if anything remains, after costs are paid. If you take labor costs out of competition, you must necessarily abolish competition, with all the benefits it brings.

Moreover, the competition in management to which Allen is said to have referred, cannot amount to very much if managements are not allowed to compete freely in the way they utilize labor. The unions do not want merely equal wage rates throughout industry; they want *total labor costs* to be equal. This means that they insist upon uniform manning requirements—the same number of men used everywhere to perform similar operations. But if management ingenuity is thus circumscribed, what area is left open to competition?

The answer is: virtually none. Thus, in the pursuit of this empty, doctrinaire ideal, the unions would, to a great extent ignorantly, destroy mankind's most effective servant, free competition.

The quest is not only pernicious—it is vain. It is vain, at any rate, in any society in which the substance of freedom remains. In order to achieve it, the unions would have to destroy all freedom; for if any is left, taking labor costs out of competition proves impossible. The strike at the Press and, more particularly, Doyle Fields, Joe Martin, Pencie Millsap, and Richard Lamaster proved that.

Back to the Middle Ages

The characteristic social features of the Middle Ages were relative rigidity and stasis. Those social features naturally determined the economic structure, for a society and its economy are largely the same thing. The medieval towns with their surrounding countryside were nearly self-contained economic units. Within the towns, custom and law decreed that status relations should prevail. Merchants and tradesmen joined together in tightly bound multi-purpose societies. One of the purposes was to protect the economic status of the members against competition from anyone outside the societies or outside the town. To this end, the societies exerted moral, political, and social pressures. There was little trade between towns, even less between what might be called "nations"; what trade of that kind there was, the authorities controlled rigorously.

The object of it all was security, of one kind or another: emotional, psychological, moral, economic. Free trade, free movement, free contract, free thought, free competition—any form of freedom—was viewed, quite correctly, as a threat to the existing "vested interests" and therefore had to be suppressed. The suppression, whatever form it might take, was always in the name of virtue and justice. The merchants who prosecuted an outsider for peddling damasks without a license from them, the bootmakers who attacked one of their members or an outsider for selling boots at a price lower than they had agreed upon—those people never thought that *they* were doing something unethical, immoral, or antisocial. If they thought so, at any rate, they never said so. They said, perhaps sincerely, that their suppressions safeguarded the community and its vital interests. Evil was the interloper, the maverick, the person exercising a natural freedom.

We know now that the medieval theories and customs were ill-advised. Life under them was short and skimpy, narrow and thin. All the dimensions were too small to contain the bursting spirit of man, his soaring aspirations, his downright, earthy needs.

In England, whence American institutions mainly derive, over the centuries the nation and eventually the world came to replace the town as the significant economic unit. Exclusive privileges and franchises gave way to universal rights in all men to compete freely. The king's courts dispensed equal justice to all men under the same rules. Free trade within the nation and largely with other nations became the way of acting, and laissez faire its philosophy.

And life grew better in every way. Little England learned that it could breed, feed, and give a long, full life to forty million Englishmen under laissez faire, as against a nasty, short, and brutish life for six million or less under the medieval way. Substituting freedom for petty security brought about a large increase in well being and an infinitely more significant security as well. Ludwig von Mises points out that but for the substitution of freedom in the place of security only one of six Englishmen would be alive today, to be preoccupied with his security.

Turning men loose to compete freely was the key—the key, as Adam Smith was to put it, to the wealth of nations. Fortunately, we in America, coming to nationhood when we did, at just about the time Adam Smith wrote, were handed the key on a silver platter. It opened the door to the extraordinarily affluent conditions that this country has always enjoyed, mainly because we were not too long afflicted with the restrictive medieval ideas. Almost from the beginning we have lived under the blessings of freedom—a virtually complete free trade within our borders, from town to town and great city to great city, from country to city, from east to west and north to south; and freedom, too, for men to enter trades or business largely at will. Some have been baffled by the American record of growth and productivity. The mystery has long been solved. Freedom, free competition, free mobility of men and capital—those are what did it.

And those are what the allied Kingsport unions seem to be trying to destroy. We saw something in Chapter VI of their determined efforts to induce publishers and boards of education to boycott the Press. The AFL-CIO convention in San Francisco passed a resolution designed to reinforce the pressures. In February, 1966, the resolution was implemented by a renewed appeal to the New York City Board of Education. On February 7, 1966, the AFL-CIO bought a half-hour of television time to back up the new appeal. Over New York City's Channel 9 Mr. Joseph Hellman, president of the New York State Allied Printing Trades Council, told viewers:

What we are acting to prevent is the loss of 100,000 jobs here in New York City, and thousands of jobs elsewhere in the United States. If an employer can take advantage of the fact that his plant is located in a depressed area, where many are unemployed, to gain an unfair competitive advantage, every section of the country lives under the threat of becoming a new depressed area. One hundred thousand New York City workers are employed in the printing industry. If their employers, paying decent wages and benefits, cannot compete successfully with low-wage oppressed area plants, 100,000 jobs are in danger of being wiped out. Those jobs are part of the economic life blood of this city. We believe it is the responsibility of all labor, all citizens and the public to protect the printing industry and every other industry from unfair competition. For that reason we take the position that it is economically and morally wrong for the Board of Education in New York City to purchase books from publishers who have work done at Kingsport Press, under conditions that are unfairly competitive.

Mr. Hellman seems to be saying fundamentally that all books used in New York City ought to be produced locally, despite his reference in the first sentence to "thousands of jobs elsewhere in the United States." He is saying this fundamentally, I submit, because the only intelligible proposition he offers, certainly the only factual one, is that the employment of 100,000 New York printers is somehow endangered.

Let us examine Mr. Hellman's statement. The first sentence sets the tone. We have heretofore been led to believe that in pressuring the New York City Board of Education, the unions are attempting to induce the Kingsport Press to come to terms with them. What terms? All the evidence indicates that they are willing to settle now for the same terms that the Press offered in March, 1963—together with the discharge of all striker replacements. We know that Kingsport wages, working conditions, and fringe benefits are not "substandard," despite the unions' assertions to the contrary. What are we then to make of Mr. Hellman's first sentence?

There is only one thing to make of it—it is drawing attention away from the real facts involved in the strike at the Press, away from the role played by the unions, and away from the true objective of the boycott. Having made a serious, even tragic mistake in calling the strike against the Press, the unions are attempting once again to hide their own culpability and shortcoming in a fog of propaganda. They are appealing to the ignorant, myopic variety of selfishness which produced the poor conditions of the Middle Ages, and trampling poor truth in the process. Let us look at some facts.

The commercial printing industry is not more than half unionized, and probably less than that. Again, wages and working conditions in the non-unionized half compare favorably with those in the unionized half. Among the highest wages in the printing industry today are those being paid by a non-union firm, R. R. Donnelley and Sons Company. Textbooks used in the New York City public schools are manufactured indiscriminately by unionized and non-unionized firms, with the choices made by the publishers. If the Board of Education should decide to join in the boycott of Kingsport Press books, there is and there can be no assurance that the books will come from New York City manufacturers, or even from unionized manufacturers elsewhere. Mr. Hellman's references to "100,000 New York jobs" and "low-wage oppressed area plants" seem better designed to frighten and confuse New Yorkers than to enlighten them as to their real interests.

There are hints in Mr. Hellman's speech of concern with depressed areas and people. Can these be taken seriously? The most effective way known to mankind of improving conditions in such areas is to open them to competition and investment. That is exactly what the founders of the Kingsport Press have done. It is also exactly what Mr. Hellman and his associates are seeking to frustrate—if, indeed, any coherent objective may be attributed to them, other than a desire to bring the Press to its knees.

What would happen if Mr. Hellman's ideas were taken seriously? What would happen if New Yorkers bought only goods manufactured by New Yorkers, in order to protect *all* jobs there, as Mr. Hellman apparently wishes to protect the jobs of "100,000 New York City workers"? The answer, of course, is that the lives of New Yorkers would become even more precarious, and conditions even more abusive, than they are now. Furthermore, if New York City is to close its doors to goods produced elsewhere, it should be equally advisable for other cities and towns to close their doors to goods produced in New York City. Jobs are important to them, too. But what would happen then, say, to the New York garment industry, the biggest employer in town? Most garments produced in New York City are sold elsewhere. More than 200,000 garment workers would lose their jobs.

The more significant response, however, is that Mr. Hellman

is not to be taken seriously as either a student or a leader of society. His remarks are naive, ignorant, and confused. If they add up to anything systematic, the sum is decay and retrogression—a reactionary wish to return to the medieval conditions which the history of mankind revealed to be not only unduly restrictive but unacceptable as well.

As a union leader, however, Mr. Hellman must be taken quite seriously, as must all union leaders. For they play a critical role today. The strike at the Press demonstrates the significance of their decisions. More than a thousand men and women and their families are in a distressing condition; the life of an American community has been drastically disrupted; a healthy, prosperous firm, contributing greatly to its local community and to the nation, has been jeopardized. All these have been brought about, fundamentally, by the incompetence and arrogance of union leaders, who seek now to throw upon others the blame which belongs to them.

Life in America, while good, has its share of problems, some economic. Of the economic problems, none is more serious than those growing out of labor relations, and the character of union leadership looms large among those. Long and bitterly fought strikes are significant mainly because they bring out the problems of union leadership so dramatically.

Of authority and power, union leaders have a great deal. The strike at the Press demonstrates that they are capable of using their authority and power quite irresponsibly upon occasion. Have our laws and policies contributed in some way to such irresponsibility? Is there something that can be done about it?

9

THE NATIONAL LABOR RELATIONS BOARD AND THE NATIONAL LABOR POLICY

The NLRB's Role in the Strike

A LITTLE LESS than eleven months after the strike began, four of the five striking unions asked the National Labor Relations Board to conduct elections at the Press. Neither the Press nor anyone else had questioned the representative status of those unions; the Press was bargaining with them whenever they asked for a meeting. Thus there seemed little point in the unions' election petition, and little chance that it would be granted. For the National Labor Relations Act gives the National Labor Relations Board authority to conduct elections only when "a question of representation" arises. Though suspecting that something odd was going on, the Press officers were not greatly concerned.

Filed on January 27, 1964, the four petitions were sent down on February 10, 1964, for a hearing before an NLRB hearing officer, Mr. Hutton S. Brandon. The hearing lasted four days, from February 20 to February 25, and the longer it went on the more peculiar it got. The conduct of both Mr. Brandon and the petitioning unions began worrying the Press management and its lawyers.

The basic purpose of the hearing was to determine whether or not a question of representation had actually arisen at the Press and, if so, whether or not the petitioning unions had legal grounds for commanding the election services of the NLRB. The question of representation could be established by proving that the Press was challenging the representative status of the unions, or that the unions had a dispute among themselves over representation rights.

Two of the petitioning unions—the Machinists and the Bookbinders—had been certified by the Board years earlier as exclusive bargaining agents in their appropriate bargaining units at the Press. If there is any definitive mode of settling representation issues among unions, such a Board certification is the mode *par excellence*. But the Pressmen's Union had intervened in the petitions for renewed certification filed by the Machinists and the Bookbinders, claiming representation rights in the units in which the latter had been certified. Looking into the Pressmen's intervention claim, the Press lawyers found much evidence that it was a sham and were sure that they could prove it to be such. All the petitions showed signs of having been framed by the same person, indeed of having been typed on the same typewriter. The unions were all joined together as the Allied Kingsport Press Unions, and they had made much of the solidarity of their relationship. That the Pressmen's Union could be seeking to raid the Machinists and the Bookbinders—especially since they were all involved one way or another in "no-raiding pacts"—defied belief.

The Press was not allowed to prove its contention of collusion. Although the whole purpose of the hearing was to determine whether or not a real question of representation existed, Mr. Brandon denied the Press and its lawyers the right to get into the record evidence that would tend to establish the bad faith of the Pressmen's intervention.

There are those who vaunt administrative agencies for their liberality, deriding the classic common law for its alleged tendency to exclude evidence on the basis of unrealistically rigid rules of relevance and cogency. It is doubtful that a common law

judge would ever have been as restrictive as Mr. Brandon was—
or as the NLRB itself and its hearing officers usually are when
it comes to attempts by employers to vindicate themselves. As
the reader will find if he looks at my book, *The Kohler Strike,*
the NLRB hearing officer in that case displayed the same one-
sidedness as Mr. Brandon did.

The hearing before Mr. Brandon terminated on February
25, and when it did Mrs. Jackie S. Stevens, the court reporter
selected and employed by the NLRB, became an important person. She was asked how long it would take to type up the record.
Estimating it at 500 pages, she said it would take ten days. She
could not promise to have it in the hands of the lawyers before
Friday, March 6, 1964. They would have to wait till then before
completing their briefs. (Arguments in briefs must be built upon
and must cite record evidence.)

The Board's Rules and Regulations grant the parties seven
days as of right for the filing of briefs. Obviously seven days after the close of the hearings would not serve when the transcript
of the record was not to be available for at least ten days. Normally it is a routine matter to get a reasonable extension in a
novel and complicated case; any court of law would grant one
without question. The Press lawyers asked for fourteen days in
addition to the seven to which they were entitled under the
Board's Rules. Mr. Brandon, however, did not feel he could
be as generous as the Press lawyers wanted him to be. If they
got the 500-page record on Friday, March 6, he didn't see why
they could not have their brief ready by Monday, March 9!

As things turned out, this ruling did not matter much. *The
NLRB decided the case before seeing the briefs—and possibly
before even seeing the record.*

Due process is defined as a fair notice, a fair hearing, and a
fair opportunity to argue one's case. *Webster's Unabridged* defines a kangaroo court as a tribunal "in which, although conducted under some authorization, the principles of law and
justice are disregarded or perverted." The Kingsport Press was
denied the right to introduce cogent and relevant evidence into
the record; it was denied a reasonable time to prepare its briefs;

the Board handed down its decision possibly without seeing the record in the case and certainly without seeing the Press's brief. It said in effect: we shall first decide and then later look at the facts and listen to the arguments.

Would it be wrong to accuse the Board of having acted like a kangaroo court? If it has done this sort of thing on numerous occasions—as it has—would it be wrong to say that it *is* a kangaroo court?

Let us recapitulate the details, if only for the historical record. Mrs. Stevens actually delivered the transcript of the record on March 5, 1964, a day earlier than she had thought she would. Mr. Brandon gave the Press till March 9 to file its brief. At 5:15 A.M. on Friday, March 6, before the brief was completed, checked, or mailed, the Press got the Board's decision. The seven-page decision had been drafted the day before, that is, on March 5.

The Board's decision, delivered on March 6, directed that elections be held as petitioned by all four unions—*"no later than March 10, 1964."* Normally, the Board insists that an election cannot be held unless for three full days prior thereto, formal, printed notices have been posted in the plant. The NLRB did not provide its formal notices of the election for posting till Saturday, March 7. With the election slated for Tuesday, March 10, only one full working day, Monday, March 9, was available for the posting of notices.

The Board proudly refers to its elections as "laboratory-pure experiments in industrial democracy," but the election at the Press on March 10 hardly bears out the claim. The Press employees had little time to let the reality of the election sink in to their consciousness or to get any information on the election issues from the only reliable source available to them, that is, the Press. For the Board has a rule silencing employers for twenty-four hours before an election. Notwithstanding the right of free speech declared in the Constitution of the United States and reaffirmed in the National Labor Relations Act, the National Labor Relations Board holds that there is no such right, and will invalidate any election in which the employer speaks his mind or discusses election issues with his employees on company time, however lawfully, during the prohibited period.

The Board advanced two arguments in justification of its precipitance. In any election held after March 10, it said, the strikers would be disqualified by law from voting. And secondly, no real harm would be done the Press, for the ballots would be impounded and remain uncounted till the Board had time to review the record of the hearing and the briefs and arguments of the parties.

The first of these arguments relates to Section 9 (c) (3) of the National Labor Relations Act. That section declares that in any election held within twelve months of the beginning of a strike, the strikers, even if they have been replaced, "shall be eligible to vote under such regulations as the Board shall find are consistent with the purposes and provisions of this Act."

The purpose of this provision is well known and widely understood. There is no doubt or controversy concerning it. Congress added it to the National Labor Relations Act in deference to complaints by union leaders of alleged abuses which existed under the previous rule. Previously, replaced economic strikers had no right to vote in elections held after a strike began. The theory of the disqualification was that legally replaced strikers— by virtue of their replacement—no longer had any legitimate interest in the wages, hours, or working conditions in the firm which they had struck. No longer employed—or entitled to employment—in that firm, what interest could they have in it? To give them a voice in selecting the bargaining agent for other employees would be like giving residents of Chicago a vote in New York City elections.

It was contended, however, that the rule permitted unscrupulous employers unfairly to get rid of unions. According to the unions, such employers would provoke their employees to strike. Then they would replace the strikers. And *then* the employers would ask for an election, in which, of course, the union would be voted out, since the strikers would be ineligible to vote.

It is difficult to believe that Congress could have taken those contentions seriously. Employers are in a position to act provocatively, but only employees and unions can strike; the choice is theirs. Moreover, an employer would have to be crazy, or very stupid, before he would provoke a strike on so precarious a set of assumptions—assumptions that he would escape serious losses and violence, that he would be able to find replacements in adequate quantity and quality, that the National Labor Relations Board would permit him to have an election whenever he wanted it, and so on. Nevertheless, Congress did respond favorably to the union complaints, and enacted Section 9 (c) (3).

But the purpose in enacting 9 (c) (3) was to discourage employers from provoking strikes and seeking elections within twelve months as means of ridding themselves of unions. As the Press lawyers argued most vigorously and pointedly, the purpose was *not* to insure that elections would be held within twelve months of the calling of a strike, whenever unions wanted them.

On the contrary, Section 9 (c) (3) was in no way designed to affect the rules establishing the appropriate occasions upon which elections might be called. It left untouched the requirement that a "question of representation" had to exist before the Board could direct an election.

The Board's haste in directing the election made the whole affair an insult to law and legal process. Two of the most complicated and critical features of representation elections were neglected: (1) determination of the appropriate bargaining units and (2) careful delineation of the voting eligibility of both the current employees and the strikers. Instead of issuing "regulations" concerning the eligibility of the replaced strikers as required by the statute—either in the proper form or, as it prefers, on an *ad hoc* basis—the NLRB left the parties in the dark. All strikers were thus in effect eligible to vote, despite the fact that under long-standing rules voting eligibility is dubious where a striker has obtained permanent employment elsewhere, has been discharged for good cause, has abandoned the strike, or has had his job eliminated for proper, lawful, economic reasons. As the Press lawyers argued, they were left without proper guideposts from the Board to challenge the right of any replaced striker to vote in the March 10 elections.

Thus, in respect of the Board's defense of its decision, only one conclusion seems justified. The Board perverted a statute designed to discourage elections within twelve months of a strike into a justification for hastily ordering an election precisely within twelve months. That this perversion was wrapped in questionable procedures, probable denials of due process of law, made it even more objectionable.

In representation cases more than in any other type of dispute under the National Labor Relations Act, the Board's powers are loosely defined. It has a great deal of discretion in such cases. Court review is largely unavailable. To the degree that it is available at all, the procedure is complex and hazardous, for the employer must deliberately risk committing an unfair labor practice as a means of establishing jurisdiction in the courts to review the Board's determination in representation proceedings.

Precisely because its powers are so broad in representation cases, the Board's responsibility to be fair and liberal is all the greater. For the importance of due process grows ever larger when the possibilities of relief or of the correction of mistakes are small. Bound by precedents of long standing, the Federal District Court and Circuit Court of Appeals both ruled in brief, almost blank decisions, that they had no power to review the Board's determinations in the election decision. They accepted the Board's contention to the effect that its powers in such cases are unreviewable.

In the circumstances, the Board should have been extraordinarily attentive to due process requirements prior to ordering the elections. Having callously dispensed with those requirements before ordering the elections, the Board was scarcely likely, after the elections were held, to find itself guilty of denials of due process, of an unseemly precipitance, and of an incorrect application of Section 9 (c) (3). And of course it did not. Its post-election decision, released after the Board had an opportunity to peruse the briefs and the record, departed in no sense from its pre-election decisions.

It is a logical possibility that the Board would have originally decided the case after a full and fair review of the briefs and record, in exactly the same way that it did without reading them. But the great service performed by the concept of due process is not limited to informing deciding tribunals; it extends also to creating community confidence in the fairness and good faith of deciding tribunals.

When the ballots were finally counted, three of the four petitioning unions—all but the Machinists—were found to have won the elections in the bargaining units in which they had sought certification. Thus those three unions, despite the bad judgment they had shown, despite the tragedy they had brought to Kingsport and to their own members, escaped without penalty. They preserved their status as exclusive bargaining agents at the Kingsport Press. This meant that they could continue to picket and to engage in other forms of harassment.

The grim irony, however, is that these same unions are now bargaining agents for workers who do not want them—and, still grimmer, for workers whom the unions wish to destroy. For the only workers presently employed at the Press are the people whom the unions call "scabs and rats." Moreover, barring some move or development which is at present improbable, they are the only workers that the Press is likely to have in the foreseeable future.

The unions are making every effort to induce the Press to get rid of the "scabs and rats." They are apparently willing to ruin the Press if they cannot force it to replace its present personnel with the bitter-end strikers. What kind of a labor policy can we call one which gives a union power to bargain for workers whom it wishes to destroy? Which rewards union leaders for making mistakes and stubbornly refusing to correct them? Is this a labor policy which benefits workers, the community, or even the "labor movement"?

One thing is certain—it is not the labor policy conceived by Congress and set forth in the National Labor Relations Act. It is the policy excogitated by the National Labor Relations Board in a long series of politically motivated, opportunistic misconstructions and perversions of the National Labor Relations Act.

Congress's Labor Policy

There are serious defects in the national labor policy as declared by Congress in such major legislation as the Norris-LaGuardia Act, the Railway Labor Act, and the National Labor Relations Act. Moreover, in recent years these legislative faults have been aggravated. However, it must be conceded that most of the Congressional mistakes reflect widely held views concerning the social desirability and effectiveness of the institution of collective bargaining. With some exceptions, the labor relations legislation compounded by the various Congresses in the last thirty-five years or so has been principled and general. It has not—again with some exceptions—been formulated in an *ad hoc,* cheap, opportunistic manner designed to placate this or that politically powerful union leader. As a matter of fact, there are elements of principled strength and dignity in the National Labor Relations Act.

Thus the NLRA does not play favorites—not intentionally and consciously, that is—between unions and employers. Its central feature is the principle of free employee choice. Employees, according to Section 7 of the Act, have equally protected rights to join or not to join unions, to bargain collectively or to refuse to bargain collectively, to participate or to refuse to participate in concerted activities.

These employee rights are protected equally—indeed in almost identical terms—from invasion by either unions or employers. Employers are told that they may not coerce employees, either physically or economically, in the exercise of their Section 7 rights. An identical provision applies to trade unions. Specific forms of conduct prohibited to employers are balanced by similar prohibitions against specific union conduct. The right of unions to strike is balanced by the right of employers to lock out their employees. By the terms of the statute, the right of employees and unions lawfully to advance the cause of unionization is balanced by the right of employers and non-union employees to oppose and resist unionization, if the means are peaceful and non-coercive.

As noted above, the NLRA has defects, serious ones. The principle of free employee choice expressed in the NLRA is a crippled one. Under the Act, employees may be compelled to join unions and pay dues to them where a valid union-shop agreement exists. Still worse, if a majority of employees in any appropriate bargaining unit choose union representation, the rest must under the NLRA accept that union as their representative whether they like it or not. This is not free employee choice, properly speaking; it is a license granted to majorities to impose their will upon the minority. True freedom, as civil libertarians continually remind us today, has a meaning different from that. It means freedom for the lone individual or for the minority, not a special privilege in majorities to suppress individual choice.

Reflecting the popular belief that collective bargaining between unions and employers is superior to the competition which goes on between employers as a means of determining wages, hours, and other terms and conditions of employment, the National Labor Relations Act has fallen into the serious error of imposing compulsory collective bargaining. It compels employers to bargain in "good faith" with unions which represent a majority of employees in any appropriate bargaining unit.

The evils associated with this compulsory bargaining principle are both serious and incurable. Compulsory bargaining is wrong in principle; in a country which regards freedom as its loftiest ideal, compelling persons to bargain is a pure anomaly. It is disastrous in practice. It has proved to be impossible to apply "good faith" standards to collective bargaining without compelling concessions, contrary to the Act's expressed disavowal of any such intention. Again, compulsory collective bargaining makes it necessary to have an agency, such as the National Labor Relations Board, with authority to rule in an arbitrary and discretionary way on such issues as the "appropriate bargaining unit." Those issues can never be resolved in an objective, principled manner; the structure of competitive industry is much too fluid and dynamic to permit of the artificial line-drawing which the concept of the "appropriate bargaining unit" inevitably involves.

This point brings us to the most profound of the defects in the national labor policy as conceived by Congress. It is possible for decent people of sound mind to argue for a long time on the pros and cons of the particular rules imbedded by Congress in the national labor policy. But I do not believe that Congress's decision to entrust the administration of the Act to the short-term political appointees who sit on the National Labor Relations Board is defensible any longer, if it ever was.

Under the NLRA, the critical power of decision rests with the National Labor Relations Board. Limited judicial review is available, but the Supreme Court of the United States, riding certain hobby horses of its own, has tended to restrict judicial review even more than Congress did in the Act. It has told the Federal courts that they must defer to the NLRB's "expertise" in labor relations, apparently never pausing to wonder how it is possible that short term political appointees, subject to fantastic political pressures, normally with little legal and no judicial experience, can acquire an "expertise" in judging superior to that possessed by men who have, by accepting Federal judicial appointment, dedicated their lives to the interpretation of fact and law.

NLRB members over the years have contended that the Board must be doing a good job on the whole because the vast majority of its decisions are approved and affirmed by the reviewing courts. Informed persons of critical and disinterested mind will not grant credit to this deceptive boasting. The Federal courts of appeals frequently affirm NLRB decisions in opinions in which, at the same time, they lament their limited powers of review, especially their limited power to review the "facts" found by the Board. Considerably more important, the courts of appeals today confront a massive accumulation of decisions by the Supreme Court which have sided with the Board and against the courts of appeals.

It would be easy to prove that the Board's proud record of affirmances by the reviewing courts is composed largely of cases in which, originally, the courts of appeals had differed, often very caustically, with the Board's legal analysis. Little by little over the past thirty years the Board's corruptions of the Act have come to take the place of the Act as Congress passed it, as a consequence of the Supreme Court's tendency, by and large, to share the ideological and political predilections which have ruled the NLRB decisions. No wonder the Board is reversed by the courts of appeals in only a minority of cases!

The NLRB's Labor Policy

Congress's labor policy may be summed up briefly as one designed to protect free employee choice and to encourage collective bargaining when majorities wish it. The NLRB has transformed that policy into one of aggrandizement of politically powerful trade unions.

The law as passed by Congress is largely neutral on the issue of union success or failure. It gives employees the right to reject or to accept unions. It recognizes a right in employers noncoercively to resist union organizational efforts. It requires collective bargaining, but carefully refrains from taking sides in the bargaining, saying in so many words that neither party is under a duty to concede anything. As already observed, the right to strike is balanced by the employer right to lock out. Under the law, furthermore, economic strikers have no right to reinstatement when they have been replaced. This means that Congress recognizes a right in employers to resist union demands and to defeat unions when they strike for wage increases in spite of the availability of replacements.

Over the years, the National Labor Relations Board has tried to pervert and corrupt each of these basic legislative principles. Sometimes it has failed, owing to the refusal of the Supreme Court to endorse its more obvious and extreme distortions of legislative policy. More often, backed by the Supreme Court, the Board has succeeded, so that the practical law of labor relations is now vastly different from the one which Congress created.

This is not the place for an exhaustive or even extensive account of the Board's version of the National Labor Relations Act. The reader will gain a sufficient conception of the Board's deeper influence on the strike at the Press from a brief description of what it has been doing with the law of labor relations.

Let us first review two of the points on which the Board's desire to transform labor policy has been frustrated to some degree by the Supreme Court. Consider, first, the Board's theory of the legality of peaceful, non-coercive lockouts, designed exclusively to back up an employer's good faith bargaining. With no basis in the language or the policy of the NLRA, the Board persisted for twenty-five years in holding that such lockouts violated the Act.

No one denied that a lockout designed to induce employees to reject unions or to evade collective bargaining would violate the Act. But there was no provision of the Act as written by Congress which could be pointed to in support of the Board's conclusion that a good faith bargaining lockout violated the Act. Such a lockout did not restrain or coerce employees in the exercise of their Section 7 rights; it did not discriminate against any employee; it did not constitute a refusal to meet and treat with the union.

Still the Board insisted that it was unlawful. Why unlawful? The Board replied: because it undercuts the right of employees to strike. The fact that there is no provision in the law and no policy prohibiting employers from "undercutting the right to strike"; the fact that the law, on the contrary, expressly recognizes the right of employers to lock out their employees in bargaining impasses—neither was sufficient to mitigate the Board's stubborn and arrogant defiance of legislative supremacy. Fortunately, the Federal courts of appeals, "expert" or not in the field, could read the statute more accurately and apply it more faithfully than the Board. On the whole, they stoutly resisted the Board's lockout view. Finally, the Supreme Court, though very late and with much agony, sided with the Federal courts of appeals. And the legislative principle to the effect that collective-bargaining lockouts are legally as valid as strikes has been vindicated.

The Board has failed, thus far, in one other attempt to substitute its policy for the one that Congress has conceived. Almost since the enactment of the Wagner Act in 1935 the Board has been trying to transform the duty to bargain into a duty to make concessions where necessary in order to strengthen unions or at least to save the face of union negotiators. As a practical matter the Board continues to impose this requirement, as we shall see a little later; but it has failed to win the endorsement of the Supreme Court. On the contrary, that Court has repeatedly reminded the Board that it must respect the Congressional policy in this area of law. Congress has said that collective bargaining implies no duty to make concessions, but despite the fidelity of the Supreme Court to Congressional purpose in this instance, the Board continues adamantly to insist that "adamancy" in collective bargaining is an unfair labor practice.

So much for the cases in which the Supreme Court has insisted upon legislative supremacy. The instances in which the Board has succeeded in substituting its policies for those of Congress have been at least as significant and far more numerous.

With the endorsement of the Supreme Court the Board has established the principle that an employer must allow unions to use company premises for organizing purposes where it would be inconvenient and expensive for them to do their organizing elsewhere. There is quite plainly no statutory or policy basis for this rule. The Act is designed to keep employers from coercively interfering with the organizing activities of employees; indeed it forbids employers to grant financial or any other kind of support to unions. To hold, in the face of these provisions, that employers must positively assist union organizers is to pervert the national policy. It is much like saying that employers must finance the organizing campaigns of unions which happen to be short of money.

Again, the Supreme Court has upheld the Board view that employers commit an unfair practice in announcing employee benefits or putting them into effect during an organizing campaign. The theory here is that such a gift is *coercive* because it reminds employees, somehow, that the "velvet glove may enfold a mailed fist."

The theory is defective. It confuses the act of influencing with the act of coercing. Of course employees may be *influenced* to vote against a union by a belief in the employer's generosity. They may come to the conclusion that they do not need unions in order to gain adequate rewards for their labor. But the Act does not forbid "influencing"; it forbids coercion. And it remains to be shown how a person is *coerced* by an attractive offer.

The Supreme Court response to this line of analysis has been vague and obscure. It has said that employee freedom of choice would be "impinged upon" if employers were allowed to grant benefits during organizing campaigns because the employees would think that the sole source of benefits would dry up if they voted against the employer's wishes. However, the Act as written by Congress does not forbid employers from "impinging upon" employee freedom of choice. To the contrary, Congress specifically and positively ordered the Board to grant immunity to employer arguments against unionization.

Aside from that, the Court's obscure view suggests considerable naiveté. If employees are somehow coerced whenever they get the idea that voting for unions will cause the employer to "dry up" as a source of benefits, one may wonder how it is possible that employees vote, as they frequently do, in favor of union representation. Do they not join unions *precisely* because they feel that unions are capable of prying out more from employers than they can secure on their own? Suppose an employer should grant increases on the Court's theory, only to withdraw them after the employees had voted against union representation. Would not such conduct induce the employees to choose union representation the next time?

The Board has enjoyed one of its greatest successes in the thirty-year war it has savagely waged against progressive, humane, and civilized attempts by company managements to solve some of their personnel problems without going through the often tortuous processes of union grievance procedures. An employer will encourage his employees to set up a more or less informal organization, electing representatives, and delegating to those representatives the function of discussing with the management anything that the employees are concerned with, anything they may have on their minds. The organization will not be called a union; it may be called an employee representation plan. It will not bargain collectively, in any sense of the word. No agreement, formal or informal, will emerge from the conferences between the employee representatives and the management. The representative may say—"John is het up over the dirt that the janitor leaves around the machines"; or he may say that "Mary thinks Jane is getting all the breaks from their supervisor." The employer will listen, but he will take action only if he thinks he should.

The Board, with the approval of the Supreme Court, automatically rules that such employee representation plans are "labor organizations," that employers commit an unfair practice in suggesting their formation and contributing any kind of support to them; and therefore that they must be "disestablished," which means that they must be destroyed. It so holds even where the employer has in no manner inhibited the employees from joining independent affiliated unions. In the leading case, indeed, the employee representation plan existed in a firm in which the employees also belonged to large outside unions, and suffered no penalty or pressure from the employer.

The Board is not pursuing Congressional policy in these cases. It is extremely difficult, if not impossible, to square the Board's holdings with the language of the statutory prohibitions upon employer coercion; and it is equally difficult to reconcile the Board's views with the basic legislative policies. These decisions, and a multitude of others which might be cited, add up to something else. They add up to a policy of suppressing all resistance to the large unions, a policy which leaves employees with only one practical choice in their quest for improvement of their condition. The employer who dares to assume that he has a right to meet his employees' needs directly is punished; if he engages actively in a program designed to convince the employees that he is on their side, that they may have confidence in his sincere interest in them, he is in for real trouble.

The NLRB and the "Communications Gap": The G.E. Case

One of the most significant examples of the Board's unremitting war against progressive employers is to be found in its 1964 decision against the General Electric Company. G.E. has long enjoyed a reputation for thoughtfully conceived and carefully executed personnel policies. Its famous vice president, Lemuel R. Boulware, took the position years ago that it is the duty of company managements not only themselves to understand that employers and employees have greater interests in common than they do in conflict, but also to convince the employees that such is the case. So General Electric has long had an effective employee-communications program, and apparently the program has borne fruit. G.E. employees seem to be aware that their wages are paid by their employer, not by their unions; that the company is sincerely desirous of good relations with the employees; and that it will always do its best for them, consistently with its equal obligations to stockholders and customers.

During the summer and early fall of 1960, G.E. and the International Union of Electrical Workers (IUE), headed by Mr. James Carey, engaged in extensive negotiations looking toward a renewal of the existing collective agreement. After a number of meetings during which the company reformulated some of its proposals, G.E. put all its proposals together into what it called a "fair and firm" offer. Mr. Carey rejected the offer, and the company, having done all it could in the meanwhile to convince the union and the employees that the offer was, indeed, fair and very, very firm, stuck with it. Thus an impasse was reached.

Mr. Carey called a strike on October 2. Twenty days later he called off the strike. Despite the usual mass picketing and violence the strike had failed to reduce production significantly, had failed to take hold in a number of plants; the employees were more interested in accepting G.E's offer than the union was. "Boulwarism" was a stunning success.

What it thus lost in the market place the leadership of the IUE determined to recoup in the political field. Carey filed charges with the NLRB, accusing G.E. of a failure to bargain in good faith. In spite of considerable evidence to the contrary, the Labor Board held that G.E. had thrust a "take-it-or-leave-it" proposition on the bargaining table and had shown no interest in bargaining at all. Good faith bargaining, according to the Board, requires recognition that collective bargaining "is a shared process in which each party, labor union and employer, has the right to play an active role." G.E.'s approach "devitalized negotiations" since it fundamentally involved a " 'fair and firm offer' . . . without holding anything back for later trading or compromising."

The Labor Board found many other things wrong with the G.E. bargaining approach. The communication program was inconsistent with good faith bargaining because it disparaged and discredited the union—and especially because it created "the impression that the employer rather than the union is the true protector of the employees' interests," whereas, according to the Board, "the employer's statutory obligation is to deal with the employees through the union, and not with the union through the employees."

One of the things that bothered the Board most, seemingly, was G.E.'s decision to communicate to the employees the final offer it made to the union earlier than Mr. Carey and the Board thought it should have. In doing this, said the Board, G.E. "consciously placed itself in a position where it could not give unfettered consideration to the merits of any proposals the Union might offer."

Having put itself in that position, G.E. convicted itself of an unfair practice, at least in the Board's conception of what is necessary to satisfy the good faith bargaining requirement. For in "good faith bargaining," as the Labor Board phrased it, "the essential thing is . . . the serious intent to adjust differences and to reach an acceptable common ground."

We have arrived here at one of the more significant legal features of the Board's decision in the G.E. case. If that last sentence is examined carefully, it will appear to establish as an *absolute requirement* for good faith bargaining that the parties must compromise when they reach an impasse. The words "serious intent . . . to reach an acceptable common ground" either mean nothing at all or they mean compromise; and compromise means concession.

Hence the G.E. decision stands for the proposition that an employer must make concessions if he hopes to operate within the law—as the Labor Board applies the law.

It can never be emphasized too much that we are now reviewing the *Labor Board's* conception of good faith bargaining—not necessarily the one which Congress defined when it wrote the law. Back in 1947, when it passed the Taft-Hartley Act, Congress was especially concerned about two trends in Labor Board decisions under the Wagner Act. It felt that the Board had gone much too far in limiting the free speech rights of employers. And it was convinced that the Board was compelling employers to make concessions to unions instead of merely enforcing the statutory duty to bargain in good faith.

This concern was formally registered in the most positive way available to Congress. The two really significant Wagner Act amendments contained in the Taft-Hartley Act dealt with the free speech issue and the duty to bargain collectively.

Congress expressly instructed the Board in Section 8 (d) that the duty to bargain in good faith was not to be stretched into an obligation to agree to any proposal or to make any concession.

The leading decision by the United States Supreme Court on the meaning of this provision was handed down in 1952 (*NLRB v. American National Insurance Co.*). Speaking for the Court in that case, Chief Justice Vinson confirmed the plain meaning of the statutory language. Reversing (and reproving) the Board, he said: ". . . it is now apparent from the statute itself that the Act does not encourage a party to engage in fruitless marathon discussions at the expense of frank statement and support of his position." Still more to the point, the Chief Justice went on to say: ". . . it is equally clear that the Board may not, either directly or indirectly, compel concessions or otherwise sit in judgment upon the substantive terms of collective bargaining agreements."

Still later, in 1960, Justice Frankfurter reviewed the background of Section 8 (d), and pointed out that it grew out of "considerable controversy over the need to objectify the elements of the duty to bargain." He then re-affirmed Vinson's view that "the history of [Section 8 (d)] demonstrates an intention to restrain the Board's power to regulate, whether directly or indirectly, the substantive terms of collective agreements."

The Supreme Court has reproved the Board in other decisions for the mistakes it has made in administering the collective bargaining features of the National Labor Relations Act, and it is certain that the precedents will get a thorough going-over in the appeals which have been filed by both the union and G.E. Here we may conclude with a review of what Congress did about the free speech abuses of which the Board was guilty under the Wagner Act. For it is quite possible that the most foreboding aspect of the G.E. decision lies in the restraints it seeks to impose upon the process of communication between employers and employees.

Congress directed the Board in Section 8 (c) of the Taft-Hartley Act to restrain itself in evaluating expressions of "views, arguments, or opinions." Such expressions, the section says, may not be regarded as unfair practices in themselves or even as evidence of other unfair practices—unless they contain threats of reprisal or force or promises of benefits.

Beyond much question, G.E.'s communication program involved the kind of argument and expression of opinion which Section 8 (c) covers. In a word, G.E. was urging the rightness, the fairness, and the firmness of its proposals. Of course it argued from its own point of view; it goes equally without saying that G.E. was intent upon establishing the justice of its own course of action, not that of the union.

But it has never been thought that the right of free speech is confined only to neutrals, or to pedants who strive endlessly to present all sides of every question. Section 8 (c) protects arguments and opinions, not academic treatises.

Finally, G.E. urged that to strike would be foolish and futile —not that it would punish anyone who chose to strike. In fact, G.E. emphatically declared its recognition of and respect for the employees' right to strike. Hence there were no threats of reprisal or force of the kind that negate the protection extended by Section 8 (c).

Nevertheless, the NLRB held that G.E.'s "total course of conduct" added up to an unfair labor practice. There can be no doubt that the G.E. employee-communications program was an integral and indispensable feature of that course of conduct. In the Board's view, the communications "discredited" and "disparaged" the union. They amounted to "bargaining with the union through the employees" rather than "with the employees through the union," in the board's phraseology. In brief, the communications program, while not held an unfair practice in itself, was held an essential aspect of the unfair practice which the Board found.

The Board's opinion does not so much as mention Section 8 (c). That omission does not, however, eliminate the obvious conflict between the Board's ruling and the will of Congress. Nor does it diminish the gravity of the Board's invasion of the right of free speech. As Board Member Leedom intimates in his dissenting opinion, the failure to grapple with Section 8 (c) serves only to emphasize the juridical weakness of the majority opinion.

Again, the Board's cease-and-desist order does not expressly command G.E. to stop communicating with its employees. A straightforward order of that kind would much too obviously flout the law. However, as an integral feature of the unfair practice which the Board found, the communications program is subject to the general cease-and-desist order issued against the unfair practice—subject, moreover, in an ambiguous and therefore extremely hampering way. If the order stands, in other words, G.E. will find itself tangled with NLRB agents operating on a carte blanche authority to challenge at will its compliance with the vague order.

There has been a tendency to underrate the "practical" importance of the G.E. decision. Some commentators have viewed it as but another example of the tendency toward greater governmental intervention in collective bargaining. But it must be remembered that in holding the G.E. bargaining method an unfair practice the NLRB laid the groundwork for holding that the strike which occurred thereafter was an "unfair-practice strike."

Unfair-practice strikers are entitled to reinstatement whenever they apply for it. If he has hired replacements, the employer must fire them if necessary to make room for the strikers. This means he cannot hold out the promise of permanent employment for replacements. And that, of course, added to the well known hazards of "scabbing," makes it extremely difficult for employers to carry on production during an "unfair-practice" strike.

Thus no comfort can be drawn from the lack of a specific finding that "Boulwarism" is an unfair practice, or from the absence of a specific order against the G.E. communications program. If the G.E. decision stands on appeal, employers will have to think very seriously before taking firm stands in union negotiations; many will certainly shy off attempts to sell their employees directly on the proposals they have submitted to the union.

The total effect of the decision is to increase still more the complexities of collective bargaining under the national labor law. Instead of promoting straightforward good faith bargaining, the NLRB seems bent on encouraging duplicity on the part of employers. Instead of promoting the development of coherent employee relations programs, the NLRB seems more interested in seeing to it that employers leave their employees in the dark, dependent solely upon union propaganda.

The NLRB and Union Arrogance: The Kohler Case

Asked to identify the worst example of the NLRB's corruption of national labor policy, the careful and disinterested student of labor law would have a difficult choice to make. There have been so many. Still, after much study and reflection, I have come to the conclusion that there is one case which exceeds all the others—which stands out as on the one hand a beckoning invitation to union arrogance, and on the other a grim warning to employers that they must tread warily in disputes with unions. I speak of the Kohler case.

I do not intend to repeat here the extensive writing I have published elsewhere on the Kohler case.* A bare account of the principal events and rulings will suffice to indicate its bearing upon our present subject.

The Kohler case began with a strike called by the Automobile Workers Union in the spring of 1954. A violent, obstructive, mass picket line of some two thousand persons heralded the strike and set the tone for the six years which were to follow before the strike was terminated. There were hundreds of instances of violence and vandalism and physical assaults. The union and its hired agents were directly identified as instrumental in many of them; the company was never so identified. Still, when the NLRB got through with the case the union emerged triumphantly unscathed while the company got hit with everything the Board had, including a tremendous financial penalty.

Consider a moment the Board's findings against the company. The trial examiner who conducted the basic hearing concluded that the company had shown more good faith than the union had in the pre-strike bargaining; yet, in its latest decision the NLRB ruled that the company had failed to bargain in good faith from the very beginning. Hence, the Board ruled, the strike was an unfair-practice strike from its inception, and thus the strikers had a right to get their jobs back, even though they had been replaced in the meantime.

In its first decision in the case, in August of 1960, the NLRB ruled that the company could lawfully have discharged every one of the strikers who had participated in the mass picketing; for,

* See *Power Unlimited: The Corruption of Union Leadership,* pp. 47–110 (New York: The Ronald Press, 1959); *The Kohler Strike* (Chicago: Regnery, 1961); "Reward the Guilty," in *Barron's* (Dec. 21, 1964), p. 1.

under the law as written, workers who participate in violent and obstructive conduct forfeit the protection of the NLRA. In its final decision, in September of 1964, the Board held that the company committed an unfair practice when it discharged fifty or more of the strikers who had been identified as having engaged in some of the more reprehensible conduct that occurred. The rationale was that Kohler's alleged refusal to bargain—a pure figment of the Board's imagination—was so flagrant a misdeed as to outweigh the evil of the strikers' conduct.

Kohler had employed some seventy temporary workers in its shell department, completing a government contract. It was understood by everyone concerned that the employment would terminate when the government contract ended. The strike intervened; some of the temporary workers stayed in, others struck. The company transferred the non-strikers to other, permanent jobs when the shell contract was fulfilled, as the original agreement envisioned. Naturally the strikers could not be so transferred; they were out on strike and declined to work either in the shell department or anywhere else. Nevertheless the NLRB held that somehow the company was guilty of an unfair practice in not providing the strikers with the transfers to permanent employment which it had given to the non-strikers!

The NLRB decisions in the Kohler case are rampant with such fantastic and virtually unintelligible rulings, and the Board's "findings of facts" were mockeries of fairness, objectivity, and truth. The questionable procedures in the Board's handling of the election petitions during the strike at Kingsport Press were bad enough; the Kohler case involved one huge and ugly perversion of the principles of due process of law from villainous beginning to tragic end.

Like the strike at the Press, the strike against the Kohler Company came about as a consequence of mistaken judgment on the part of the union leadership. Within months many strikers had returned to work and "new hires" were available to the Kohler Company in abundance because Kohler was, in the eyes of people in the surrounding area, a good place to work. In short, the union called a strike which it should never have called, and that stern and just arbiter of economic decision, the free market, demonstrated both the error and the irresponsibility.

However, the National Labor Relations Board, administering its private National Labor Relations Act, rescued the union leadership from the consequences of its mistakes. The NLRB's guiding principle in the Kohler case was that an employer must never make union leaders look bad in the eyes of the public or in the eyes of employees; and that, above all, unions must never lose strikes, no matter how badly, how irresponsibly, they exercise their authority as bargaining agents.

The NLRB's Responsibility in the Press Mess

I do not believe that the members of the National Labor Relations Board are evil men, any more than I believe that the leaders of the Allied Kingsport Press Unions are evil men. On the contrary, from what I have seen of both groups they strike me as decent persons. The accusation I make against the National Labor Relations Board is that it is bringing to labor relations not the peace, order, and accommodation which national labor policy strives to establish, but turmoil, confusion, and tragedy. It is producing these results by pampering trade union leaders on the one hand and, on the other, by creating in conscientious and law-abiding employers a fear so great that they are immoblized. Employees are as a result exposed all too often to only one side of the story; they make mistakes of judgment because they are inadequately informed and educated in respect of their own deepest interests.

The strike at the Press should never have been called, and, once called, it should have been terminated within weeks. It *would* have ended in weeks had not the union leaders fallen into the habit of thinking that they were invincible. And it probably would never have been called in the first place had the Press not been scared out of its wits by the repressive policies of the National Labor Relations Board.

A confident, aggressive employee-communications program by the Press management would most likely have brought home to the bulk of the employees the facts which were always evident to the more informed and intelligent among them: the stupidity and vanity of striking; the desirability of work at the Press relative to other opportunities in the area; the heavy unemployment prevailing around Kingsport; the fallacy of the "labor solidarity" mythology.

But it would be unfair to criticize the Press for not having engaged in an extensive program of employee education. Had it done so, as the Kohler and G.E. cases indicate, the NLRB might very well have held it guilty of an unfair practice; and the situation might then have been worse all around than it is now. Thus the strike at the Press owes much to the NLRB's ill-conceived and illegitimate usurpation of policy-making power.

The NLRB's policies are doing no one any real good—not even the union leaders. Unionization makes no long-run gains when the mistakes and abuses of union leaders are disguised by political devices. The proof lies in the increasingly skeptical attitude toward unions expressed by both the general public and workingmen. The Automobile Workers leadership may have come out on top in the Kohler case, and the Electrical Workers leadership in the G.E. case. But one way or another the tragic mistakes they make impress themselves upon the public and upon the workingmen immediately involved. I am reminded of Jack Salyer's friend—the striker who could not bring himself to cross the picket line but who swore, nevertheless, that he would never join a union again. The relevant fact here is that the large, affiliated unions have been standing still in this country, even going backwards, for almost twenty years. The political favoritism which they have striven for and largely achieved has not done them any good. You can not fool all the people all the time.

I believe it would be expecting too much to ask the National Labor Relations Board to reform its ways, to begin to administer the national labor policy fairly and even-handedly. The members are short-term political appointees. As such, they must bow to political pressures. If they do not, they will find themselves out of a job.

So, at bottom, the responsibility does not really fall to the

Board. It falls, instead, to the Congress of the United States and
to the people who elect congressmen and senators. The Congress
must come to the realization that the Constitution was right, after
all, in insisting that the judicial power of the United States be
vested only in the Federal courts, administered by men who have
life tenure in office and who, therefore, need not bow to political
pressures in order to hold their jobs. Perhaps this is the greatest
single lesson taught by the strike at the Press.

The Press has to this day a spotless record of scrupulous respect for the labor policy established by *Congress*. Indeed, the
"communications gap" which Clifton Fritschle mourns and
which must share some of the blame for the strike indicates
scrupulous respect by the Press management for the *NLRB's*
labor policy as well.

After the strike was called the unions filed unfair-practice
charges, obviously in order to add to the pressures on the Press
and to provide the NLRB with an opportunity to win for the
unions, as it did in the Kohler case, a strike which the unions
could not themselves win on the merits. These unfair-practice
charges were dismissed in the NLRB regional office. The dismissal in the regional office is a fair indication that they were
considered extremely weak, for the NLRB regional offices are
not inclined to dismiss charges which show any merit at all.

The strange thing is that now, as of this writing in March,
1966, those charges, though dismissed in the regional office in
August, 1965, are still pending in the Washington offices of the
NLRB.* What is taking so long? There has been a "field investigation," leading to dismissal of the charges. The current charges
against the Press involve no new and tricky legal questions.
They involve, instead, the same old vague, tired generalizations
about "refusal to bargain in good faith"—charges which the
history of the marathon negotiations between the Press and the
unions should refute out of hand.

Let me hazard a guess. In my opinion, the charges are hang-

* After withdrawing the charges during the summer of 1966, the
unions later refiled them. Again the charges were dismissed in the NLRB
regional office and are now—in 1967—once again hanging fire in the
Washington offices of the NLRB.

ing fire for these many months for two reasons: first, as additional pressure on the Press management, designed to frighten it into submission; second, in the hope that the Press will miss its footing somewhere on the treacherous ice and thus provide an opportunity for the NLRB's killer whales to engulf it.

The union people around Kingsport remarked to me on more than one occasion that they would never let the Press go. One way or another, they were confident, the NLRB would get back at the Press officers for their insolence in exercising the rights of free Americans when confronted with the unions' demands.

Let the reader recall here the remarks made by Mr. Walter Reuther at the AFL-CIO Convention in San Francisco in December of 1965. Mr. Reuther was talking about the effect that the situation at Kingsport and at Kohler was likely to have on other managements "who will flirt with this idea that they can defy organized labor." The plain fact, of course, is that he was engaging in the vainglorious bragging and distortion that have become typical of some union leaders. For in the fair and square battle of wit and courage that the free market poses, both the Press and Kohler trimmed the pants off their union opponents.

The union did not win against Kohler; the government of the United States, wielding the power supplied it, all unknowing, by the people of the United States, beat and bullied the Kohler management into submission. Quite obviously the unions are also not winning against the Press. But are we to be witnesses again in the Kingsport Press case to the kind of massive intervention by government that occurred in the Kohler case?

What is to happen to Americans, to consumers and to workers, if Walter Reuther's ambitions are realized? What is to happen to us all when and if employers conclude that it is hopeless to "defy organized labor"?

Mr. Reuther's position is in my opinion a vain and foolish one. The trade unions are not about to take over this country now, and they never will. But union leaders consider themselves politically powerful enough to ride roughshod over the rights of others. They have acquired that opinion largely through the favoritism shown by the Federal government in general and by the

NLRB in particular. Much of the Press Mess is directly attributable to the irresponsibility of the union leadership involved, and indirectly attributable to the NLRB, whose political susceptibilities have caused it to transform the national labor policy into a machine for the creation of inept and arrogant union leaders.

10

THE LAW AND THE STRIKE

The Premises of Labor Policy

POLICY TRENDS for fifty years or more have been built upon the premise that the field of labor relations is a new phenomenon, raising new problems, and thus perforce calling for new solutions. Those who have led the trends deplore direct dealing between employers and employees. Preferring collective bargaining and government intervention, they concluded that the common law had to be discarded since its property and contract principles made it possible for employers and anti-union employees to resist unionization and collective bargaining, and thus flatly conflicted with the measures which a government bent on active intervention into labor relations would have to adopt.

Accordingly, legislative principles of the kind described in the preceding chapter were substituted for the free-contract principles of the common law. Unions grew mightily in numbers, and collective bargaining became an active and widespread institution. Today more than 15,000,000 employees belong to large, aggressive trade unions, and something on the order of 70,000 collective agreements are negotiated every year or so.

Since World War II, collective bargaining has come in for the kind of re-examination that individual and direct dealing between employer and employee had been subjected to previously. The strike record had been bad during World War II, and it became considerably worse after the War. Many were proposing at the time that the government take a stronger hand in determining wages and conditions of employment. There were proposals for compulsory arbitration of major disputes.

In passing the Taft-Hartley Act in 1947 the Congress to some extent reflected the new attitude. While shrinking from compulsory arbitration it increased the role of government. This increase took two forms. First, the National Labor Relations Act was amended to establish controls upon unions similar to those which the Wagner Act of 1935 had imposed upon employers. Second, the Congress empowered the President of the United States to seek and the federal courts to grant temporary injunctions against certain large-scale strikes.

Congress was accused at the time of wishing to "bust unions" and "to turn back the clock" to earlier conditions. Incorrect then, those accusations seem clearly out of order now. The Taft-Hartley Act repealed none of the special privileges which the Wagner Act had given labor organization, and it preserved the principle of compulsory collective bargaining under the administration of the National Labor Relations Board. The perspective provided by subsequent events indicates that the Taft-Hartley Act should be viewed as an attempt by Congress only to make compulsory collective bargaining work.

The aim was not to destroy unions but simply to prevent them from acquiring so much power that still greater and more direct intervention by government would be the only recourse. Restraints were placed upon unions in the hope that their demonstrated capacity to exploit workers and the economy might be reduced and thus that direct administration of employer-employee relations by government agencies would not be necessary.

The Taft-Hartley Act did not achieve its aims, in part because the National Labor Relations Board did not administer the law faithfully.* Union growth halted, but union excesses of all kinds increased, as the investigations of the McClellan Committee disclosed. The pressures for new controls increased with them, and the Congressional response came in the Landrum-Griffin Law of 1959. That law attempted to correct the NLRB's distortions of

* See my books: *How the NLRB Repealed Taft-Hartley* (Washington, D.C.: Labor Policy Association, 1958); *Power Unlimited: The Corruption of Union Leadership* (New York: Ronald Press, 1959).

the Taft-Hartley controls upon unions. It also went off in part on a new tack. For the first time, Congress regulated the internal affairs of trade unions in an attempt to restrain the abuse of union members which the McClellan Committee had disclosed. Landrum-Griffin did not, however, provide for any more direct governmental control over wages, hours, and terms of conditions of employment than the Wagner Act or the Taft-Hartley Act had established.

The quest for solutions continues. Few would contend that the Landrum-Griffin Law has been any more successful than the Taft-Hartley Act in restraining union oppression of employees. The National Labor Relations Board continues to compress almost to the point of invisibility the law's controls upon unions while expanding immensely the older legislative restrictions upon employers.

Since 1959, pressures for increased governmental intervention have intensified. The long steel strike of 1959, the long New York newspaper strike of 1962–63, the subway strike of 1966, and any number of other strikes and disputes—all these have kept concern alive and turned worry into panic at times. We hear another refrain. Direct dealing between employers and employees has failed. Compulsory collective bargaining (erroneously referred to as "free" collective bargaining) has also failed. Something new must be tried: the government must step in to see that labor disputes are resolved without the wastefulness and dislocation of strikes, and in a manner which protects the public against the hazards of wages which are either "too low" or "too high." The "guidelines" which the government has been advancing since 1961—that is, the formula for 3.2 per cent wage increases, usually ignored by the trade unions—are probably best regarded as the first tentative steps toward a politically administered "incomes policy."

Continuance along the line of the dominant trends of the last thirty years is bound to result in direct administration of the economy by politicians and bureaucrats. Today, in the spring of 1966, this seems a certainty even to the union leaders who have led the campaign for government intervention in labor disputes.

The newspapers are full of Mr. George Meany's "revolt" against the Presidential guidelines. President Lyndon B. Johnson and his Labor Secretary, Mr. Willard Wirtz, are reportedly concerned over the possibility that the "labor movement" may defect from the Democratic Party.

If government takes over responsibility for determining wages it will have to concern itself with prices as well. When politicians and bureaucrats administer wages and prices the integrity of the market economy will be seriously compromised. An economy in which product and labor prices do not move freely in accordance with the decisions of the persons directly involved is indeed not a market economy at all.

The present danger of government control of the economy traces directly to the legislative policies of the last thirty years or so, and those policies are a product of the premises which I have summarized. Trade unions could not possibly have reached their present size or acquired their present abusive character without the special privileges which interventionist legislation accorded them. In the absence of that legislation they would not now be in a position to threaten and to dislocate the economy. In turn, the case for still more direct governmental control of the market, such as it is, would be untenable.

Examine the Premises

When a course of development threatens a destructive conclusion, the thing to do, as Ayn Rand has said, is to re-examine the premises upon which that course is based. Let us do so now with the premises of labor policy.

The employer-employee relationship necessarily breeds situations of friction and conflict. Differences must arise concerning wages, hours, conditions of employment, treatment on the job, advancement and promotions, and so on. Some of these sources of friction are accurately viewed as peculiar to the employer-employee relationship—for example, the rate of pay or the number of persons to be employed on a machine. Others are merely characteristic of all human relationships—for example, whether or not affairs in the shop or the office are conducted with a decent consideration for the sentiments and feelings of the persons involved. Promotions, upgrading, and other such matters are likewise inherent in organized society, where competition among persons for "preference"—for the relatively scarce and relatively desirable conditions or positions—is a fixed and unremovable aspect of the nature of things. Whether in Communist Russia or capitalist America, in home or office or shop, polite and humane consideration is necessary in order to achieve harmony, and competition for the more desirable conditions is likewise bound to exist.

As to the more purely economic features of the employment relationship—namely wages, hours, and such things as manning or work loads—developments in this century have introduced nothing new. In fact, even the Industrial Revolution introduced nothing really new. Some people have worked for others since the dawn of society, since the beginning of the division of labor, specialization, and exchange. Populations have increased, and some productive units have grown in size and numbers. In such cases the employment relationship has tended to become more complex and even more impersonal, from one point of view. The relationship between the lowest-rank employee and the ultimate employer in a large corporation, namely, the stockholder, is tenuous, highly distended, totally impersonal. But then, upon closer scrutiny, it will be seen that even in the largest corporation, there are subdivisions of various kinds. Thus while John Doe might be described as only one of the hundreds of thousands of employees of the General Motors Corporation, he might also and more pertinently be described as one of a hundred or so employees in a given section of a given department of the Tarrytown plant of the Chevrolet Division of G.M., working under a supervisor with whom he is as familiar as he would ever be if that supervisor were his ultimate employer.

Thus it was wrong to assume, even in respect of the largest firms, that something radically new in the employment relationship was introduced in the twentieth century or by the Industrial Revolution. At any rate, it was wrong to assume that then, for the first time in history, direct dealing between employers and employees was bound to bring about socially unacceptable results. For the proper remuneration for work has always posed problems.

The error was perhaps pardonable. Employment units had grown in size. This growth had aimed at and achieved increased productivity. With more wealth thus created, the sensibilities of more people were heightened, and these heightened sensibilities were turned to gaze in horror upon the conditions within which the less fortunate lived and worked. Though those conditions were no worse than conditions in past ages, though indeed they were much better, the more sensitive observers lacked for one reason or another as vivid a conception of past conditions as they had of the then current state of affairs. They concluded that something had to be done, and the developments which we have traced were the result.

As a matter of fact, conditions in England and America for the average working person improved steadily from the eighteenth century onward.* The "sweatshops" may have been bad relative to circumstances nowadays or to those of other people at the time. But they were not bad relative to the past conditions of people at the bottom of the social scale. On the contrary, they were substantially better. In an earlier age, people at the bottom of the social scale lived short lives of unbounded misery, and their children had nothing better in store for them; whereas many persons of wealth and high position today are the children of parents who worked in "sweatshops."

It is understandable, too, that the concept of "inequality of bargaining power" should have taken hold of the minds of many. John Doe, one of hundreds of thousands, looks pretty puny when measured against General Motors. It is difficult to see, at that focus, how he has any bargaining power at all. Sure he can quit, but G.M. will have little difficulty replacing him; not nearly so much difficulty replacing him as he will have finding another job as good as the one he holds at General Motors.

The trouble, however, is that the focus is wrong. The wages

* See Paul Mantoux's great study, *The Industrial Revolution in the Eighteenth Century.*

paid by General Motors are not determined in any important degree by negotiations between G.M. and its employees, whether in individual, direct negotiations or in negotiations between G.M. and the United Automobile Workers. They are also not subject in any substantial degree to the discretion of the G.M. management.

Wages are determined in another place and in another way. The contest is among all the employers of the economy. Even the employers are only contestants, however. Somebody else makes the final decision on wage levels. The final judge is the consumer.

General Motors is not in a position, even in the absence of unionization of its employees, to pay just any level of wages that suits its fancy. When contemplating the Tarrytown operation, for example, G.M. had to calculate in terms of wages which would attract competent workers in the vicinity. It was able to pay such wages *only* because and so long as consumers were willing to pay enough for G.M. automobiles to warrant those wages, and because G.M. was run efficiently enough to make money at the wage levels and price levels at which *the market* compelled the company to operate. There may be those in the G.M. management who believe that they have greater discretion in setting wage levels than I have just indicated. After all, not too long ago the chief executive of a large steel company testified before a congressional committee that his firm could price steel largely at will. But if corporate executives still believe this, they are simply mistaken. Let them try to set wages appreciably lower than the prevailing rates and see how many and what kind of workers they will get.

It is true that wages are "indeterminate" within a certain range. However, that range becomes narrower and narrower as the economy develops, as worker mobility increases, as education and intelligence grow, as businessmen become more and more aggressive, as a society amasses in widely diverse forms the capital which makes for ever increased competition among employers.* Already, in our day, the ranges of indeterminacy are

* See Murray N. Rothbard, *Man, Economy, and State*, II, 629 et seq., especially at pages 629–30 (Princeton: D. Van Nostrand Co., 1962).

narrow indeed. A few cents per hour will make the difference between profits and losses for most employers.

The theory that compulsory collective bargaining was necessary in order to remove inequality of bargaining power and the idea that it would serve the public interest by "bringing wages up to fair levels" were as mistaken as the observation upon which they were based. There is only one way in which unions are capable of raising wages above the levels they would reach in the competition among employers for workers. That way is illustrated by the abortive attempt of the Allied Kingsport Press Unions in the strike at the Press.

Unions are capable of raising wages above market levels only by brutally and unlawfully preventing workers from taking the jobs offered at market levels. Had the Allied Unions been successful in preventing the Press from operating during the strike, the chances are that the Press would have yielded a bit more in wages. That concession, however, would have had certain consequences. The Press would not have been able to bid as successfully for printing work as it could have at the lower wage levels that it was willing to pay. In other words, printing prices quoted by the Press would have been higher; but since the demand for printing work is to some extent elastic, the Press would have been able to secure fewer orders. Its plans for expansion would have been aborted. If the same thing occurred throughout the printing industry, the result would be the same universally: less printing, less employment in the printing industry.

Nothing in the foregoing analysis suggests that there is something fundamentally wrong with labor organizations or with collective bargaining. The implication is only that it is incorrect to take the position that unions are necessary if employees are to be paid what they are worth.

This implication should not be surprising. After all, most employees in the United States—in fact, more than three-quarters of all persons employed—are not represented by unions. And I am not aware of any great feeling that they are worse off than the organized workers. They vote persistently against union representation and resist it in many other ways.

If investors and employers wish to make money, they must

hire people to work for them. In order to get workers they must pay at least the prevailing wages for workers in the categories they seek. If workers prefer to have unions represent them in wage negotiations, that is their right in a free country. Moreover, if they wish to withdraw their labor in concert by striking, that is their right, too. Their rights do not extend, however, to preventing other people from offering their labor. All the principles which make for decent living together in society—the principles of law, of morality, of economics—dictate that the terms of the employment contract be determined in the same peaceful, consensual way that applies to other terms of trade.

Consider the matter more broadly. Suppose the corner grocer should suddenly insist on a substantial increase for his wares while other grocers continue to offer those wares at the old price. Would it serve society to permit him to blockade the other grocers? Suppose the corner grocer had supplied the people on the street for years—had extended credit—had been a friend to all —and participated in neighborhood affairs. Would he then have acquired the right to prevent his old customers from shifting their patronage to other grocers?

Society as we know it—*and,* as we all desire it—could not survive such a mode of operation generally in the area of human relations involving economic exchanges, for that area comprehends much of human relations.

The considerations applicable to the more clearly economic aspects of employment must apply perforce to the others as well. Human decency, kindness, courtesy, cooperation, consideration, fairness—these virtues are as essential in minimizing friction on the job as they are in family life or in any other purely social situation. It is true that the employment relationship is a limited one, but so too are all other relationships, even the most intimate ones. Two hearts never do beat continuously as one, no matter what songwriters say.

Able men of business have always known that the principles of decency helpful in human affairs generally can be even more critically important in the employment relationship, where the stakes are unusually high. Of course it is true that not all businessmen are models of fairness and consideration; but neither are all husbands, fathers, lovers, children, wives, aunts, and uncles. And there is this difference, in favor of competitive business and businessmen: they developed theories of systematic "scientific" management a hundred years ago or more, long before unions became important in this country. Those theories were profit-oriented; the idea was to encourage team spirit and cooperation in the plant in order to promote productivity. But that should make no difference. Profit of one kind or another is the spur to all action. The important thing is that contemporary personnel practices in any well run firm, tracing back to the pioneers of systematic management, are humane, decent, civilized.

It is quite possible that the stronger unions tend to inhibit the potentials of development inherent in management theory. Such unions normally seek in effect to take over the work of personnel departments. They consider themselves to be entitled to take charge of worker grievances. When they are unable to agree with management decisions on grievances they insist that outside arbitrators be given the final authority.

Grievance arbitration has enjoyed a great vogue for many years. It is today a feature of most collective agreements. This is probably an undesirable trend. It tends to make both unions and managements less responsible. I know one industrial relations director of a very large company who argues in favor of grievance arbitration. He once said to me that the union and the arbitrator very often get the company "off the hook" in difficult or embarrassing grievance cases. I said to him that I objected to arbitration for that very reason—it is wrong for a responsible executive to agree to a systematic procedure for relieving himself of his essential responsibility.

Despite the foregoing observations, I do not mean to suggest that there is anything necessarily wrong in union participation in grievance procedures. As in the case of bargaining over wages and as in the case of strikes, employees have a right to entrust the prosecution of their grievances to unions. And unions in turn have a right to insist upon arbitration as the means of settling grievances in the last resort.

What I do mean to suggest is that employers are no more

justly subject to criticism when they refuse to submit to union demands for grievance procedures and arbitration than when they refuse to concede other union demands. On the contrary, there is a great deal to be said for such employers. Far from being primitive and reactionary, they are in fact seeking manfully to shoulder one of the most trying of management responsibilities.

The trends and tendencies previously sketched are leading toward an end which is certain to prove incompatible with many of our basic desires. First compulsory collective bargaining replaced direct dealings between employers and employees and voluntary collective bargaining in important parts of the economy. Now the trend moves on to promote government resolution of wage disputes and disposition of employee grievances by outside arbitrators. Freedom and responsibility are being drastically reduced and thinned out in the process, and they are the vital bases of all that is good in American life.

The situation is by no means desperate as yet. America remains preponderantly a free country with an active, productive free enterprise system, still today the most productive the world has ever known.

The important thing, while recognizing the trends that exist, is to fix attention firmly on the sound principles of freedom and responsibility which constitute the basic framework of the system and account for its strength and productivity.

The strike at the Press illustrated those principles in motion. The unions made demands which they had a right to make, however unwise they may have been; the Press resisted those demands, as it had a right to do. The unions called a strike, as they had a right to do; the Press decided to continue operations, as it had a right to do. The stage was set for a clean-cut, peaceful decision by the only really disinterested arbiter available for economic disputes: the consumer, reaching a decision freely on free markets. Aside from the imperfections introduced by a defective labor relations policy and the still more defective administration of that policy by the National Labor Relations Board, the most serious violation of the principles of freedom and responsibility, therefore, lay in the conduct of the strike: the obstructive and provocative picketing and mob demonstrations, the assaults, the bombings, and the vandalism.

Terror, chaos, and anarchy took the place of freedom, responsibility, and order. That is no way to resolve a labor dispute, any more than it is a way to resolve a dispute among grocers. Present trends toward government intervention in wage disputes and toward arbitration in grievance cases will some day come to an end, when the public realizes the incompatibility of those trends with more important objectives. But the problem of violence in labor disputes will still have to be resolved. Perhaps we can learn something about that from further analysis of the violence in Kingsport and the efforts of the legal authorities.

Violence and Law Enforcement— And Public Opinion

We have already described the violence and vandalism that went on in Kingsport for more than a year. Let us now analyze their components. These may be divided into two large categories—overt and covert, or mob and individual.

By overt mob violence I mean the mass picketing and the mass demonstrations which took place near the plant. These mob activities were undoubtedly planned and arranged and therefore had a purpose, for people do not expend such energies without some end in view. They must have been planned or arranged because it is impossible to believe that a large and diverse assemblage could have spontaneously congregated at particular places and particular times, especially for the particular purpose that had brought them together. That purpose was to prevent the Press from operating, more particularly to discourage people from taking employment with the Press.

We know fairly well at least some of the animating convictions of the mob: that jobs at the Press "belonged" to the strikers; that the "scabs and rats" were traitors and evil people who were not exercising rights of their own but invading the rights of the strikers; that the Press was out to "bust" the unions; that in all the circumstances the mob had a "right" to prevent the "scabs and rats" from stealing jobs and the Press from operating.

As observed in Chapter VIII, we cannot in fairness hold the union leadership guilty of directly and deliberately inciting the mob to particular unlawful acts such as throwing stones, ball bearings, and eggs, and spreading nails. We do know, however, that union leaders recommended "jeering" and that jeering is provocative, indeed highly so. We know also that the union leadership had much to do with indoctrinating the mob in the beliefs just summarized; and that with their vast experience they expected "things to happen which should not happen."

The covert violence and vandalism—the pursuit of and individual assaults upon striker replacements, the tear gas, the bombings, the shooting-up of cars, the breaking of windows—undoubtedly were stirred up to a large extent by the same animating convictions and purposes. Some of it, no doubt, was produced by the sheer malignity unleashed by the general conditions of terror and violence.

The authorities in Kingsport voiced a correct attitude toward what was going on. Mr. R. L. Eisenbise, Kingsport's Safety Director, issued a statement on June 16, 1963, which said, among other things:

> Many people . . . feel that due to the present labor dispute they are immune from any arrest or prosecution. Quite the contrary, when a group of people assemble for the purpose of disturbing the peace of the city, or that of others, by violence, tumultuous or offensive conduct, or by loud and unusual noises or language calculated to provoke a breach of the peace, many laws are applicable. . . . When respect for the laws of our land are no longer honored [sic] and the law of the day is mob rule, we are then an anarchy state. (*Kingsport Times-News,* June 16, 1963.)

The sentiments professed by law-enforcement officers were one thing, their performance another. For three months or more, mass pickets and mobs were allowed to congregate. When picketing was finally limited to ten at each plant gate, the pickets were allowed to continue with their provocative name-calling and jeering. The police were quick to warn off a person who tried to take pictures of the pickets, I observed, but did nothing to prevent the pickets from their constant, annoying, and insulting name-calling; and tacks and nails were being spread at approaches to the Press as late as March, 1966. In December of 1963, the Tennessee Supreme Court finally upheld Chancellor Jackson C. Raulston's limitations on the picketing. A day or so later, Raulston's home was again hit by vandals.

There is only one thing to do with an agitated mob, and every peace officer worth his salt knows what that is. If civilized conditions are to be maintained, the mob must be dispersed—instantly, and with whatever force is necessary.

Judges must swiftly, and if necessary with no notice or hearing at all, issue orders restraining people generally from congregating in numbers at the scene of a labor dispute. No rights are infringed upon by such *ex parte* orders, for there is no such thing as a right to obstruct and intimidate—which is all that mobs do, and all that they are intended to do. An order limiting pickets during a strike to one, or at most two, at each entrance, adequately safeguards such rights as the extremely punctilious may feel are involved. The order should absolutely prohibit all jeering and name-calling. The rights of free men do not include a license to insult and provoke people. Moreover, society has an independent interest in keeping the peace—its interest in self-preservation. For in the absence of peace, society cannot exist. If it is necessary to keep one or more police officers stationed constantly at each picket post, then that is what should be done. A decent, self-respecting social order can do no less.

As for covert acts of individual aggression, they call for the same policing jobs as in the usual case of furtive crime: patrolling, detection, apprehension, and prosecution. To some small degree the policing is simplified during strikes by the restricted and predictable character of the victims, for they will usually be strike defectors and replacements. Still, the prevention of furtive crime will always be a difficult job.

The best hope of preventing furtive crime associated with strikes lies in the same measure which, at bottom, must be resorted to in connection with mob violence. Public opinion rules society. If labor disputes are to be resolved peacefully and consensually, public opinion must insist upon the protection of individual rights during strikes.

Domestic Tranquility and the Great Society

Law enforcement officials—judges and peace officers—cannot be expected to do their jobs properly during strikes when public opinion is uncertain about the basic rights involved and ignorant of the consequences of the abandonment of law and order. We have been hearing much in recent years about the Great Society. But no society, great or small, is possible except when domestic tranquility prevails, so that peaceful, productive people are free to pursue their productive interests, to build, undistracted by the invasions of thugs and bullies, the dignity and wealth which are necessary to a life worth living.

The civilized members of the community are going to have to get to work on their ancient task with even more determination and more courage. They must teach the rest of the community, including politicians and law-enforcement officials, that the basic principles of civilization apply equally to all; that no pressure group, however aggressive, no "cause," however appealing, no mob demand, however exigent, is entitled to a special exemption from the moral and legal rules which make society possible and life good. Sir Henry Sumner Maine, in his book, *Popular Government,* written almost a hundred years ago, said what there is to say on the subject:

> The venerable legal formulas, which make laws to be administered in the name of the King, formulas which modern Republics have borrowed, are a monument of the grandest service which governments have rendered, and continue to render, to mankind. If any government should be tempted to neglect, even for a moment, its function of compelling obedience to

law—if a Democracy, for example, were to allow a portion of the multitude of which it consists to set some law at defiance which it happens to dislike—it would be guilty of a crime which hardly any other virtue could redeem, and which century upon century might fail to repair.